The Cheap Bastard's™ Guide to
NEW YORK CITY

Start saving
your pennies and
any that you find along
the way! Love,
Kristin ~ Tom
5-10-03

Help Us Keep This Guide Up to Date

Every effort has been made by the author and editors to make this guide as accurate and useful as possible. However, many things can change after a guide is published—establishments close, phone numbers change, facilities come under new management, and so on.

We would love to hear from you concerning your experiences with this guide and how you feel it could be improved and kept up to date. While we may not be able to respond to all comments and suggestions, we'll take them to heart and we'll also make certain to share them with the author. Please send your comments and suggestions to the following address:

The Globe Pequot Press
Reader Response/Editorial Department
P.O. Box 480
Guilford, CT 06437

Or you may e-mail us at:

editorial@globe-pequot.com

Thanks for your input, and happy travels!

The Cheap Bastard's Guide to
NEW YORK CITY

A NATIVE NEW YORKER'S SECRETS OF
LIVING THE GOOD LIFE—FOR FREE!

Rob Grader

GUILFORD, CONNECTICUT

The prices and rates listed in this guidebook were confirmed at press time. We recommend, however, that you call establishments to obtain current information before traveling.

Copyright © 2002 by Rob Grader

Text and map design: M. A. Dubé
Spot art: Image Club
Lyrics on page 27 from "Grand Central Station, March 18, 1977" by Steve Forbert, reprinted by kind permission of Welk Music (ASCAP, adm Lichelle Music Co.).

Library of Congress Cataloging-in-Publication Data
Grader, Rob.
    The cheap bastard's guide to New York City : a native New Yorker's secrets of living the good life — for free \ Rob Grader. —1st ed.
        p. cm.
    Includes index.
    ISBN 0-7627-2352-1
     1. New York (N.Y.) — Guidebooks. I. Title
    F128.18.G69 2002
    917.47'10444—dc21   2002069312

Manufactured in the United States of America
First Edition/Third Printing

Dedication

For Dad, the one, the true, the Original Cheap Bastard
and for Mom, though not always cheap, one true original in her own right.

Contents

> "Misers aren't fun to live with, but they make wonderful ancestors."
> — David Brenner

ACKNOWLEDGMENTS

N O ONE BECOMES A Cheap Bastard on their own, and here are the names to prove it. There are many people I need to acknowledge who've helped me along the way. From the very beginning, I had training from the best, the ultimate Cheap Bastard himself, my dad, Jack Grader. Thanks also to Mom, Bernice Grader, and everyone in my family for their support, encouragement, and suggestions while I was putting this opus together. In particular, thanks to Scott Grader (with two t's, right?) for all the free legal counseling, to Trish Lande Grader for the free publishing know-how, and to all the rest of the Graders: Jessica, Michelle, Emily, Sally, Jonas, Jeff, Lisa, Stu, and Ellen. Special thanks to Shari Springer Berman and Bob Pulcini for all the free writing advice and consultations. I am also indebted to Steve Harper for the free proof-reading services (and the constantly free ear!), to

Harry Mizrahi of American Spectrum Realty for the free use of the office equipment and for giving me plenty of free time while I was working for him, to Hans Kriefall and his mom for the free Latin lesson, and to Chiori Miagowa, Suzi Takahashi, Nilaja Sun, Ignacio Lopez, Ken Bolden, Danny Weiss, Patricia Kelley, Bill Quigley, Bill Driscoll, Mark Farnan, Sue Barret, Helen Mandlin, Karen Raksis (the best things in life *are* free!) for all giving so freely of your spirits. My gratitude also goes out to Mark S. Roy and Brian DeFiore of DeFiore and Company, and to Laura Strom, Shelley Wolf, and everyone at The Globe Pequot Press for your invaluable assistance. There is also a little nasty little secret about New Yorkers I must expose: Contrary to popular belief, they truly are the friendliest, smartest, most generous and helpful people in the world. Innumerable friends, acquaintances, associates, and strangers helped me out in countless ways throughout the development of this book. I'm sorry I cannot name you all, but please know you are appreciated. Thanks to all—you're a wonderful bunch of Bastards!

> *"Truly, our greatest blessings are very cheap."*
>
> —Henry David Thoreau

INTRODUCTION:
THE LAND OF THE FREE

A FEW YEARS BACK while I was visiting England, I found myself low on cash—but still wanting to see the sights. Not to be deterred by this minor detail, I proceeded to figure out ways to sneak into some of the Brits' most expensive and heavily guarded tourist attractions. My proudest feat was making my way into the impenetrable Tower of London. Take that, William the Conqueror! I was having such a good time getting around the system that I thought this would make a great first in a series of books—Getting Around London: How to Sneak into Anywhere. Upon further consideration (and after speaking with my brother the lawyer), it seemed there might be an array of legal problems with this kind of book. But somehow the idea wouldn't go away.

Then back home in New York, I watched the Pulitzer Prize–winning play *Wit* one evening for free (and legally!). After the show, I stopped by a favorite haunt of mine to get a little snack (free, thank you), and made it home to my spacious Upper West Side apartment (for which I pay $521 a month in rent and found without paying any broker's fee). As I sat relaxing in my leather easy chair (free, too!) and thinking about my yoga class the next morning (you guessed it, free), it dawned on me—I am one cheap bastard. I also understood that I have a mission in life to figure out how I can get or do practically anything I want without paying one red cent, and usually on the up and up. And I felt compelled to share this—my life's work—with the world. So I humbly offer to you *The Cheap Bastard's Guide to New York City*.

The *CB Guide* is not only a collection of specific destinations, listings, and tips on how to get almost anything imaginable for free or ridiculously cheap (more on my definition of these later); it's also a celebration of life on the cheap. The myth is that New York is a great place to live or visit if you have the money to enjoy it. The truth is, no place offers more for free than New York, but only if you know how to find it. And once you find it, oh the joy! Anyone can pay their way into a Broadway show, but when you get in for free somehow the lights are brighter, the songs are sweeter, the drama so much more heartbreaking. There is no thrill in buying a dinner, but the taste of a free Buffalo wing is spiced with adventure, the crunch of a crisp free Granny Smith apple is the sound of triumph, and the kick of getting a free cup of coffee puts just that extra spring in your step.

A big part of the value of getting something for nothing is the story that goes with it—the history, the event. What can you tell me about any piece of furniture in your house that you bought? *I went to the store. I liked it. I bought it.* But everything in *my* house comes with a heritage. Every time I sit in my leather easy chair, I'm reminded of how I came to own this piece of furniture that by all rights I could never afford to buy. I was walking along a few blocks away from my apartment, my arms loaded down with books I was donating to my local library, when I saw a chair sitting in the curb waiting to be picked up by the next sanitation truck. While at first glance it looked like it might truly be ready for the trash heap, with its torn-up seat cushion, I knew right away I wanted it. Still, I couldn't stop to grab it then. I hurried to the library, dropped off my books, and rushed back to the chair. Of course, someone else was checking out the merchandise by the time I got back. I thought I had lost it. Who would pass up such a great find? I waited on the corner sending evil thoughts his way . . . and miraculously, he walked away. *Great, it's mine!* When I was in the middle of inspecting my chair, seeing if the cushion really was beyond repair, another guy walked up to offer his advice. "Eh, you don't want that, it's falling apart," he said. I thanked him for his words of wisdom and continued to poke and prod at the chair. He then walked away, and I noticed him heading back to his double-parked van just down the block. *Nice try, buddy,* I thought. I knew I had to grab it now or kiss it good-bye. I heaved it over my head, managed to lug it the few blocks home—and the rest is history. All I had to do was to fashion a new cover for the cushion, which cost me no more than $30. The chair has now served me well for more than five years.

Each and every listing in this book offers you an opportunity for something more valuable than money: a memory, an experience, a story (and of course, the chance to save a boatload of cash ain't such a bad thing, either).

The listings in this book can be split into two categories: Free and Ridiculously Cheap, with the vast majority of the listing being free. So let's define what I mean by these terms.

Simply stated, *free* is getting something without having to pay any money for it. So, here are some of the things you will *not* find in this book: "Buy One, Get One Free"; "First Month Free"; "Mention the Cheap Bastard and get in for half price"; or any other scheme that is ultimately about getting cash out of your wallet. What kind of free listings *will* you find in this book? Two basic kinds: free-free and free-with-a-catch. *Free-free* is just that: no-strings-attached, give-it-to-me-but-I'm-not-giving-you-anything free. For example, you can get a professional facial for free at Shiseido Studio in Soho, no strings attached. *Free-with-a-catch* generally means you'll need to exchange some time or effort to get that something for free. For example, you can see almost any Off Broadway and some Broadway shows for free by being a volunteer usher. Show up an hour early, help seat the paying folks, and watch the show for nothing. I have tried to clearly lay out any catch you may need to know about by including the category The Catch (ingenious, eh?) wherever necessary.

Ridiculously cheap listings are those things that, yes, you will have to lay out some money to get. Still, the cost is so minimal that when you're asked to pay, you do it quickly for fear they'll realize their mistake. For example, does $25 a year for a gym membership sound pretty ridiculous to you?

Let me also mention what makes someone a Cheap Bastard. I see *Cheap Bastard* as a proud term referring to someone who enjoys the thrill of the hunt, not someone whose end-all and be-all is not spending money. This isn't someone who will deny himself or anyone else anything simply because it will cost some money. Most importantly, this isn't someone who is looking to cheat another person; nor is it to be confused with *stingy*. A Cheap Bastard is not out to beat another person out of a few cents; he is out to beat the system.

This book is intended for visitors and natives alike. Whether you're a backpacker from Australia who has just shown up in the city at the end of your round-the-world jaunt with less cash than you planned; a born-and-bred New Yorker who needs to stretch that paycheck a little farther; someone who's just moved to the city and working his first (low-paying) job out of college; a college student who needs to figure out how to make that student loan last all year; or even one of those folks for whom money is no worry, but, hey, you just like getting something for nothing (and who doesn't?)—this book is for you.

Finally, all the information in this guide is accurate as of press time, but things change quickly in New York, so I have included as much contact information as possible for each listing. Always call, check the Web site, or stop by to make sure all the information in this book is still accurate. If you have any thoughts, comments, corrections, or suggestions for future volumes, I would love to hear from you. Please send all correspondence to thecheapbastard@email.com (you guessed it, that's a free e-mail address).

I've had a ball putting this book together, and I hope it helps you get the most out of the greatest city in the world.

Live Well, Live Free,

Rob Grader
The Cheap Bastard
New York City

Section 1:

ENTERTAINMENT IN NEW YORK

"Of all men, physicians and
playwrights alone possess
the rare privilege of charging
money for the pain they
inflict on us."

—Santiago Ramón y Cajal

THEATER: FREE SPEECH

FROM THE BRIGHT LIGHTS of Broadway to the cutting-edge antics of the downtown performance world, New York is the undisputed capital of the theater world. Any day of the week, there are literally hundreds of performances going on in every corner of the city. And while the top ticket prices for a Broadway show have surpassed $100, you can spend endless evenings in the theaters of New York without spending a cent. By taking on the role of a volunteer usher, you can make your way into some Broadway shows and almost any Off Broadway show, absolutely free. You can also keep yourself very busy attending any of the many just-plain-free performances at theaters throughout the city. These run the gamut from full productions to staged readings of new plays and musicals.

VOLUNTEER USHERING

Every time you walk into a theater to see a show, some kind person takes your ticket and shows you to your seat. Often you find that these folks are just thrilled to be doing this job. Ever wonder why? Well, this isn't their regular job; they're just there to see the show, like you. The only difference is, they haven't paid a cent to get in. Yes, they're volunteer ushers, and you'll find them at almost all Off Broadway and some Broadway theaters. Considering the ticket price of these shows (from $25 to $95), volunteer ushers get "paid" very well for basically one hour's work, so why wouldn't they be pretty darn happy? And it's easy to join their ranks.

Each theater has its own protocol, but essentially all that's involved is making a reservation a week or two in advance, then showing up an hour before the curtain rises. The house manager will give you a quick rundown on the seating plan (warning: you do need to be able to count to twelve to understand this; sometimes you even need to count backward), then you help seat the paying folks. During the performance, enjoy the show. Ushers get to watch from seats that remain empty as the show is about to start. There are almost always good seats—many times the best seats in the house—for you to fill, even if the show is officially sold out. On the very rare occasion that there are absolutely no seats available, they will set up chairs for you, or in extremely rare cases ask you to sit in the aisles. Occasionally you need to stay a couple of minutes after the show to help pick up stray playbills. It's as simple as that.

Dress the Part

While no special skills or training are needed to be a volunteer usher, a nice pair of black pants and a crisp white shirt are often required. Many theaters do ask you to look the role, even though you're only playing the part for one evening. The dress codes vary from black and white (black pants and a white shirt) to all-black; some just ask you to look respectable (don't worry, no ties required). Be sure to ask what to wear when making reservations. Most theaters are flexible in these requirements, but some do take them very seriously and will not let you usher if you aren't dressed properly.

Why do theaters do this? Economics. It's cheaper to let you in for nothing than it is to hire a full-time ushering staff. You can even bring a friend. Most theaters need at least two ushers per show (some as many as ten) and are happy to let you reserve more than one slot. Even some theaters that officially only use one usher per show will let you bring a companion to usher with you if you ask nicely. Talk about your cheap dates!

BROADWAY

THE ROUNDABOUT THEATRE COMPANY
The American Airlines Theater
227 West 42nd Street (between Eighth Avenue and Broadway)
(212) 719–9393
www.roundabouttheatre.org
Ushers per performance: 6
After years of hopping from theater to theater, one of New York's most renowned theater companies has found a permanent home on Broadway. And since they remain a not-for-profit theater, this is one of the few opportunities to volunteer usher on Broadway. They also maintain the Broadway production of *Cabaret* and the Off Broadway performances at the Gramercy (see below for information on these theaters). Their productions often attract star performers and are almost always of a high caliber (particularly the musicals). To book a slot at the American Airlines Theater, go to the box office any Monday through Friday between 10:00 A.M. and 6:00 P.M. to sign up for the date you want. They generally schedule them about two to three weeks in advance, depending on the popularity of the show. They are very serious about the black-and-white dress code for ushers.

CABARET
Studio 54
534 West 54th Street (between Broadway and Eighth Avenue)
(212) 719–9393
www.roundabouttheatre.org
Ushers per performance: 10
This is the 1998 Tony-winning production directed by big-shot Brit director Sam Mendes (the Oscar-winning director of *American Beauty*) set in the spectacular club atmosphere of Studio 54. These guys certainly do make you jump through hoops to see the show, but it's absolutely worth the effort. First, you need to go the theater on any Saturday between 5:00 and 6:00 P.M. to schedule a performance. On the day of the performance, you

need to show up an hour and a half before showtime to help seat the audience. For this show, your responsibilities do not end at curtain time. During the intermission, they ask you to stand your position to direct patrons to the bar, rest rooms, and so on, and at the end of the show, you need to help hand out the playbills. (Why at the end of the show? Evidently, it's part of the director's concept of giving the audience the full cabaret club experience.) While the show is on, just sit back and enjoy.

OFF-BROADWAY

AMERICAN PLACE THEATRE
111 West 46th Street (between Sixth and Seventh Avenues)
(212) 840–2960, ext. 7
www.americanplacetheatre.org
Ushers per performance: 3 in the main theater, 1 in the first-floor theater.
One of the stalwarts of the Off Broadway theater scene since 1963, American Place Theatre has made a name for itself by recognizing and being among the first to produce many leading American artists. Some of the playwrights APT was among the first to produce include Sam Shepard, Steve Tesich, Maria Irene Fornes, William Hauptman, Emily Mann, and Richard Nelson. The performers who have graced their stages include Eric Bogosian, Bill Irwin, John Leguizamo, Roscoe Lee Browne, Michael Douglas, Faye Dunaway, Morgan Freeman, Richard Gere, Joel Grey, Dustin Hoffman, Sam Waterson, and Sigourney Weaver. Call the ushering line to leave a reservation. They also present free readings of plays in development occasionally; call the theater for details.

ASTOR PLACE THEATRE
434 Lafayette Street (between East 4th and 8th Streets)
(212) 254–4370
www.blueman.com
Ushers per night: 4
Home to the long-running Off Broadway industry Blue Man Group. You've seen them on the Intel commercials, Jay Leno, David Letterman, and every other talk show imaginable, and if you still haven't seen enough of them, come on down to the theater where the whole thing started and see them for free (they don't need any more money). They will also ask you to stay about fifteen minutes after the show is over to clean up. Warning: It's a messy show. To make a reservation, call about a week in advance, Monday through Friday from 10:00 A.M. to 6:00 P.M.

ATLANTIC THEATER COMPANY

336 West 20th Street (between Eighth and Ninth Avenues)
(212) 645–8015
www.atlantictheater.org
Ushers per performance: 2

Founded by followers of the David Mamet school of acting and known for producing his works and others of the same ilk. Productions all have limited runs, and ushering slots fill quickly. They start taking ushering reservations three weeks prior to the start of performances and are usually "sold out" by the time the reviews come out.

CENTURY CENTER THEATER

111 East 15th Street (between Union Square East and Irving Place)
(212) 982–6782, ext. 11
Ushers per performance: 2

This theater has been home to a number of popular Off Broadway plays, including *The Play about the Baby,* the Pulitzer Prize–winning *How I Learned to Drive,* and *The Complete Works of William Shakespeare (Abridged).* Call the house manager to make a reservation Wednesday through Friday after 7:00 P.M., Saturday between 2:00 and 11:00 P.M., Sunday between 3:00 and 5:00 P.M. and Monday between 7:00 and 9:00 P.M. Call two weeks to a month in advance for reservations.

THE CHERRY LANE THEATRE

38 Commerce Street (between Bedford and Hudson Streets)
(212) 989–2020
www.cherrylanetheatre.com
Ushers per performance: 3

Since 1924, this theater has been home to many of the early works of such playwrights as Edward Albee, Beckett, Ionesco, Mamet, Pinter, Lanford Wilson, and Sam Shepard. In recent years it has played host to such successful Off Broadway shows as *Fully Committed, Nunsense, True West, Blown Sideways through Life,* and many others. Call a week to a month in advance. Very casual and easygoing atmosphere for ushers.

CLASSIC STAGE COMPANY

136 East 13th Street (between Third and Fourth Avenues)
(212) 677–4210, ext. 30
www.classicstage.org
Ushers per performance: 3

For more than thirty years, CSC has built a reputation for reinventing classic works of the theater—some well known, others less so. They have attracted a loyal following by working with some of the best-known actors, directors, and writers from New York, Hollywood, and around the country. Call for reservations a week to a month in advance of the performance.

ENCORES
City Center
West 55th Street (between Sixth and Seventh Avenues)
(212) 247–0430, ext. 202
www.citycenter.org
Ushers per performance: 6–9
Presenting series of highly produced staged readings of musicals with star performers, Encores is considered one of the hottest tickets in town. Call far in advance to put your name on a list of volunteers to hawk CDs and other paraphernalia in the lobby to get into the shows.

ENSEMBLE STUDIO THEATRE
549 West 52nd Street (between Tenth and Eleventh Avenues)
(212) 247–4982
www.ensemblestudiotheatre.org
They use ushers on an as-needed basis. They are always in need of ushers during their Octoberfest and Spring Marathon.

45 BLEECKER THEATER AND GALLERY
45 Bleecker Street (between Bowery and Lafayette Streets)
(212) 253–9983
www.45bleecker.com
Ushers per performance: 2
Since opening its doors in 1999, 45 Bleecker has played host to such shows as *Bombity of Errors, And God Created Great Whales,* and *The Game Show* in its two performance spaces. Call the box office to leave a message with the house manager about ushering and they will call you back to make a reservation.

GRAMERCY THEATER
127 East 23rd Street (between Park and Lexington Avenues)
(212) 777–4900
www.roundabouttheatre.org
Ushers per performance: 6
The Roundabout Theater Company's Off Broadway house has played host to such plays as *Hotel Suite, Juno and the Paycock, Blue,* and *A Skull in Connemara.* They will soon be moving to the American Place Theatre on West 46th Street. Call the main Roundabout office (212–719–9393) for information. Call the theater on Tuesday, Thursday, or Friday between

noon and 4:00 P.M., or Wednesday, Saturday, or Sunday between noon and 2:00 P.M. to set a date. Dates are often available within the week (depending on the popularity of the show).

HERE PERFORMANCE ART CAFE
145 Sixth Avenue (between Spring and Broome Streets)
(212) 647–0202
www.here.org
Ushers per performance: 1–2
Here is a downtown art center bringing together theater, performance art, music, dance, and visual art into one complex. With an ever-changing rotation of productions of all sorts in their three theaters and intriguing work on the walls and floors of their gallery, there is always something worthwhile to see Here. Call a couple of days to a week in advance to reserve an ushering slot.

IRISH ARTS CENTER
553 West 51st Street (between Tenth and Eleventh Avenues)
(212) 757–3318
www.irishartscenter.org
Ushers per performance: 1
Presents a full season of productions by and about the Irish experience, as well as playing host to many imports from Ireland. Call to add your name to the list of volunteer ushers and they will call when they need you.

IRISH REPERTORY THEATRE
132 West 22nd Street (between Sixth and Seventh Avenues)
(212) 727–2737
www.irishrepertorytheatre.com
Ushers per performance: 2
Call Tuesday through Saturday after 12:30 P.M. to schedule a date. This company has built a strong reputation for presenting the works of (believe it or not) Irish and Irish American writers, both classical and contemporary. They have three theaters, and you may usher in any of them. Call at least two weeks in advance for a reservation, more if you need a specific date.

JANE STREET THEATRE
113 Jane Street (between West and Washington Streets)
(212) 255–2921
Ushers per performance: 2
Call to set up a date, but you may have more luck if you drop by the box office and ask to speak to the house manager. The theater has been the home of such shows as *Hedwig and the Angry Inch* and *Tick, Tick . . . Boom!*

JEAN COCTEAU REPERTORY (BOUWERIE LANE THEATRE)

330 Bowery (at 2nd Street)
(212) 677–0060
www.jeancocteaurep.org
Ushers per performance: 2
For more than thirty years, their resident acting company has presented a season of classics by the likes of Shakespeare, Shaw, Sophocles, Strindberg, Chekhov, Molière, Wilde, Tennessee Williams, Harold Pinter, and others. Call about a week in advance to make an ushering reservation.

JOHN HOUSMAN THEATER

450 West 42nd Street (between Ninth and Tenth Avenues)
(212) 967–7079
Ushers per performance: 2
Call Monday through Friday, 10:00 A.M. to 6:00 P.M. to make a reservation from one day to two weeks in advance. This theater has been home to many popular shows recently, including *Lobby Hero* and *Puppetry of the Penis*.

THE JOYCE THEATER

175 Eighth Avenue (at 18th Street)
(646) 792–8355
www.joyce.org
Ushers per performance: 8
The leading theater for dance companies, the Joyce plays host to practically every major company from around the country and around the world. They begin taking reservations two weeks before each performance.

THE LAMB'S THEATRE

130 West 44th Street (between Sixth Avenue and Broadway)
(212) 575–0300
This church theater has played host to many Off Broadway productions, including *The Countess* and *Dames at Sea*. It's currently undergoing renovations and may not return to being an Off Broadway theater. If it does, they will use volunteer ushers; call for details.

LUCILLE LORTEL THEATER

121 Christopher Street (between Hudson and Bleecker Streets)
(212) 924–2817, ex. 207
www.lortel.org
Ushers per performance: 3
This venerable Off Broadway theater has been the home of many major productions over its fifty-year history, such as *Cloud 9, Steel Magnolias,*

Three Penny Opera, As Bees in Honey Drown, and many others. Call anywhere from a few days to a few weeks in advance to make a reservation, depending on the popularity of the show.

MANHATTAN ENSEMBLE THEATER (MET)

55 Mercer Street (between Broome and Grand Streets)
(212) 925–1900
www.met.com
Ushers per performance: To be announced.
This new theater company founded by the former artistic director of Cocteau Rep specializes in dramatizing classic literary works. At press time the company was still setting up its ushering procedures; call for details. They also plan to have regular free readings on Monday night in this new Soho theater space.

MANHATTAN THEATRE CLUB

City Center (theater and box office)
West 55th Street (between Sixth and Seventh Avenues)
311 West 43rd Street, Eighth Floor (administrative offices)
(212) 247–0430, ext. 240
www.mtc-nyc.org
Ushers per performance: 4 on Stage 1, 1 on Stage 2.
MTC is a major producer of new plays, many of which end up transferring to Broadway theaters including *Proof, The Tale of the Allergist's Wife, Ain't Misbehavin',* and many others over the years. See them before they move, because you can't usher for them once they hit the Great White Way. Call Tuesday through Saturday after 9:30 P.M. anywhere from one to three weeks in advance once the show is running. If you reach the voice mail, don't bother leaving a message; just keep calling back until you reach an actual human being on the other end to make a reservation. Be persistent.

MCC THEATER

120 West 28th Street (between Sixth and Seventh Avenues)
(212) 727–7722
www.mcctheater.org
Ushers per performance: 3
MCC is a small but popular Off Broadway company that has made a name for itself by producing such plays as the Pulitzer Prize–winning *Wit* and has worked with such actors as Calista Flockhart, Bridget Fonda, Thomas Gibson, Kyra Sedgwick, Marisa Tomei, Allison Janney, and Lili Taylor over its fifteen year history. Make reservations a week or two before performances begin. Slots fill up quickly.

MINT THEATER COMPANY
311 West 43rd Street, 5th Floor (between Eighth and Ninth Avenues)
(212) 315–9434
www.minttheater.org
Ushers per performance: 1
This small, well-respected company concentrates on rediscovering lost classics from the nineteenth and twentieth centuries. Recent productions have included *The Voysey Inheritance, House of Mirth,* and *Mr. Pim Passes By.* Ushering slots do get filled quickly; call two to three weeks before performances begin to be assured of a reservation.

THE NEW GROUP THEATER
The Theater at St. Clements
423 West 46th Street (between Ninth and Tenth Avenues)
(212) 691–6730
www.newgrouptheater.com
Ushers per performance: 2
A high-profile company with many productions that have won all the awards and transferred to long runs at major Off Broadway theaters, including *This Is Our Youth, Ecstasy, Another American Asking and Telling,* and others. Call two weeks in advance for reservations.

NEW YORK THEATRE WORKSHOP (NYTW)
79 East 4th Street (between Second Avenue and Bowery)
(212) 780–9037
www.nytw.org
Ushers per performance: 5
NYTW produces some of the most daring and artistically challenging productions of any Off Broadway theater; it was the original producer of such Broadway hits as *Rent* and *Dirty Blond.* Ushering slots can be reserved anywhere from the day of a performance to three weeks in advance, depending on the popularity of the show. Be sure to get on their ushering mailing list and they will send you out reminders for each new show. They also throw in free coffee or tea at the concession stand for ushers.

THE PEARL THEATRE COMPANY
Theatre 80
80 St. Marks Place (between First and Second Avenues)
(212) 598–9802
www.pearltheatre.org

Ushers per performance: 4
One of the only true classical repertory companies remaining in New York. Their seasons concentrate on the works of Shakespeare, Chekhov, Coward, the Greeks, and other Dead European White Men. Their productions are almost never startlingly original, but almost always respectably done. Call one to two weeks in advance for reservations.

THE PERFORMING GARAGE

33 Wooster Street (between Broome and Grand Streets)
(212) 966–3651
www.thewoostergroup.org
Ushers per performance: 2–3
Home of many experimental theater companies, most notably the Wooster Group (Willem Dafoe and others). The productions often sell out; call far in advance for an ushering slot.

PLAYHOUSE 91

316 East 91st Street (between First and Second Avenues)
(212) 831–2000
Ushers per performance: 2
The theater was the longtime home of the Jewish Repertory Theater and many other companies and productions over its more-than-thirty-year history. It's now an independent commercial theater and has been home to such productions as *The Syringa Tree, A Bronx Tale,* and others. Stop by the box office from 1:00 P.M. to 7:00 P.M. Monday through Friday or call the house manager between 6:30 P.M. and 7:00 P.M. to reserve an ushering slot. There are usually dates available within two weeks.

PLAYWRIGHTS HORIZONS

416 West 42nd Street (between Ninth and Tenth Avenues)
(212) 564–1235
www.playwrightshorizons.org
Ushers per performance: 1–3
Produces a season of new plays and musicals by well-known and up-and-coming playwrights, many of which transfer to larger Off Broadway or Broadway theaters. Past productions have included *Driving Miss Daisy, The Heidi Chronicles, Once on This Island,* and James Joyce's *The Dead.* They maintain a large list of ushers and send out mailings before each show begins performances. Call far in advance; slots fill up quickly.

PRIMARY STAGES

354 West 45th Street (between Eighth and Ninth Avenues)
(212) 333–4052 or (212) 840–9705
www.primarystages.com
Ushers per performance: 1
Presents a season of new plays by notable contemporary American playwrights like David Ives, Donald Margulies, Charles Busch, and many others. Begins taking ushering reservations three weeks before performances
begin.

PROMENADE THEATRE

2162 Broadway (at 76th Street)
(212) 580–1313
Ushers per performance: 2
This large Off Broadway theater has been home to many major productions
including the original productions of *Godspell, Hurlyburly, A Lie of the
Mind, Pacific Overtures,* and *The Lisbon Traviata.* Call Tuesday through
Saturday from 8:30 to 9:30 P.M. to make a reservation. Call one week to a
month ahead of time to reserve a slot, depending on the popularity of the
show.

P.S. 122

150 First Avenue (at East 9th Street)
(212) 477–5829, ext. 306
www.ps122.org
Ushers per performance: 2 (possibly more)
The longtime home of experimental and cutting edge theater and dance,
P.S. 122 continues to host many well-known and emerging performance
artists, including Eric Bogosian, Spalding Gray, John Leguizamo, and
Karen Finley. You never know what you're going to catch there, but it's
always daring and innovative. Call the week of the performance to book
an ushering slot in one of their two theaters.

RATTLESTICK THEATRE

224 Waverly Place (off Seventh Avenue at 11th Street)
(212) 627–2556
www.rattlestick.org
Ushers per performance: 1
This up-and-coming Off Broadway theater has begun to build a strong
name for itself producing contemporary playwrights. Past productions have
included *Down South, Whale Music,* and *Killers and Other Family.* Call a

week in advance for reservations. Also holds free play readings on Tuesday afternoon and evening.

SECOND STAGE THEATRE
307 West 43rd Street (at Eighth Avenue)
(212) 787–8302, ext. 216
www.secondstagetheatre.com
Ushers per performance: 4
Hailed in past years by the *New York Times* as "the season's most indispensable theater," Second Stage produces a season chock-full of theater heavyweights like August Wilson, Stephen Sondheim, Edward Albee, and many others. Leave a reservation on the ushering hot line one week to one month in advance, depending on the popularity of the show.

THE SIGNATURE THEATRE COMPANY
Peter North Space
555 West 42nd Street (between Tenth and Eleventh Avenues)
(212) 244–7529
www.signaturetheatre.org
Ushers per performance: 5
Specializes in highly regarded productions focusing each season on the works of a single American playwright. Past seasons have included Arthur Miller, Edward Albee, Maria Irene Fornes, and Sam Shepard. Call at least two weeks in advance. Free coffee, tea, and hot chocolate for ushers!

SOHO PLAYHOUSE
15 Vandam Street (between Spring and Prince Streets)
(212) 691–1555
Ushers per performance: 1
This theater has been home to such productions as *Killer Joe, Grandma Silvia's Funeral,* and others. Make reservations a few days to a week in advance by calling the box office noon to 7:00 P.M., Tuesday to Saturday.

THE TRIAD THEATRE
158 West 72nd Street (between Broadway and Columbus Avenue)
(212) 362–2590
Ushers per performance: 2
This Upper West Side cabaret theater is the home of fun and musical pieces like *Hello Muddah, Hello Faddah,* and other toe-tapping favorites. Call a week or two in advance for reservations.

UNION SQUARE THEATRE
100 East 17th Street (between Union Square East and Irving Place)
(212) 505-0700
Ushers per performance: 5
A large Off Broadway house that has played host to such shows as *Wit,
The Laramie Project, BatBoy,* and others. Call one to three weeks in
advance.

VARIETY ARTS THEATER
110 Third Avenue (between 13th and 14th Streets)
Ushers per performance: As needed
This theater has a regular ushering staff and uses volunteers only on an
as-needed basis. To sign up for a date, you need to drop by the theater
when the house manager is available. This means near or during a performance. The best time to stop by is about 8:30 or 9:15 Tuesday through
Saturday, and 3:30 or 4:15 on Saturday and Sunday. Usually hosts high-
profile Off Broadway shows such as the Pulitzer Prize–winning *Dinner with
Friends.*

THE VINEYARD THEATRE
108 East 15th Street (between Union Square East and Irving Place)
(212) 353-3366, ext. 226 (usher hotline)
www.vineyardtheatre.org
Ushers per performance: 2
The Vineyard produces and develops new works by many major figures
in the American theater. They have brought to life such shows as *Fully
Committed,* the Pulitzer Prize–winning *How I Learned to Drive,* and *Three
Tall Women.* Make reservations one to three weeks in advance.

WESTBETH THEATRE CENTER
151 Bank Street (Washington Street and West Side Highway)
(212) 691-2272
www.westbeththeatre.com
Ushers per performance: 3
Presents and develops theater and music performances, many of which end
up transferring to larger theaters around New York, regional theaters, and
around the world. Notable performances have included Eddy Izzard, Sandra
Bernhard, Marc Maron, *Hedwig and the Angry Inch,* Billy Connelly, Ray
Davies, the Losers Lounge, Lypsinka, and Margaret Cho. They don't use volunteer ushers for every show; call for details.

Off the Menu

If there's an Off Broadway show that you're interested in seeing and the theater isn't on this list, just ask at the box office if they use volunteer ushers for that show. There are always new venues popping up, and nontraditional performance spaces being used for new shows. Staff are very much used to answering this question. Nine times out of ten, they will say yes and tell you how to go about making a reservation.

WOMEN'S PROJECT THEATRE

Theatre 4, 424 West 55th Street (between Ninth and Tenth Avenues)
Administrative offices: 55 West End Avenue
(212) 765–1706
www.womensproject.org
info@womensproject.org
Ushers per performance: 6
Dedicated to producing and developing the talents of women playwrights, over its twenty-year history this theater has been among the first to work with such artists as Eve Ensler, Maria Irene Fornes, Anna Deavere Smith, Liz Diamond, Tina Landau, and Joyce Carol Oates, among others. To get on their ushering list, send a note or an e-mail to the administrative office. They send out notices six weeks before performances begin. Also holds "First Looks"—free reading series—most Mondays at 4:00 P.M. at their studio (55 West End Avenue, between 61st and 62nd Streets).

YORK THEATRE COMPANY

St. Peter's Church
619 Lexington Avenue (at 54th Street)
(212) 935–5824, ext. 19
www.yorktheatre.org
Ushers per performance: 2
Over the last thirty years, York has produced such award-winning musicals as *The Grass Harp, Pacific Overtures, She Loves Me, Company, 110 in the Shade, Sweeney Todd, Carnival,* and *Merrily We Roll Along.* Many of its productions have made the move to Broadway and larger Off Broadway theaters. Call two weeks ahead to make ushering reservations. The theater also presents free staged readings of new musicals most Monday nights at 7:30 P.M.

THE ZIPPER THEATRE

336 West 37th Street (between Eighth and Ninth Avenues)
(212) 563–0480
Ushers per performance: 4–6
This new, fun, and funky theater space located in a converted zipper factory plays host to a variety of no-holds-barred, screw-traditional-theater
productions. Call for ushering reservations anywhere from a couple of days
to three weeks in advance, depending on the popularity of the show.

CHEAP SEATS

Truth be told, the following listings are not exactly my idea of bargains. I
mean, if you have to put out some actual cash for something, what's the
point? But the rest of the world thinks these are good deals, so I'd be
remiss if I didn't include this information. Here are a few worthy organizations that can get you good seats in loads of Broadway and Off Broadway theaters and concert halls for a minimum of cash.

AUDIENCE EXTRAS

109 West 26th Street, #3B (between Sixth and Seventh Avenues)
(212) 989–9550
www.audienceextras.com

$85 yearly membership fee, $15 refundable deposit on membership card, and $30 personal reserve fund toward the $3.50 service charge per ticket.

This company's sole purpose is to get living, breathing bodies into the
seats of concert halls and theaters around the city. When a production
needs a crowd—either because critics will be reviewing the production
that night, or because it's early in the run and they want a full house to
gauge audience response—producers turn to these guys to "paper the
house" (translation: fill the seats). The bulk of the tickets offered are for
the big-name and edgier Off Broadway theaters and classical concerts at
such places as Lincoln Center. They occasionally also have tickets for
Broadway shows, as well as Off Off Broadway. They charge a membership
fee, and you are charged a $3.50 service fee per ticket (which is deducted
from your "personal reserve fund"); otherwise the tickets are "free."

PLAY BY PLAY

165 West 46th Street, Suite 412 (between Sixth and Seventh Avenues)
(212) 575–9808
www.play-by-play.com

 $99 yearly membership, and $3.00 service fee per ticket

Exactly the same service as Audience Extras, with the only difference being that Play by Play sometimes offers tickets to a larger variety of performances and possibly more opportunities for Broadway shows. Just like AE, the bulk of the shows they offer tickets for are Off Broadway and classical concerts, with the occasional Broadway or Off Off Broadway show, but they also regularly offer tickets to stand-up comedy, cabarets, and movie screenings. Once you've paid the yearly membership fee ($99.00), any performance will only cost you $3.00 per ticket.

TKTS BOOTH

Theater Development Fund (TDF)
Duffy Square (47th Street and Broadway)
(212) 221–0013
www.tdf.org

Sells tickets for 25 or 50 percent off ticket price plus a $2.50 service charge per ticket.

"We'll get tickets at the booth" has been the cry of many a spontaneous theatergoer for more than twenty-five years. The TKTS booth sells tickets to Broadway, Off Broadway, music, and dance events the day of the performance at 25 or 50 percent off the ticket price (plus a $2.50 service charge per ticket). They post the available shows outside the booth on boards, which change throughout the day. They accept payments only in cash or traveler's checks. As a rule, you can be sure you won't find tickets available to the newest, hottest show. The lines can be long, particularly on weekends and holidays. The tickets, however, are for some of the best seats in the theaters. There is also a downtown location, which is temporarily located in Bowling Green Park Plaza because of the September 11 attack (call for location details). At the downtown location only, you are able to buy matinee tickets the day before the performance. The downtown hours are Monday through Friday, 11:00 A.M. to 5:30 P.M.; Saturday, 11:00 A.M. to 3:30 P.M. The Duffy Square hours are Monday through

Saturday, 3:00 to 8:00 P.M. (for evening tickets); Wednesday and Saturday, 10:00 A.M. to 2:00 P.M. (for matinee tickets); and Sunday, 11:00 A.M. to closing (for matinee and evening tickets).

JUST PLAIN FREE THEATER

THE ACTORS STUDIO ACTING SCHOOL
159 Bleecker Street (between Thompson and Sullivan Streets)
(212) 479–1778
www.newschool.edu/academic/drama
From the end of January through May, the Actors Studio presents a repertory season of performances by their graduating MFA students who are completing a three-year training program. Each evening consists of three pieces; many are well-known classic and contemporary plays as well as original material written by the graduate writing students. All performances are free, but reservations are required.

AMERICAN ACADEMY OF DRAMATIC ARTS
120 Madison Avenue (between 30th and 31st Streets)
(212) 686–9244, ext. 313
www.aada.org
Some of the most legendary stars of stage and screen have trained at this institution, including Lauren Bacall, Spencer Tracy, John Cassavetes, Grace Kelly, Cecil B. De Mille, Danny DeVito, Colleen Dewhurst, Anne Bancroft, Ron Leibman, Jason Robards Jr., Kirk Douglas, and many others. To date academy alumni have received nominations for seventy Oscars, fifty-four Tonys, and 181 Emmys. From September through February the Academy Company—made up of third-year students—presents a season of free productions. Here's a chance to say you saw them when. Click on "Programs" on the Web site or call for dates and schedules.

AMERICAN THEATER WING
CUNY-TV, 365 Fifth Avenue (at 34th Street)
(212) 765–0606
www.tonys.org or www.cuny.tv
The folks who bring you the Tony Awards also present a free series of seminars called "Working in the Theater" that examines the making and the state of the American theater. The seminars take place in April and October and bring together the New York theater community's most respected and accomplished actors, playwrights, directors, designers,

composers, producers, and agents. The conversations are often very candid and interactive, giving anyone interested in the how-tos of Broadway a great behind-the-scenes view of the theater world.

CHERRY LANE ALTERNATIVE
38 Commerce Street (between Bedford and Hudson Streets)
(212) 989–2159
www.cherrylanetheatre.com
Cherry Lane's Mentor Project presents a series of readings and showcase productions of new plays by emerging playwrights who have worked one-on-one with such established writers as Tony Kushner, Wendy Wasserstein, Alfred Uhry, Craig Lucus, and others. The readings and productions happen February through June; call or check the Web site for details.

CIRCLE EAST
(212) 252–5510
www.circleeast.com
This theater company with a vast list of talented writers and performers hosts free workshops of new plays Monday evening at 7:00 P.M. and intimate salon readings on Thursday at 3:00 P.M.. Some of the writers in the company include Lanford Wilson, Craig Lucus, William Hoffman, Terrence McNally, Paula Vogel, as well as many lesser-known, but equally talented folks.

52ND STREET PROJECT
Ensemble Studio Theater
549 West 52nd Street (between Tenth and Eleventh Avenues)
(212) 642–5052
www.52project.org
A program through Ensemble Studio Theater that creates short theater pieces by or for the children of Hell's Kitchen in collaboration with professional theater artists. While these may not be Broadway productions, they are surprisingly well put together and offer an evening that is always full of laughter, original music, and a lot of talent (community and professional).

HB PLAYWRIGHTS FOUNDATION
124 Bank Street (between Greenwich and Washington Streets)
(212) 989–7856
Established by acting legends Herbert Berghoff and Uta Hagen in 1965 as an offshoot of their renowned (and low cost!) acting school, the theater presents four productions a year (always free) and has featured many well-

Standing Room Only

Dying to see that boffo Broadway hit, but you don't have the hundred bucks for the ticket or can't wait the six months until one becomes available? Standing room is what you're looking for. Many, but not all, Broadway theaters sell standing room tickets. They're available only on the day of the performance and only if the show is completely sold out. It will cost you somewhere between $15 and $25 for the honor of standing to watch the show. The good news is that you'll have a great view: Standing room is directly behind the orchestra seating. And if you get tired, keep your eyes peeled for an empty seat for the second act. Check with the specific box offices for details.

established writers, actors, and directors. In recent years the company has given birth to such productions as *Mrs. Klein, Collected Stories,* and others that have moved to larger pay-for-your-ticket venues. The best way to find out about the performances is to call the office during business hours and ask to be added to their mailing list.

JEAN COCTEAU REPERTORY (BOUWERIE LANE THEATRE)

(see page 10 for details)
Monday evenings at 7:00 P.M.
A series of readings of plays considered "New Classics," with symposiums and receptions often following.

THE JUILLIARD SCHOOL

60 Lincoln Center Plaza (Broadway and 65th Street on plaza level)
(212) 769–7406
www.juilliard.edu

 You must call to get on the drama division's mailing list to find out about the productions.

See tomorrow's stars of stage and screen today. This is considered the preeminent conservatory for actors in the country, and they present a full schedule of productions throughout the school year featuring students at every level of development. Often productions are put together by well-

known directors—both faculty members and guest artists. All performances in the fall and early spring are free, though tickets are required and
go fast. Call to put your name on the drama division's mailing list to get
information on the free performances. Every spring they remount all of
these productions for a spring Repertory, but they charge for those tickets ($15). To get the free tickets, line up at the box office on the day
they become available, usually two weeks before the performances begin;
otherwise you'll probably be sold out of the event. You can also line up
an hour before the show to try to get in on a standby basis. Performances
by the music division are also free, though not those by the dance and
opera departments.

NEW DRAMATISTS
424 West 44th Street (between Ninth and Tenth Avenues)
(212) 757–6960
www.newdramatists.org
New Dramatists is an organization devoted to developing playwrights, both up-and-coming and established, along with their
material. They conduct an ongoing series of readings and workshops
of new plays, musicals, and screenplays staffed with many leading
actors and directors from the New York theater scene. Performances
take place throughout the week (Monday through Friday) in the late
afternoon or evening. All readings are free, and almost all are open
to the public. Check the Web site or call for a calendar of events.

NEW YORK SHAKESPEARE FESTIVAL/THE
PUBLIC THEATER
425 Lafayette Street (at Astor Place)
(212) 260–2400
www.publictheater.org
From the people who bring you Shakespeare in Central Park every
summer come other free theater events throughout the year. The
"Conversations With . . ." series is usually held on the third Sunday
of each month, showcasing new and emerging talent through discussions, performances, symposia, and other events. These conversations often use the talents of those involved in productions on the
stages of the Public. Every spring they hold a two-week festival of
readings and workshops called New Work Now!; many of the pieces
presented here have later ended up on their main stage, including
the plays *Stop Kiss, References to Salvador Dali Make Me Hot,
Topdog/Underdog,* and others.

NEW YORK THEATRE WORKSHOP
(see page 12 for information)
"Mondays at 3" is an ongoing play-reading series of new plays, musicals, and performances in development. It often includes the works of leading artists of the American theater. Also look out for the Just Add Water Festival of new play readings every spring and fall. In-depth discussions with the playwright often follow the readings.

NEW YORK UNIVERSITY GRADUATE ACTING PROGRAM
721 Broadway (between Waverly and Washington Streets)
111 Second Avenue (between 6th and 7th Streets)
(212) 998–1921
www.nyu.edu/tisch/gradacting/html/calendar.html

THE CATCH Only second-year productions are free.

One of the most respected graduate acting programs in the country has a distinguished alumnus list that boasts the likes of Billy Crudup, Camryn Manheim, Marcia Gay Harden, Barry Bostwick, Tony Kushner, and many others. See full productions of classics and contemporary plays mounted by the second-year students (they charge for the third-year student productions). Tickets are available one week before performances begin and sell out very quickly for these intimate performance spaces. Check the Web site or call for schedule and details.

PERFORMANCE SPACE NBC (PSNBC)
Here Performance Art Café
145 Sixth Avenue (on Dominick, between Spring and Broome Streets)
(212) 647–0202, ext. 301
www.nbc.com/psnbc
Monday through Thursday at 7:30 P.M.
Sponsored by NBC (the TV network), this space is designed to develop and nurture writers, actors, and comedic performers and eventually make use of them on the small screen. All performances are free and worth checking out. Reservations are required. Tuesday night always features an alternative stand-up show; other evenings can be anything from one-acts to improv to who-knows-what.

RATTLESTICK THEATRE COMPANY
(see page 14 for information)
Two free readings every Tuesday as part of their Exposure Festival—at 3:00 and 8:00 P.M.

WOMEN'S PROJECT THEATRE
(see page 17 for information)
"First Looks" is a free reading series most Mondays at 4:00 P.M.

YORK THEATRE COMPANY
(see page 17 for information)
Presents free staged readings on new musicals most Monday nights at 7:30 P.M.

FREE WILL(IAM): FREE THEATER IN THE PARKS

SHAKESPEARE IN CENTRAL PARK
New York Shakespeare Festival/The Public Theater
Delacorte Theater
Turtle Pond (midpark at West 81st or East 79th Street)
(212) 539–8750
www.publictheater.org

The granddaddy of all Shakespeare in the Park festivals, now in its fifth decade of free performances in Central Park. They present star-studded productions each summer (at least one of which is always a Shakespeare play). They start handing out the free tickets at 1:00 P.M. each day at the Delacorte in Central Park, and from 1:00 to 3:00 P.M. at the Public Theater (425 Lafayette Street between East 4th Street and Astor Place). In recent years they have also started handing out tickets in various locations throughout the five boroughs; call for details. These tickets are always in demand, so plan to spend a while on line. But don't let that deter you: This event attracts a great cross section of people, and waiting on line is often as much fun, if not more, than the show itself. If you don't have the time to wait, take a chance and stop by the Delacorte box office at 7:30, when they release many reserved tickets.

Here are some other companies that bring the Bard and other works to a neighborhood near you. All the performances are free, but some of these companies are not shy about passing the hat at the end of the night. Call or check their Web sites for shows, times, and specific locations:

BOOMERANG THEATRE COMPANY, Prospect Park and other parks; (212) 501–4069; www.angelfire.com/ny3/boomerang.

CYPRECO THEATER GROUP, various parks and libraries throughout the five boroughs; (718) 626–7896.

GORILLA REP, Washington Square Park, Fort Tryon Park, and other locations; (212) 330–8086; www.gorillarep.org.

KINGS COUNTY SHAKESPEARE COMPANY, various Brooklyn parks; (718) 398–0546.

LITE THEATRE COMPANY, Prospect Park; (212) 414–7773; www.theliteco.org.

NEW YORK CLASSICAL THEATRE, West 103rd Street and Central Park West; (212) 252–4531.

SHAKESPEARE IN THE PARK(ING LOT), Ludlow Street (between Delancey and Broome); (212) 358–5096; www.expandedarts.com.

THEATER FOR THE NEW CITY, parks throughout the five boroughs; (212) 254–1109; www.theaterforthenewcity.org.

THEATREWORKS/USA, call for theater location; (212) 627–7373, www.theatreworksusa.org.

2TEXANS THEATRE COMPANY, Tompkins Square Park (East 7th Street between Avenues A and B); (212) 561–1815, www.2texans.com.

"I'll open my case, and I
might catch a coin, but all
ears may listen for free."

—Steve Forbert
"Grand Central Station, March 18, 1977"

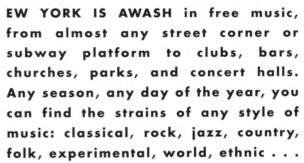

MUSIC: OF FREE I SING

NEW YORK IS AWASH in free music, from almost any street corner or subway platform to clubs, bars, churches, parks, and concert halls. Any season, any day of the year, you can find the strains of any style of music: classical, rock, jazz, country, folk, experimental, world, ethnic . . . if you can hum it, you can find it somewhere in New York for free. Particularly during the summer months, you can hardly turn around without being enticed into another amazing free performance at one of the many free concert series all over the city. This being New York, these venues attract top-name artists whom you'd usually have to pay top dollar to see. And I'm not talking about one great show a summer; this goes on week after week, all summer long. One thing to be aware of when attending free shows at many bars and clubs is they do often have a one-, two- or more-drink minimum, which could add up to a tidy sum. Check out the prices before you order, too; sometimes even a Coke could cost as much as $5.00.

ROCK, POP, FOLK AND ALTERNATIVE

ARLENE GROCERY
95 Stanton Street (between Ludlow and Orchard Streets)
(212) 358–1633
www.arlene-grocery.com

 Free shows Sunday through Thursday only.

This converted grocery store now serves up variety packs of every brand of music, with three to five bands a night playing styles including indie rock, alt, grunge, folk, ska, or heavy metal.

THE BACK FENCE
155 Bleecker Street (at Thompson Street)
(212) 475–9221
www.thebackfenceonline.com

 They charge admission on Saturday night only.

Straw on the floor, peanuts at the bar, and free classic, country, and folk rock six nights a week.

THE BAGGOT INN
82 West 3rd Street (between Thompson and Sullivan Streets)
(212) 477–0622
www.thebaggotinn.com

No cover or minimum for shows Sunday through Wednesday night only.

During the week you will find nights of bluegrass jams, acoustic open mike, blues, country, and rock.

B3 LOUNGE
33 Avenue B (at 3rd Street)
(212) 614–9755
www.b3restaurantandlounge.com

The downstairs lounge is a little like hanging out at your next-door neighbor's unfinished basement rec room . . . except this rec room comes with a full bar. This intimate performance space offers a variety of music and comedy performances throughout the week, including the popular Saturday-night open mike. The crowd can be loud (and not particularly interested in listening to the music). There is no minimum or cover ever.

THE C-NOTE
157 Avenue C (at 10th Street)
(212) 677–8142
www.thecnote.com

 ONE-DRINK MINIMUM PER ACT signs are posted, but not enforced.

This slim bar is all about the music, and the music is all over the place. On any given night you can hear five to seven acts playing any combination of acoustic, rock, folk, jump, jazz, fusion, funk, or Latin. On rare occasions, they do charge a cover, but primarily it's free music seven nights a week.

DEMPSEY'S PUB
61 Second Avenue (between 3rd and 4th Streets)
(212) 388–0662
www.thebaggotinn.com/dempseys
Grab your penny whistle and uilleann pipes and come on down to Dempsey's every Tuesday for a traditional Irish music seisun (jam session) at 8:00 P.M. Musicians and listeners welcome.

HANK'S SALOON
46 Third Avenue (at Atlantic Avenue)
Brooklyn
(718) 625–8003
www.hankstavern.com
Free live country/rock/rockabilly music Wednesday through Sunday night at this Brooklyn dive. Sunday night, don't miss the free barbecue. No cover, no minimum.

LAKESIDE LOUNGE
162 Avenue B (between 10th and 11th Streets)
(212) 529–8463
www.lakesidelounge.com

A honky-tonk bar with a band in the back room late nights. It's free, but sometimes you get what you pay for. They book some good rock bands who try their damndest to play above the roar of the crowd. No cover, no minimum.

THE LIVING ROOM

84 Stanton Street (at Allen Street)
(212) 533-7235
www.livingroomny.com

 One-drink minimum per act, loosely enforced.

Intimate, welcoming storefront bar/lounge. While it's a bit sparsely furnished for a Living Room (only one cozy chair and a lot of plain old restaurant tables and chairs), you'll find that the spirit of the spot lives up to the name. They book an eclectic lineup of acoustic and indie music types and attract a fun and attentive audience. This is a great place to hear music. They never charge a cover.

LUNA LOUNGE

171 Ludlow Street (between Houston and Stanton Streets)
(212) 260-2323
www.lunalounge.com

Loud, young, and pulsing with free live indie Rock six nights a week. (Monday features comedy, but they charge for that.) The bar's spacious (by New York standards) back room plays host to a number of bands every night. No cover, no drink minimum.

PADDY REILLYS MUSIC BAR

519 Second Avenue (at 29th Street)
(212) 686-1210
www.paddyreillys.com

 Free shows/no minimum Sunday through Thursday night (except some Tuesdays).

The definitive home of Irish music in New York. You'll find everything from Irish rock to traditional Irish music seisun on the schedule. Musicians are always welcome to join in on the seisun.

PARKSIDE LOUNGE

317 East Houston Street (at Attorney Street)
(212) 673–6270
www.parksidelounge.com

 Two-drink minimum that they do try to enforce—but "we're not gonna trow ya out if ya don't drink."

A local bar complete with pool table, pinball games, and a hip jukebox, along with a snazzy back room with live shows every night. You'll find a lot of local rock/alternative/blues bands most nights. They also have a comedy night every Tuesday and a very popular salsa night every Friday; bring your own instrument and join in. Shows are almost always free (except for the two-drink minimum).

POSTCRYPT COFFEEHOUSE

Columbia University
Basement of St. Paul's Chapel
116th Street and Broadway
(212) 854–1953
www.columbia.edu/cu/postcrypt/coffeehouse

This is one of the great hidden treasures of New York City. Since 1964, every Friday and Saturday night during the school year this small performance space (only about twenty-five seats) has been filled with the sounds of some of the top names in folk and acoustic music. Past performers have included David Bromberg, Jeff Buckley, Shawn Colvin, Ani DiFranco, John Gorka, Patty Larkin, Lisa Loeb, Ellis Paul, Martin Sexton, Tony Trischka, Suzanne Vega, Jerry Jeff Walker, and Dar Williams. No place in the city presents this music in a more pure form. Here acoustic means *acoustic*—no mikes, no nothing. Always brings in a crowd that is serious about hearing the music. They also serve cheap beer and brownies, but best of all, the popcorn is always free.

THE RED LION

151 Bleecker Street (between Thompson Street and Laguardia Place)
(212) 260–7979
www.goredlion.com

Free shows Monday through Thursday night.

A full schedule of rock bands attracts a very young crowd.

JAZZ AND BLUES

ARTHUR'S TAVERN
57 Grove Street (off Seventh Avenue South)
(212) 675–6879
www.arthurstavernnyc.com

Since 1937, Arthur's Tavern has been serving up a variety of music for every taste: straight-ahead jazz, New Orleans–style jazz, real Chicago blues. On Monday night for more than thirty-five years, it's been home to the same Dixieland jazz band. Stop by any time of night; there's always something going on. Never a cover or minimum.

DECADE
1117 First Avenue (at 61st Street)
(212) 835–5979
www.decadeNY.com

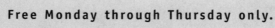 **Free Monday through Thursday only.**

This very swanky restaurant/bar offers up free jazz during the week from 6:00 to 9:30; the dance floor opens up for a DJ spinning dance hits from the 1950s to today. No cover, no minimum during the week.

DETOUR
349 East 13th Street (between First and Second Avenues)
(212) 533–6212
www.jazzatdetour.com

Two-drink minimum per set.

Seven nights a week the jazz flows freely from the stage of this intimate and cozy East Village bar. You'll hear everything from sweet soul jazz to postbop from a talented crew of local musicians. The music starts at 9:00 P.M. during the week, and 9:30 on the weekend.

55 BAR
55 Christopher Street (between Seventh Avenue South and 8th Street)
(212) 929–9883
www.55bar.com

Free shows on Sunday and Tuesday evenings only.

Since 1919, this Prohibition-era dive has been presenting top-of-the-line jazz, funk, and blues with no cover, minimum, or attitude every Sunday and Tuesday evening. They charge $3.00 to $15.00 cover on other nights, but the popcorn is always free.

Underground Music

For years the platforms of the New York City subway system have been the place to hear a varied, eclectic mix of music from all parts of the world played by some of the most talented (and sometimes not-so-talented) musicians around, all playing their hearts out for a handout. And for just as long, the police and MTA wished these folks would stop clogging up the subway's platforms and tunnels. They tried everything from ticketing to arresting offenders to get rid of them. It didn't work. The musicians stayed, and the quarters kept being tossed.

Finally, though, someone smart at the MTA convinced the city to give in to the old adage "If you can't beat 'em, join 'em" and organized the MTA Arts for Transit Music Under New York (MUNY) program. So now you'll find jazz bands, folk singers, didjery do players, steel drummers, tap dancers, break dancers, blues singers, salsa, and of course the ever-present Ecuadorian pan flute bands playing throughout the MTA system. MUNY holds auditions every spring at Vanderbilt Hall in Grand Central Station (open to the public) and has twenty-three locations where there are more than 150 performances every week. Some of the most popular sites are Grand Central Terminal, Penn Station, Times Square Station, 42nd Street (Sixth and Eighth Avenue stations), Grand Central Shuttle, Columbus Circle Station, Union Square, and Astor Place. Performances take place throughout the day and into the late night. For more information, check out www.mta.nyc.ny.us/mta/aft/muny1.htm or call (212) 878–7452.

Of course, you'll still find plenty of other musicians littered throughout the system. My personal favorite is singer-songwriter Kathleen Mock (www.mockmusic.com), whose haunting melodies and beautifully resonant voice ring out in stations around the Upper West Side. When you're waiting for that late-night train to finally arrive, you'll be glad these folks were there to help you through the long wait.

GROOVE
125 MacDougal Street (at West 3rd Street)
(212) 254–9393
www.clubgroovenyc.com
Live rhythm and blues, funk, and hip hop. Free admission every night.

101 ON SEVENTH
101 Seventh Avenue South (at West 4th Street)
(212) 620–4000
Live rhythm and blues 7 nights a week.

PARLOR ENTERTAINMENT
555 Edgecombe Avenue, Studio 3F (between 159th and 160th
Streets)
(212) 781–6595
Occasionally you come across one of those events that you feel privileged to
have been a part of. Well, that's exactly what goes on every weekend at Ms.
Marjorie Eliot's North Harlem apartment. Marjorie graciously welcomes you
into her living room, hallway, kitchen, and anyplace else you can find some
space to listen to some of the purest, sweetest, swingin'est jazz you will hear
anywhere and for any price. And here, of course, there isn't any price. The
music begins at 4:00 P.M. with an informal jam session on Saturday and a pol-
ished performance on Sunday. Every week Ms. Eliot brings together an
ensemble of guest musicians and fifty or more of her closest friends for an
afternoon of joyful music. And anyone who attends quickly becomes one of
those dear friends. The atmosphere is so warm and comfortable, and the
music played so intimately, you'll think you're sitting in a friend's house listening to some of your favorite tunes. Which, in fact, you are.

CLASSICAL MUSIC

BROOKLYN HEIGHTS MUSIC SOCIETY
(718) 499–2025
www.brooklynheightsorchestra.org
Currently in search of a permanent home, this well-respected community
orchestra made up of amateur, student, retired, semiprofessional, and professional musicians brings symphony and chamber music concerts to
libraries, churches, and temples around Brooklyn. You are also welcome to
bring your own bassoon, tuba, or triangle and join in on their open
rehearsals every Monday night. Check the Web site for details. Performances
and rehearsal are always free, but they are happy to accept contributions.

CARNEGIE HALL NEIGHBORHOOD CONCERT SERIES

Locations throughout the five boroughs
(212) 903–9670
www.carnegiehall.org
For more than twenty-five years, the distinguished hall has presented over eighty concerts a year (September through April) in neighborhoods throughout the five boroughs in libraries, churches, and community centers. The series presents a mix of classical, jazz, pop, and folk music; all shows are free and open to all. For schedule and location information, call or click on the "Education" menu at their Web site.

DONNELL LIBRARY CENTER

20 West 53rd Street (between Fifth and Sixth Avenues)
(212) 621–0619
www.nypl.org
This library presents an extensive calendar of musical performances throughout the week, including classical, jazz, show tunes, opera, and more. All performances are free.

THE INTERCHURCH CENTER

475 Riverside Drive (between 119th and 120th Streets)
(212) 870–2933
www.interchurch-center.org
This interdenominational center for all faiths offers free concerts every Wednesday at 12:05 P.M., September through May. Performances last about thirty minutes; the programs range from string quartets to woodwind ensembles, traditional African folk music to Celtic songs and dances, medieval to jazz, vocal soloist to choir, piano to organ, emerging artists to established professionals.

THE JUILLIARD SCHOOL

60 Lincoln Center Plaza (Broadway and 65th Street on the plaza level)
(212) 769–7406
www.juilliard.edu

Free tickets go quickly.

See the leading artists of tomorrow, today. This is the preeminent conservatory for classical musicians in the country, and they present a huge array of classical, chamber music, and jazz concerts by students and faculty throughout the year. Most of the performances are free, though some require tickets. To get tickets for these events, stop by the box office on

How Do You Get to Carnegie Hall?

Forget about practicing—just join Norman Seaman's Concert/Theater Club and he can get you there (and into Lincoln Center, Merkin Hall, and others) for hundreds of concerts a year for free. The Concert/Theater Club is a mom and pop organization that has been filling seats at major concert halls and theaters all around the city for more than fifty years. Primarily offering the best seats in the house to classical performances, the club also offers its members the chance to attend the occasional Broadway production, Off Broadway play, and film screenings. One-year memberships to the club will run you $29.00 for single tickets to all events, $39.95 for two tickets to all events, or $49.95 for four tickets to all events. For more information call (212) 330–7932 (daily offering hotline) or (845) 279–8296. To join send a check to Norman Seaman's Concert/Theater Club, 130 Saint Edwards Street, Brooklyn, NY 11201.

the day they become available; otherwise you may be sold out of the event. You can also line up an hour before the show to try to get in on a standby basis. Venues are throughout Lincoln Center and the Juilliard School, and scheduled in the afternoon and evening all week long. Check the Web site or pick up a copy of the performance schedule at the box office. Performances by the drama division are also free, though not the dance and opera departments.

MANHATTAN SCHOOL OF MUSIC

120 Claremont Avenue (between 121st Street and Seminary Row)
(212) 749–2802, ext. 4538
www.msmnyc.edu
A full schedule of free classical and jazz concerts.

MANNES COLLEGE OF MUSIC

150 West 85th Street (between Columbus and Amsterdam Avenues)
(212) 496–8524
www.mannes.edu
A full schedule of free orchestral, chamber music, and jazz concerts throughout the school year.

TEMPLE EMANU-EL
10 East 66th Street (between Fifth and Madison Avenues)
(212) 744–1400
www.emanuelnyc.org
This largest house of Jewish worship in the world offers eight to ten free classical concerts from October through May. The performances include a young artists series, chamber orchestras, and opera. Call to get on their mailing list.

TRINITY CHURCH
74 Trinity Place (Broadway at Wall Street)
(212) 602–0747
www.trinitywallstreet.org

 $2.00 suggested contribution, but nothing required.

Their "Noonday Concert" series offers performances every Monday at noon at St. Paul's Chapel (Broadway and Fulton Street) and Thursday at 1:00 P.M. at Trinity Church. Both of these churches are steeped in American history and National Historic Landmarks.

OUTDOOR SUMMER CONCERTS

During the summer months New York is the Mecca, Medina, Jerusalem, and Emerald City of free music. Almost any open green space transforms into a concert hall for an amazing array of established stars and cutting-edge performers of practically every genre of music. Many of these venues have become quite popular over the years—which means you should be sure to show up early to claim your space on the lawn or in the stands.

BATTERY PARK PLAZA SUMMER CONCERT SERIES
1 Battery Park Plaza (between Pearl and Bridge Streets, Whitehall Street side)
(212) 407–2429
Wednesday at 12:15 P.M.
Local musicians of every sort (Dixieland, folk, rock, classical, and more) entertain the lunchtime crowd every Wednesday.

BROOKLYN CONSERVATORY OF MUSIC

58 Seventh Avenue (at Lincoln Place)
Park Slope, Brooklyn
(718) 622–3300
www.brooklynconservatory.com
Friday at 5:00 P.M., June through August.
One of the country's oldest community music schools. Their "Garden Concert" Series (which takes place on the front stoop—so much for the garden) offers a schedule of mostly jazz and some classical performances by the faculty of the conservatory.

BRYANT PARK

Sixth Avenue between 41st and 42nd Streets
(212) 768–4242
www.bryantpark.org
Known mostly for the hugely popular film series on Monday night, the park also hosts a great deal of concerts and performances throughout the summer. You will find the likes of the B52s, Carly Simon, the Beach Boys, and other big-name groups performing in the park for the TV show *Good Morning America*. Also, classical, jazz, and Broadway performances in the afternoon and evening. Check the Web site for the extensive schedule.

CELEBRATE BROOKLYN

Prospect Park Bandshell (Prospect Park West and 9th Street)
Park Slope, Brooklyn
(718) 855–7882, ext. 45
www.celebratebrooklyn.org
June through August.
Brooklyn's popular free series presents a star-studded schedule of everything from free films to spoken word and dance performances, rock, jazz, Latin, folk, and world music.

CENTRAL PARK SUMMERSTAGE

Rumsey Playfield
72nd Street, midpark
(212) 360–2756
www.summerstage.org
June through August.
If New York is the Promised Land of free concerts during the summer, this is the Wailing Wall. The schedule runs the entire length of the summer, with performances almost every night of the week and a wildly varied schedule that runs the gamut from opera to hip-hop, from world to teeny-bopper pop.

You're likely to find names you're familiar with—like Joan Jett, Randy Newman, David Byrne, or the Indigo Girls—and just as likely to be wowed by performers whose names you never would have come across if not for SummerStage's daring programming. There are also evenings devoted to spoken word and dance. Seating is on a first-come, first-served basis; for some of the more popular shows, the line starts hours before the gates open.

FREE CONCERTS IN PARKS
Neighborhood parks throughout Brooklyn, the Bronx, and Manhattan
(212) 360–8290
www.cityparksfoundation.org
July and August.
The name says it all. The free concerts (in Parks) are a mix of well-known oldies rock and roll, rhythm and blues, funk, and Latin groups. Call or check the Web site for locations and schedule.

HARLEM MEER PERFORMANCE FESTIVAL
Charles A. Dana Discovery Center
Central Park (110th Street and Central Park North)
(212) 860–1370
www.centralparknyc.org
Sunday at 4:00 P.M., June through August.
Upper Central Park makes a beautiful backdrop for this free concert series showcasing established and emerging jazz, Latin, dance, and gospel artists.

HARLEM WEEK/HARLEM JAZZ AND MUSIC FESTIVAL
Throughout Harlem and Manhattan
(212) 862–8477
www.discoverharlem.com
August.
What started out as a one-day event has grown into a monthlong celebration of African American life in America. The festival offers many concerts throughout the month in different locations around Harlem and Manhattan, as well as films, lectures, sporting events, street fairs, and more. Most events are free. Check the Web site for this year's schedule.

JAZZMOBILE
154 West 127th Street (between Lenox and Seventh Avenues)
(212) 866–4900 or (212) 866–3616 (concert hot line)
www.jazzmobile.org
Various locations around the five boroughs.

Since 1964, Jazzmobile has been bringing the music to the people by presenting a lineup of world-class musicians in parks, libraries, schools, and street corners all around New York and the surrounding areas. They also offer free Saturday workshops and master classes for students, ages seven and up at PS 197 in Harlem with such artists as Max Roach, Branford Marsalis, and Donald Byrd. Check the Web site for details.

LEGENDS AT LUNCHTIME
Metrotech Center (between Flatbush Avenue, Jay, Johnson, and Willoughby Streets)
Downtown Brooklyn
(718) 636–4100
www.bam.org
Thursday at noon, June through August.
Brown-bag it over to Brooklyn every Thursday during the summer for the Rhythm and Blues Festival at Metrotech. The series lives up to its name with shows by the likes of Dr. John, Bo Diddly, The Robert Cray Band, and Burning Spear.

MARTIN LUTHER KING JR. CONCERT SERIES
Wingate Field (across the street from Kings County Hospital)
Winthrop Street (between Brooklyn and Kingston Avenues)
(718) 469–1912
www.brooklynconcerts.com
Monday, July and August.
Stars of gospel, soul, funk, and jazz perform. Performers have included Mighty Clouds of Joy, Teena Marie, Stephanie Mills, the O'Jays, and the Gap Band.

MET IN THE PARKS
Parks throughout the five boroughs
(212) 362–6000
www.metopera.org
June.
For three weeks in June, the world-renowned Metropolitan Opera Company sheds the pomp and pretense of the opera hall and presents concert performances to the masses in Central Park and other parks throughout the five boroughs. Check the Web site for schedule and locations.

MUSIC AT CASTLE CLINTON
Battery Park
(212) 835–2789
www.downtownny.com
July 4th and Thursday evening in July and early August.
The season opens with a large open-air concert in Battery Park on the Fourth of July weekend, drawing thousands of listeners; then the shows move into the smaller space at Castle Clinton. Tickets are required (free, but limited) for the Castle Clinton shows and given out on a first-come, first-served basis at 5:00 P.M. on the day of the show. Past performers have included Crash Test Dummies, Taj Mahal, Mark Cohen, Billy Bragg, Emmylou Harris, Shawn Colvin, and Junior Brown.

NAUMBURG ORCHESTRAL CONCERTS
Naumburg Bandshell (Fifth Avenue and 72nd Street)
(212) 262–6927
Tuesday evening, late June to early August.
It may not be the biggest or the most well known, but it is the oldest continuous series of free outdoor concerts in the United States. It includes performances by the New York Chamber Symphony, Empire Brass, and others.

NEW YORK PHILHARMONIC
Concerts in the Parks
(212) 875–5709
www.newyorkphilharmonic.org
July.
For more than thirty-five years, the Philharmonic has brought millions of people into the parks for what they call "Priceless Music Absolutely Free." With guest musicians and conductors, they present two programs of classical and popular music in city parks throughout the five boroughs and always cap the evening off with a spectacular fireworks display.

RIVER MUSIC
Battery Park City Parks
Robert F. Wagner Jr. Park (at Battery Place)
(212) 267–9700
www.bpcparks.org
Thursday evening, July and August.
Bring a picnic diner and enjoy the spectacular sunset views of the lower Hudson while you enjoy these jazz, blues, funk, and fusion performances. Past performers have included Hiram Bullock, Glen Velez, and Howard Fishman.

SEASIDE SUMMER CONCERT SERIES
Asser Levy Park (Sea Breeze and Ocean Avenues)
Brighton Beach, Brooklyn
(718) 469–1912
www.brooklynconcerts.com
Thursday evening, July and August.
Travel out to the heart of Brooklyn and travel back in time to this series that features many of the biggest names in music and comedy from the 1950s, 1960s, 1970s and 1980s (golden oldies, disco, rock, and stand-up comedy). In past years they have featured appearances by Gladys Knight, Jay Black and the Americans, Todd Rundgren, Pat Benatar, Kenny Rogers, the Temptations, David Brenner, the Village People, and others.

SOUTH STREET SEAPORT
Pier 17 (at Fulton and South Streets)
(212) SEA–PORT (732–7678)
www.southstreetseaport.com
Tuesday through Sunday noon and 5:30 P.M., May through September.
Starting with a huge Cinco de Mayo Festival and running throughout the spring and summer, the South Street Seaport presents lunchtime and after-work concerts in every style of music, from country, folk, and rock to gospel, jazz, and Latin. The performers often include well-known acts as well as up-and-coming artists. Many summer weekends are also filled with full-day music, sports, and other festivals. Any day you can count on running across your fair share of jugglers, mimes, magicians, and other buskers to keep you entertained. Monday is the only day they don't schedule any official programs. Call or check the Web site for up-to-date information.

SUMMER IN THE SQUARE
Union Square (14th to 17th Streets between Park Avenue and University Place)
(212) 460–1208
www.unionsquarenyc.org
Wednesday at 12:30 P.M., June through August.
Stop by the park for a midday, midweek jolt of music. Every week brings something completely different, including jazz, classical, blues, Brazilian, theater, and more. Make a day of it with storytelling at 5:00 P.M. and dance performances at 6:00 P.M.

WALL STREET CONCERT SERIES
Various locations around Lower Manhattan
(212) 835–2789
Monday and Wednesday, noon–2:00 P.M.
Local jazz and classical musicians entertain a lunchtime crowd.

MUGGER: "Don't make a move. This is a stick-up. Your money or your life! . . . Look, bud, I said your money or your life"

JACK BENNY: "I'm thinking it over."

FILM: CHEAP SHOTS

NOW THAT WORLD WIDE Cinemas is a distant memory (what most cheap New Yorkers used to lovingly refer to as "the three-dollar theater") and prices are topping $10 a ticket, there has never been a greater need to find places to see movies without spending the moolah. If you've ever been among the throngs of people camped out at Bryant Park on a summer Monday evening, you know what I mean. Well, Bryant Park is only the beginning of the cheap cinema offerings throughout the city. From outdoor screenings under the stars during the summer to bars, libraries, and even theaters throughout the year, here is your list of where to get your fix of free flicks.

FREE MOVIES BY THE WEEK
(YEAR-ROUND)

TIME	MONDAY	TUESDAY	WEDNESDAY	THURSDAY	FRIDAY	SATURDAY	SUNDAY
MULTIPLE SCREENINGS: Call for schedule		French Institute (with membership)					
2:00 P.M.			St. Agnes Library Baychester Library (every other week)	Bloomingdale Library	58th Street Library	Van Nest Library	
2:15 P.M.							
2:30 P.M.			Donnell Library				
2:45 P.M.							
3:00 P.M.							
3:15 P.M.							
3:30 P.M.							
3:45 P.M.							
4:00 P.M.							
4:15 P.M.							
4:30 P.M.					MoMA (after 4:30 P.M.)		
4:45 P.M.							
5:00 P.M.							
5:15 P.M.							
5:30 P.M.			New Amsterdam Library				
5:45 P.M.							
6:00 P.M.	Jefferson Market Library			Instituto Cervantes at CUNY Sony Wonder (every other week)			
6:15 P.M.			Instituto Cervantes at King Juan Carlos I Center				
6:30 P.M.							
6:45 P.M.							
7:00 P.M.		Halcyon			Deutsches Haus (selected weeks)		
7:15 P.M.							
7:30 P.M.							
7:45 P.M.							
8:00 P.M.		Axis Company	Void	Czech Center (every other week)			
8:15 P.M.							
8:30 P.M.							
8:45 P.M.							
9:00 P.M.							
9:15 P.M.							
9:30 P.M.			The Pourhouse (last Wednesday of the month)				
9:45 P.M.							

FREE FLICKS

AXIS COMPANY
1 Sheridan Square (West 4th Street between Sixth and Seventh Avenues)
(212) 807–9300
www.axiscompany.org
Tuesday at 8:00 P.M.
"Free Movie Tuesdays" happen every week here throughout the year. The films run the gamut from classics *(Jaws, Willy Wonka and the Chocolate Factory)* to almost recent releases. The films are shown on a big screen in this small theater, and are always preceded by a trailer for their upcoming theater projects (that's why they try to get you in there). The box office opens at 7:30 P.M. for an 8:00 start. Sometimes there's even some free popcorn thrown into the deal.

BROOKLYN BRIDGE PARK FILM SERIES
Empire–Fulton Ferry State Park (between the Brooklyn and Manhattan Bridges)
(718) 802–0603
www.brooklynbridgepark.org
Thursday night, June through August.
Under the shadow of the Brooklyn Bridge, watch films that either were shot in, are about, or were made by people from . . . Brooklyn! *(Do the Right Thing, Saturday Night Fever, Moonstruck,* and more . . . .)

BRYANT PARK SUMMER FILM FESTIVAL
West 40th to West 41st Streets (between Fifth and Sixth Avenues)
(212) 512–5700
www.hbobryantparkfilm.com or www.bryantpark.org
Monday at nightfall, June through August.
This is the granddaddy of all free film screenings in New York. It has become incredibly popular, and as a result you need to get there mighty early if you have any hope of claiming a piece of the greenery for your own. They start letting people onto the lawn at 5:00 P.M. Since HBO foots the bill for this event, you can be sure you'll get a preview of something coming soon to a friendly cable network near you. There is always a cartoon before the feature, and then you can join the crowd dancing to the HBO trailer just before the film begins (don't ask me why). The features on the huge screen range from cinema classics *(Doctor Zhivago, Rear Window, An American in Paris)* to kitschy favorites *(Viva Las Vegas, The Wild One).*

FREE MOVIES BY THE WEEK
(SUMMER)

TIME	MONDAY	TUESDAY	WEDNESDAY	THURSDAY	FRIDAY	SATURDAY	SUNDAY
6:00 P.M.				Sony Wonder (every week)			
NIGHTFALL	Bryant Park		Movies under the Stars	Brooklyn Bridge	Chelsea		
	Flying Saucer		DEBNA	Celebrate Brooklyn	Open Cine		

CELEBRATE BROOKLYN
Prospect Park Bandshell (Prospect Park West and 9th Street)
Park Slope, Brooklyn
(718) 855–7882, ext. 45
www.celebratebrooklyn.org
Thursday at 8:00 P.M., June through August.
Brooklyn's popular free series presents everything from free films to spoken word and dance performance, rock, jazz, Latin, folk, and world music. Classic and silent films are often accompanied by live contemporary music and performers.

CHELSEA SUMMER CLASSIC FILM FESTIVAL
Pier 63 (Twelfth Avenue and 23rd Street)
(212) 989–9090
Friday at 8:00 or 8:30 P.M., from July 4 to Labor Day.
Located on a still somewhat undiscovered pier along the Hudson, this outdoor film series is one that keeps you safe from the elements with an awning for the bandshell—no rainouts here. They show classic films of the 1940s, 1950s, and 1960s, and even throw in a program with extensive historic articles about the films. A bar and kitchen are available for you to buy reasonably priced drinks, dinner, and, of course, popcorn.

CZECH CENTER
1109 Madison Avenue (at 83rd Street)
(212) 288–0830
www.czechcenter.com
Thursday at 8:00 P.M. Every other week throughout the year.
Shows new and old films from the Czech Republic with English subtitles.

DEUTSCHES HAUS
42 Washington Mews (near University Place)
(212) 990–8660
www.nyu.edu/deutscheshaus
Selected Fridays at 7:00 P.M., and other times.
This cultural center for all things German regularly holds free films screenings. Recent series have focused on film versions of Kafka's novels, gay films in early German cinema, and the films of Marlene Dietrich, as well as contemporary films from Germany. Most screenings are held on Friday evening, but there are others scattered throughout the week on their schedule. Often films are accompanied by lectures and live performances. Call or check the Web site for schedule and details.

DUKE ELLINGTON BOULEVARD NEIGHBORHOOD ASSOCIATION (DEBNA)
La Perla Garden
105th Street (between Manhattan and Columbus Avenues)
(212) 340–8067
Wednesday at dusk, June through August.
This small uptown community garden plays host to a big selection of films, from fun cult classics to Hollywood blockbusters.

FLYING SAUCER
494 Atlantic Avenue (between Nevins Street and Third Avenue)
Brooklyn
(718) 522–1383
Monday night at Dusk, June through August.
This coffeehouse shows fun sci-fi films *(Barbarella, When Worlds Collide)* in their outside garden during the summer.

FRENCH INSTITUTE/ALLIANCE FRANÇAISE
Florence Gould Hall
55 East 59th Street (between Madison and Park Avenues)
(212) 355–6160
www.fiaf.org
Tuesday afternoon and evening.

You must be a French Institute member.

While not exactly free, for fans of French films this is a pretty worthwhile deal. If you're a member of the French Institute ($75.00 for a single or $115.00 for a family), you can attend the weekly Cine Club screenings every

Who Wants to Be a Moviemaker?

Do you ever find yourself walking out of a movie thinking I could do better than that? Or do you just know you could be the next Scorsese, if you knew where to start? Well, here's your chance to put your money (or should I say time?) where your mouth is. By volunteering your time at schools and facilities like Film/Video Arts (50 Broadway, between Exchange Place and Morris Street; 212-673-9361) or Downtown Community Television Center (87 Lafayette Street, between White and Walker Streets; 212-966-4510), you are able to take classes and use their equipment and facilities free of charge. Both ask for a commitment of approximately sixteen hours a week doing administrative or production work in exchange for the free ride. For more information, see the chapter titled Education: Cents-Less Smarts.

Tuesday for free (otherwise it costs $8.00 each week). This usually consists of a double feature, often of recent popular favorites as well as classics and lesser-known films. All films are shown in French with English subtitles.

HALCYON
227 Smith Street (between Butler and Douglas Streets)
Carroll Gardens, Brooklyn
(718) 260-9299
www.halcyonline.com
Tuesday at 7:00 P.M.
Stop by for Keepin' It Reel Tuesdays at this hip-loungy bar/restaurant/record shop. Every week it's another cult classic *(Spinal Tap, Clockwork Orange, Liquid Sky, Blade Runner)*. Admission and the popcorn are always free, and the movie is followed by a DJ spinning a creative blend of house music until midnight. Call or visit to find out what's going on this week.

INSTITUTO CERVANTES
King Juan Carlos I Center, 53 Washington Square South (between Thompson and Sullivan Streets); Wednesday at 6:15 P.M.

CUNY Graduate Center, 365 Fifth Avenue (at 34th Street); Thursday at 6:00 P.M.

(212) 689-4232
www.institutocervantes.org

For lovers of Spanish and Latin American films or English-language films that deal with those parts of the world, there is no better destination than these two weekly film series put together by the Cervantes Institute. They also offer free panel discussions, lectures, and a great library (see page 179). For more information on other activities, call or check their Web site.

IRIS & B. GERALD CANTOR FILM CENTER AT NYU

36 East 8th Street (between Broadway and University Place)
(212) 998–4100
Every week during the school year, the center holds many screenings of international films, Hollywood hits, and student films. Some events are limited to NYU students; others are free and open to the public. Call or drop by for a schedule.

MOVIES UNDER THE STARS

Erie Lackawanna Train Plaza (Hudson River and N.J. Transit train station)
Hoboken, New Jersey
(201) 420–2207
www.jerseycityonline.com/hoboken
Wednesday at 8:00 or 8:30 P.M., June through August.
For the cost of a ride on the PATH train ($1.50), hop over to Hoboken where they show many recent hits and blockbusters in this summer series.

MUSEUM OF MODERN ART (MoMA)

11 West 53rd Street (between Fifth and Sixth Avenues)
(212) 708–9480
Free Friday, 4:30–8:15 P.M.
The museum has two movie theaters that are free with admission to the museum—and on Friday afternoon and evening, that's free, too (well technically it's "pay what you wish," but . . .). They show classic and contemporary independent and art films. Call for a schedule.

OCULARIS

Galapagos Art and Performance Space
70 North 6th Street (between Wythe and Kent Streets)
Williamsburg, Brooklyn
(718) 388–8713
www.ocularis.net
Ocularis runs a number of art film series in Williamsburg, Long Island City, and Astoria, many outdoors during the summer and others continuing

Everyone's a Critic

Here's your chance to let Hollywood know what you think of their films. Many major film studios run private screenings of soon-to-be-released films. They're hoping to gauge response, figure out how to market the movie, learn what changes might be needed, or simply see if the movie's any good. There's no way to necessarily get on a list to see these previews, because they want a random sampling of people, but they are constantly going on and there are ways to increase your chances of getting an invitation.

You'll often find people handing out screening passes in front of multiplexes around New York (particularly Loews Lincoln Square–Broadway between 67th and 68th Streets) and Tower Records (66th Street and Broadway location). If you see someone handing out passes, don't be afraid to approach and ask for one. These folks are paid by the number of people they can get to show up at the screenings. If you promise to show up, they want you. They are usually (though not always) looking for people between the ages seventeen and thirty-four, but they don't check IDs. And they won't let anyone involved in the entertainment industry into the screenings. If that's you, when they ask what you do for a living, remember to embrace your inner accountant.

indoors throughout the year. The screenings are in conjunction with institutions like P.S. 1 Contemporary Art Center, the Asia Society, the African Film Festival, and others. They show documentaries, experimental and avant-garde films, contemporary and emerging artist flicks, as well as features from around the world (in other words, you are not going to see *Terminator 3* here). Screenings are often accompanied by live music and dance. Some films are free, others are not; check the Web site for a detailed schedule.

OPEN CINE
De Salvio Playground (at Mulberry and Spring Streets)
www.opencine.com
Friday night, June through September, at nightfall.
This is absolutely the Anti–Bryant Park. A splat of white paint on the far end of a basketball court wall serves very well as a screen (that is, once the basketball games subside). A small crowd gathers every Friday night to view films with a gritty, urban feel to them. Some are well known *(Mean*

Streets, Taxi Driver), some not so well known, and some foreign. The evening always starts with a couple of choice silent shorts with a soundtrack of car horns and neighborhood voices. This is a pure New York Experience not to be missed.

THE POURHOUSE

790 Metropolitan Avenue (at Humboldt Street)
Williamsburg, Brooklyn
(718) 599–0697
www.thepourhouse.com
The last Wednesday of every month, 9:30 P.M.

This cozy neighborhood bar that strives to be a "community center with alcohol" hosts a film night once a month in the comfort of its back room. They show classic flicks (projected on real sixteen-millimeter film), and the popcorn is always free. Stop by on Sunday for the free bagels, too.

SONY WONDER TECHNOLOGY LAB

550 Madison Avenue (at 56th Street)
(212) 833–7858
www.sonywondertechlab.com
Thursday at 6:00 P.M. (every week during the summer, every other week during the school year).

They screen recent and some less recent Hollywood favorites *(The Wedding Planner, Peggy Sue Got Married, Muppets from Space)*, on their amazing high-definition screen. They accept reservations the week of the film, and give out any remaining tickets at 5:45. Get there early and enjoy the four floors of interactive activities—everything's free.

VOID

16 Mercer Street (between Howard and Canal Streets)
(212) 941–6492
www.voidltd.com
Wednesday at 8:00 P.M. (closer to 8:15).

Void multimedia lounge and bar presents an eclectic collection of classic and contemporary films on their large video screen. Every Wednesday this artsy Soho bar lowers the lights and attracts a mixed crowed of artists, hip neighborhood types, students, and film aficionados. The drinks can be pricey, but there's no minimum or cover ever (and I've even seen folks bring in their own dinner from nearby Chinatown noodle shops). They also have an extensive schedule of free DJ, performance, and other film events throughout the week; check the Web site for details.

BETTER THAN THE BOOK

NEW YORK PUBLIC LIBRARIES
www.nypl.org/branch/events/

Many public libraries throughout Manhattan and the Bronx show regularly scheduled films every week. These films could include black-and-white classics from the 1930s and 1940s, documentaries, foreign films, and recent features. Here's a list of the branches with screenings every week; call or check the Web site to confirm schedules.

MANHATTAN BRANCHES

58TH STREET LIBRARY, 127 East 58th Street (between Lexington and Park Avenues); (212) 759–7358; Friday at 2:00 P.M.

BLOOMINGDALE LIBRARY, 150 West 100th Street (between Columbus and Amsterdam Avenues); (212) 222–8030; Thursday at 2:00 P.M.

DONNELL LIBRARY CENTER, 20 West 53rd Street (between Fifth and Sixth Avenues); (212) 621–0618; Wednesday at 2:30 P.M.

JEFFERSON MARKET LIBRARY, 425 Sixth Avenue (at 10th Street); (212) 243–4334; Monday at 6:00 P.M.

KIPS BAY LIBRARY, 446 Third Avenue (at East 31st Street); (212) 683–2520; call for details.

NEW AMSTERDAM LIBRARY, 9 Murray Street (between Broadway and Church Street); (212) 732–8186; Wednesday at 5:30 P.M.

ST. AGNES LIBRARY, 444 Amsterdam Avenue (between 80th and 81st Streets); (212) 877–4380; Wednesday at 2:00 P.M.

BRONX BRANCHES

BAYCHESTER LIBRARY, 2049 Asch Loop North; (718) 379–6700; every other Wednesday at 2:00 P.M.

VAN NEST LIBRARY, 2147 Barnes Avenue (at Lydig Avenue); (718) 829–5864; Saturday at 2:00 P.M.

ALIEN: "On this cable system, we receive over one million channels from the farthest reaches of the galaxy."

BART: "Do you get HBO?"

ALIEN: "No, that would cost extra."

—The Simpsons

TELEVISION TAPINGS: PUBLIC ACCESS

AFTER HOLLYWOOD, NEW YORK is home to the most small-screen shows. While Los Angeles is the place to be if you want to see tapings of sitcoms, the kinds of programs that are based in New York have a mix of everything, including talk shows, game shows, variety shows, comedies, and courtroom shows. It's possible to get tickets to many of these shows the week of the taping, but many of the more popular shows have long waiting lists and require you to request tickets from a couple of months to up to a year in advance. All television tapings are free, but be warned that some do require a substantial commitment of time. The upside is that there's usually a very funny comedian working the crowd trying to keep you entertained while you sit around waiting for the official fun to begin.

The audience is an important part of the show, so they want to keep you lively for when they need you to hoot, holler, and applaud wildly. And one of the best ways they have found to keep you interested is through bribery. Often these shows offer giveaways for the audience. You could receive anything from key chains and T-shirts to Broadway tickets, CDs, and books.

THE ANANDA LEWIS SHOW
528 West 57th Street (between Tenth and Eleventh Avenues)
(212) 817-5550
www.theanandalewisshow.com
Tape days: Tuesday, Wednesday, and Thursday at 12:30 and 3:00 P.M. (arrive ninety minutes earlier). Audience-participation talk show. Call for tickets anytime up until the day of taping.

THE CAROLINE RHEA SHOW
NBC Studio
30 Rockefeller Plaza (49th Street, between Fifth and Sixth Avenues)
(212) 664-3056
www.nbc.com
Tape Days: Monday through Thursday, 10:00–11:00 A.M. Caroline Rhea takes over for Rosie O'Donnell for the lively morning chat show. It was almost impossible to get advanced tickets when it was Rosie's show because of the load of goodies she gave away every day to the audience members, but call the ticket request line to try your luck now that Caroline Rhea has taken the reins. You can always try for standby tickets, which are given out at 7:30 A.M. at the NBC Studio lobby by lottery (there is no need to arrive much earlier then 7:30). Standby tickets are not a guarantee of tickets to the show; it will depend on how many people with reserved tickets do not show up for the taping later that day.

CHANGE OF HEART
Chelsea Studios
221 West 26th Street (between Seventh and Eighth Avenues)
(877) 485-7144
www.changeofheart.warnerbros.com
Tape days: Friday and Saturday at 11:30 A.M. and 3:30 P.M. each day (arrive 90 minutes early). The *Dating Game* with a twist. Call anywhere from the day of taping to a week ahead for tickets.

CROSSING OVER WITH JOHN EDWARDS
(800) 962–9960
www.scifi.com/johnedward
John talks with your dearly departed. Tickets are very hard to come by. They only accept requests through their hot line the first Saturday of every month between 2:00 and 5:00 P.M.

THE DAILY SHOW WITH JON STEWART
513 West 46th Street (between Tenth and Eleventh Avenues)
(212) 586–2477
www.comedycentral.com/dailyshow
Tape days: Monday through Thursday, from 5:30–7:30 P.M. (arrive at 4:30). Emmy-winning news satire/comedy talk show. Call a month ahead for tickets. You must be over eighteen. No day-of standby tickets, but you can call on Friday at 11:30 to see if there are any cancellations for the next week's shows.

EMERIL LIVE
604 West 52nd Street (between Eleventh and Twelfth Avenues)
"Bam!" It's a cooking show with a live band and celebrity guests. They tape shows at various times throughout the year and only give tickets away through a lottery system. Send a postcard with your name, address, and phone number to Emeril Live Tickets, P.O. Box 550, Salem, VA 24153. This is the only way to get tickets; there are no standby tickets.

GOOD MORNING AMERICA
West 44th Street and Broadway
www.abcnews.go.com/sections/GMA/index.html
Tape days: Monday through Friday 7:00–9:00 A.M. Hang out with Diane Sawyer and Charles Gibson in their Times Square studio as they talk about world events, chat with celebrities and tell you the best way to clean your dust bunnies. Send for tickets through the Web site about a month in advance. Plan to arrive at 6:00 A.M.; the show is on the air from 7:00 to 9:00. You can also always join the crowd on the street outside the studio.

JUDGE HATCHETT
www.judgehatchett.com
The judge settles your disputes. Fill out a request form at the Web site.

LAST CALL WITH CARSON DALY
NBC Studio
30 Rockefeller Plaza (49th Street, between Fifth and Sixth Avenues)
(212) 664–3056
www.nbc.com

Tape days: Vary from week to week, but they usually tape two nights per week with shows at 7:00 and 9:00 P.M. Late-night talk show with the MTV star interviewing hipsters from music, film, and sports. Call to request advance tickets one to three weeks before the date you want. Standby tickets are available at 9:00 A.M. at the NBC Studio lobby and given out on a lottery basis (so there's no need to arrive much earlier than 9:00 A.M.). Standby tickets do not guarantee you'll get into the show; it will depend on how many people with reserved tickets fail to show up at the taping later that day.

LATE NIGHT WITH CONAN O'BRIEN
NBC Studio
30 Rockefeller Plaza (49th Street, between Fifth and Sixth Avenues)
(212) 664-3056
www.nbc.com/conan
Tape days: Tuesday through Friday, 5:30–6:30 P.M. Join Conan for his late-night wise-ass interviews. Call the ticket request line for reservations two to three months in advance. Standby tickets are given out at 9:00 A.M. at the NBC Studio lobby by lottery (again, there's no need to arrive much earlier than 9:00 A.M.). Standby tickets do not a guarantee you'll get into the show; it will depend on how many people with reserved tickets fail to show up at the taping later that day.

THE LATE SHOW WITH DAVID LETTERMAN
The Ed Sullivan Theater
1697 Broadway (between 54th and 55th Streets)
New York, NY 10019
(212) 975-1003 (general info)
or (212) 247-6497 (standby tickets)
www.cbs.com/latenight/lateshow
Tape days: Monday through Thursday at 5:30 P.M. (4:15 arrival time), and Thursday at 7:00 P.M. (5:00 arrival time). It's the top ten list, viewer mail, Stupid Pet Tricks, Paul, Dave, and you all together in a very chilly studio (bring a sweater!). For advance tickets, send a postcard with your name, address, phone number, and number of tickets requested, or go to the CBS Web site (limit two per person). Send for tickets at least two months in advance. To get standby tickets on the day of the taping, call the standby phone line at 11:00 A.M.. There is no in-person standby line.

LIVE WITH REGIS AND KELLY
7 Lincoln Square (at 67th Street and Columbus Avenue)
(212) 456-3054
www.tvplex.go.com/buenavista/livewithregis

Tape days: Monday through Friday at 9:00 A.M. (arrive at 8:00). Regis tries not to lose it, Kelly tries to understand it, and Gelmen tries to keep it all together on this morning chat show. For advance tickets, send a postcard with your name, address, phone number, the date you would like tickets for, and the number of tickets requested (limit four per person). Send ticket requests to Live Tickets, Ansonia Station, P.O. Box 23077, New York, NY 10023. Requests can take up to a year to be filled. To try for standby tickets on the day of taping, arrive at the studio as early as 7:00 A.M., tickets are given out on a first-come, first-served basis.

THE MAURY SHOW
New York's Hotel Pennsylvania
401 Seventh Avenue (between 32nd and 33rd Streets)
(212) 547-8421
www.themauryshow.com
Tape days: Tuesday, Wednesday, and Thursday at 8:30 A.M., (arrive by 8:15). Audience-participation talk show. Call for tickets anytime up until the day of taping. If you don't have tickets, they say you can always come to the studio the day of the taping; they'll probably be able to get you in.

THE MONTEL WILLIAMS SHOW
433 West 53rd Street (between Ninth and Tenth Avenues)
(212) 989-8101
www.montelshow.com
Tape days: Wednesday and Thursday at 10:00 A.M., 1:00 P.M., and 4:00 P.M. Audience-participation talk show. Call for tickets anytime up until the day of taping.

THE PEOPLE'S COURT
401 Fifth Avenue, eighth floor (at 37th Street, between Fifth and Madison Avenues)
(888) 780-8587
Tape days: Tuesday and Wednesday at 10:00 A.M. and 2:00 P.M. (be prepared to stay for three hours). Courtroom reality show. Call for tickets anytime up until the day of taping.

THE RICKI LAKE SHOW
Chelsea Studios
226 West 26th Street (between Seventh and Eighth Avenues)
New York, NY 10001
(212) 352-8600
www.ricki.com

Tape days: Wednesday, Thursday, and Friday at 1:30 P.M. and 3:30 P.M. Audience-participation talk show. For advance tickets, call, write, or go to the Web site about a month ahead. For standby tickets, go to the studio at least ninety minutes before the taping times to wait on line.

THE SALLY JESSY RAPHAEL SHOW
The Hotel Pennsylvania
15 Penn Plaza (West 33rd Street, between Sixth and Seventh Avenues)
(212) 244–3595
www.sallyjr.com
Tape days: Monday, Tuesday, and Wednesday at 10:30 A.M. and 1:30 P.M. (arrive one hour early). Audience-participation talk show. Call or fill out a request form for tickets at the Web site anytime from the day of taping to a month in advance. Stay for both shows in a day and they'll feed you!

SATURDAY NIGHT LIVE
NBC Studio
30 Rockefeller Plaza (49th Street, between Fifth and Sixth Avenues)
(212) 664–3056
www.nbc.com/snl
Tape days: Saturday, September through June. The original late-night comedy sketch show, with popular guest stars and top-of-the-charts musical guests. They run a lottery every August to give away tickets for the upcoming year of shows. Check the Web site for details. You may have better luck getting standby tickets, which are distributed every Saturday at 7:00 A.M. at the NBC Studio lobby by lottery (so you don't need to camp out there all night for a shot). Standby tickets do not guarantee you'll get into the show; it will depend on how many people with reserved tickets fail to show up later for the dress rehearsal at 8:00 P.M. or the live show at 11:30.

T.R.L.
45th Street and Broadway
(212) 398–8549
www.mtv.com/onair/trl
Tape days: Monday through Friday at 3:30 P.M. You pick the hits, and Carson plays the videos. Call for tickets three months ahead of time. To be a member of the studio audience, you must be at least sixteen years old and "appear" to be no older than twenty-four. For standby tickets on the day of the show, line up at the 44th Street entrance at about 2:00 P.M. If you don't make it into the studio, join the throngs of screaming fans out-

side on Broadway between 44th and 45th Streets, Monday through Friday at 3:30 P.M.

THE VIEW
320 West 66th Street (off West End Avenue)
New York, NY 10023
(212) 456–0900
www.abc.go.com/theview
Tape days: Monday through Friday at 11:00 A.M. (plan to arrive by 10:00 A.M.). Barbara and the gals talk about everything from terrorism to bra sizes. Send a postcard with your name, address, phone number, and number of tickets requested or fill out a request form at the Web site. Tickets will be sent for dates about four to six months from the date they are received. They often have room for you the day of the show, however: Stop by the studio no later than 10:00 A.M. and put your name on the standby waiting list. These tickets are distributed on a first-come, first-served basis. You must be at least 18 years old to attend.

WHO WANTS TO BE A MILLIONAIRE
30 West 67th Street (at Columbus Avenue)
(212) 838–5901
www.abc.com
Tape days: Monday through Thursday at 4:00 P.M. and sometimes at 12:30 P.M. Regis is the host with the most (money!). Send a postcard with your name, address, day and evening phone numbers, and the number of tickets you would like (limited to four per request), or fill out a request form at the Web site. You must be at least eighteen years old to attend. Send to Who Wants to Be a Millionaire, Columbia University Station, P.O. Box 250–225, New York, NY 10025. Tickets are sent out for tapings about one to two months from the date requests are received. For day-of-taping standby tickets, you must arrive at the studio on or before 1:30 P.M. for the 4:00 shows, or 10:00 A.M. for the 12:30 P.M. shows.

"I've been asked to say a couple of words about my husband, Fang. How about "short" and "cheap"?"

—Phyllis Diller

COMEDY: CHEAP JOKES

I COULD SAY THAT THE PRICE of comedy shows in New York is no laughing matter, but that would be too obvious, so I'll just say the cost of laughing in the city is no joke (sorry, couldn't resist). Suffice it to say, yucks cost bucks (okay, I'm done). But you can have the last laugh by stopping in at one of these free comedy nights. Many feature newcomers taking their first shots at stand-up or are opportunities for more established comics or improv troupes to try out new material—or more likely a combination of the two. The schedules do change from time to time, so be sure to call to confirm information before showing up.

COMEDY BY THE WEEK

TIME	MONDAY	TUESDAY	WEDNESDAY	THURSDAY	FRIDAY	SATURDAY	SUNDAY
4:00 P.M.							
4:30 P.M.	New York Comedy Club						
5:00 P.M.							
5:30 P.M.							
6:00 P.M.							
6:30 P.M.							
7:00 P.M.							
7:30 P.M.	PSNBC	PSNBC	PSNBC	PSNBC			
8:00 P.M.		The Parlour Bar 169					
8:30 P.M.	Xando						
9:00 P.M.	Asylum	Absolutely 4th	B3 Lounge				
9:30 P.M.							Upright Citizens Brigade
10:00 P.M.							
10:30 P.M.						Ye Olde Tripple Inn	

ABSOLUTELY 4TH
228 West 4th Street (between Seventh Avenue and West 10th Street)
(212) 989–9444
Tuesday at 9:00 P.M.

One-drink minimum.

The trio of Noelle, Becky, and Abby put together a fun evening of stand-up and sketch comedy every Tuesday.

ASYLUM
149 Bleecker Street (at Thompson Street)
(212) 254–8492
This dive does comedy every Monday at 9:00 P.M.

BAR 169
169 East Broadway (between Jefferson and Rutgers Streets)
(212) 473–8866
www.169bar.com
Tuesday at 8:00 P.M.
The weekly show of stand-ups is called "Rape & Pillage," so you know you're in for a fun night.

B3 LOUNGE
33 Avenue B (at 3rd Street)
(212) 614–9755
www.b3restaurantandlounge.com
Wednesday at 9:00 P.M.
The downstairs lounge is a little like hanging out at your next-door neighbor's unfinished basement rec room . . . except this rec room comes with a full bar and cozy couches to lounge on while you're entertained by a variety of comedy upstarts and veterans.

NEW YORK COMEDY CLUB
241 East 24th Street (between Second and Third Avenues)
(212) 696–5233
Monday, 4:30–8:30 P.M.

 "We couldn't possibly charge you to watch the open mike."

Once a week this stand-up club opens its microphone to anyone who has $5.00 and thinks he's the next Seinfeld. You never know what you're going to see during this show. It might be painful, it might be sad, it might be offensive, and it might even occasionally be funny, but if you want to try your luck, watching is free: There's no charge, and no drink minimum (though you may need a couple of shots of something to make it through).

THE PARLOUR
250 West 86th Street (between Broadway and West End Avenue)
(212) 501–4845
www.livingroomlive.com
Tuesday at 8:00 P.M.
Live from the Upper West Side, it's Tuesday Night! For more than five years, the sketch comedy troupe Living Room Live has been dishing out fresh helpings of laughs every Tuesday in the comfortable confines of this Irish pub's basement lounge. In addition to the eight regular cast members, they also include guest performances every week from some of the best stand-up comics around New York.

PERFORMANCE SPACE NBC (PSNBC)
Here Performance Art Café
145 Sixth Avenue (on Dominick between Spring and Broome Streets)
(212) 647–0202, ext. 301
www.nbc.com/psnbc

Toyota Comedy Festival

Every June the Toyota Comedy Festival brings a cacophony of chuckles to New York with a festival of established and rising stars from the comedy world. While this festival isn't free (and in fact many of the show are pretty darn expensive), in past years they have always offered free shows as part of the celebration. The free shows vary from year to year, from an entire series of midday stand-ups at Bryant Park to selected panel discussions and performances at smaller venues around town. Check out the Web site for schedule and information: www.toyotacomedy.com.

Monday through Thursday at 7:30 P.M.
Sponsored by NBC (the TV network), this space is designed to develop and nurture writers, actors, and comedic performers and eventually make use of them on the small screen. All performances are free and worth checking out. Reservations are required. Tuesday night always features an alternative stand-up show; other evenings can be anything from one-acts to improv to who-knows-what.

UPRIGHT CITIZENS BRIGADE
161 West 22nd Street (between Sixth and Seventh Avenues)
(212) 366–9176
www.ucbtheater.com
Sunday at 9:30 P.M.
A comedy improv troupe (late of Comedy Central) hosts a wild and freewheeling performance every Sunday evening at 9:30. In addition to the regular citizens of the brigade, they always have guest improvisers from the casts of such shows as *Saturday Night Live, Conan O'Brien,* and others. Free tickets are given out at 8:15; no reservations accepted. Folks start lining up at about 6:30, so try to get there by 7:30 to be guaranteed a ticket—or show up at about 8:45 to try your luck with the standby line. They always have a full house for the show, and the evening is well worth the effort.

XANDO COFFEE AND BAR
2160 Broadway (at 76th Street)
(212) 595–5616
Monday at 8:30 P.M.

It's a relaxed evening of lattes and laughs as local comedians work out their new material in the intimate confines of the basement lounge in this coffeehouse/bar.

YE OLDE TRIPPLE INN
263 West 54th Street (between Broadway and Eighth Avenue)
(212) 245–9849
Saturday at 10:30 P.M.

An evening of comedy doesn't get much better than Felber's Frolics every Saturday night at the Tripple Inn no matter how much you pay for it—and here you don't have to pay for it! Each week the brother-and-sister team of Susie and Adam Felber (of NPR's *Wait, Wait, Don't Tell Me*) rustle up a bunch of their friends—who all happen to be A-list and up-and-coming comedians—to put together a truly riotous evening. Expect guests who've appeared on *The Daily Show,* Comedy Central, *Late Night with Conan O'Brien,* and many others. Expect spontaneous songs from the Felbers. Expect audience participation and even prizes. But most of all, expect to laugh, a lot!

"Dancing: The highest intelligence in the freest body."

—Isadora Duncan

DANCE: FREE EXPRESSION

AYBE IT'S BECAUSE New Yorkers are always on their feet—racing along the sidewalks, crammed together in the subways, or trudging up a five-story walk-up—but it seems that everyone in New York dances in one way or another. Or perhaps it's the palpable energy of the city that draws dancers from every corner of the planet. Whatever the reason, New York is like a dance itself, and its clubs, public spaces, and studios abound with opportunities for you to strut your stuff without unstuffing your bank account. If you prefer to watch, New York is home to some of the world's leading dance companies and conservatories, so the talent on display at no cost is unrivaled anyplace in the world.

WATCHING IT

BRYANT PARK SUMMER CONCERT SERIES
West 40th to West 41st Streets (between Fifth and Sixth Avenues)
(212) 512–5700
www.bryantpark.org
Friday night June through August.
Presents a variety of dance styles and companies along with an eclectic selection of opening bands.

CELEBRATE BROOKLYN
Prospect Park Bandshell (Prospect Park West and 9th Street)
Park Slope, Brooklyn
(718) 855–7882, ext. 45
www.celebratebrooklyn.org
Friday evening, June through August.
Brooklyn's popular free series presents everything from free films and dance performances to world music and readings. Dance performances are usually on Friday evening.

CENTRAL PARK SUMMERSTAGE
Midpark (enter at East or West 72nd Street)
(212) 360–2777
www.summerstage.org
June through August.
A complete schedule of free performances throughout the summer, from big names to cutting edge in music, opera, dance, spoken word, and more. This is a very popular venue; claiming a spot on line early is recommended. Dance performances most Friday evenings.

DANCING IN THE STREETS
55 Avenue of the Americas, Suite 310
(212) 625–3505
www.dancinginthestreets.org
Commissions and presents all forms of dance and movement performances throughout the city. All productions are site-specific performances in various parks, open spaces, and indoor spaces. Most performances are free.

JOYCE SOHO
155 Mercer Street (between Houston and Prince)
(212) 431–9233
www.joyce.org/soho.html

Work as a volunteer usher to see the performances for free.

This downtown sister of the Joyce Theater (below) presents a schedule of cutting edge independent choreographers and not-for-profit professional dance companies. Call two weeks in advance to reserve a spot as a volunteer usher to see the shows for free.

THE JOYCE THEATER
175 Eighth Avenue (at 19th Street)
(646) 792–8355
www.joyce.org

 Work as a volunteer usher to see the performances for free.

The leading theater for dance companies, the Joyce plays host to practically every major company from around the country and around the world. Call to set up dates to be a volunteer usher and see the show for free. They begin taking reservations two weeks in advance.

THE KITCHEN
512 West 19th Street (between Tenth and Eleventh Avenues)
(212) 255–5793, ext. 15
www.thekitchen.org

 Work as a volunteer usher to see the performances for free.

Although its location has moved farther uptown in recent years, the Kitchen remains firmly downtown in ethos. For the last thirty years, it has been home to such nontraditional, uncategorizable performers as Philip Glass, Laurie Anderson, Bill T. Jones and Arnie Zane, Eric Bogosian, David Byrne with the Talking Heads, Meredith Monk, Brian Eno, John Lurie, Robert Mapplethorpe, Cindy Sherman, and many others. Performances strive to combine music, dance, video, spoken word, and any other forms an artist feels like playing with at the moment. Call about three weeks in advance to reserve a spot as a volunteer usher.

LINCOLN CENTER OUT OF DOORS FESTIVAL
65th Street and Broadway
(212) 876–5766
www.lincolncenter.org

Throughout August.
This eclectic performance music and dance festival every August features leading modern, ethnic, and cutting-edge dance companies, as well as music from around the world in almost every genre, and a great selection of children's performances.

MOVEMENT RESEARCH
Judson Memorial Church
55 Washington Square South (West 4th and Thompson Streets)
(212) 539-2611
www.movementresearch.org
Monday at 8:00 P.M., September through June.
Presents free modern, improvisational, adventurous dance performances every Monday night at 8:00 P.M., September through June, by leading downtown movement artists.

NEW YORK UNIVERSITY
Tisch School of the Arts—Graduate Dance School
111 Second Avenue (between 6th and 7th Streets)
(212) 998-1982
www.nyu.edu/tisch/dance
October through May.
The graduate dance department offers free contemporary dance performances throughout the school year, often with notable guest choreographers.

DOING IT

DANCE TANGO
Central Park midpark at 66th Street (at the Shakespeare statue); Saturday 6:00 to 8:30 P.M.

South Street Seaport, Pier 16 (between the Ambrose and Peking ships); Sunday 6:00-9:00 P.M.

(212) 726-1111
www.dancetango.com
May through September.
Put a rose in your mouth and head down to Central Park (Saturday) or South Street Seaport (Sunday) for free tango lessons and dancing to live and recorded music under the stars.

DANCING ON THE PLAZA
Charles A. Dana Discovery Center, Central Park
110th Street and Central Park North
(212) 860–1370
www.centralparknyc.org
Thursday at 6:00 P.M., August.
The Harlem Meer makes a stunning backdrop for you to dance beneath the stars at this free summer dance series. Each week it's a new style of live music to dance to: swing, salsa, rock and roll, disco, or ballroom. Free lessons begin at 6:00 P.M., live bands at 7:00 P.M.

MIDSUMMER NIGHT SWING AT LINCOLN CENTER
65th Street and Broadway
(212) 875–5766
www.lincolncenter.org
July.
Yes, you too can be a dancer at Lincoln Center. Beginning in late June and running through July, the plaza at this famed performance center turns into the best dance floor in New York City. Every night they present top names from every sort of dance music, including American regional, Latin, Caribbean, African, ballroom, rhythm and blues, and, of course, swing! You can pay your way onto the official dance floor ($12), which is usually pretty overcrowded, but the savvier folks spread out on the vast Lincoln Center plaza to Savoy shuffle to their heart's content. Dance lessons begin at 6:30 P.M., dancing at 8:00 P.M.

MOONDANCE
Pier 25, Hudson River and North Moore Street
(212) 533–PARK (7275)
www.hudsonriverpark.org
Sunday evening, July and August.
Like all the events down at Pier 25, this one is all free! Swing, tango, and cha-cha away every Sunday night under the stars with live music from New York's hottest bands. Free lessons begin at 6:30 P.M., and the dancing keeps going until 10:00. Hey, why not arrive early and warm up with some free Ping-Pong before you hit the dance floor?

PARKSIDE LOUNGE
317 East Houston Street (corner of Attorney, between
Avenues B and C)
(212) 673–6270
www.parksidelounge.com
Friday night, 10:00 P.M.–3:00 A.M.

Two-drink minimum that they do try to enforce— but "we're not gonna throw ya out if ya don't drink."

A local bar complete with pool table, pinball games, and a hip jukebox, along with a snazzy back room with live shows every night. Join local musicians and neighbors in a celebration of the salsa beat every Friday night. While not officially a dance club (due to those stingy cabaret laws), people have been known shake a little something to the infectious rhythms, and I'm not just talking about maracas.

SANDRA CAMERON DANCE CENTER
199 Lafayette Street (between Broome and Kenmore Streets)
(212) 674–0505
www.sandracameron.com
The last Friday of every month.
This popular dance studio offers classes to the masses in swing, salsa, ballroom, and tango. Stop in for the guest night every month and get a free introductory swing class, some hot dance performances, and open swing, salsa, and ballroom dance sessions. There's even free wine and cheese!

TRIANGULO SCHOOL OF ARGENTINE TANGO
Chelsea Market
75 Ninth Avenue (between 15th and 16th Streets)
(212) 633–6445
www.tangonyc.com
Saturday 4:00–7:00 P.M., September through May.
What was once the birthplace of that most American of icons, the Oreo cookie, is transformed into a truly international atmosphere every Saturday afternoon. This gourmet marketplace is filled with the sights and sounds of Argentina as it plays host to a free *milonga* (tango salon) every week. When you need to take a break for the dancing, stop in and grab a few free samples at many of the gourmet shops in the market.

SO YOU WANT TO BE A DANCER: WORK-STUDY DANCE CLASSES

New York is the place to be if you hope to join those tapping feet on 42nd Street—but it's not a cheap dream to pursue. Dance classes can cost as much as $15 per hour. But fear not, there are ways for you to make it to the Great

White Way without spending such a great green amount. Many of the leading dance studios around New York offer scholarships, internships, or work-study options in exchange for free classes, or to greatly reduce the cost of classes.

BROADWAY DANCE CENTER
221 West 57th Street (Broadway and Eighth Avenue)
(212) 582-9304
www.broadwaydancecenter.com
Classes in jazz, ballet, tap, modern, tumbling, and aerobics with leading teachers from Broadway and around the world. There are three possibilities for free and low-cost classes at the studio. One is the Ellner Scholarship, offered to students seriously dedicated to their training. To get a scholarship, students must be recommended by a faculty member. Scholarship recipients do not have to fulfill any work commitments at the studio and receive ten free classes a week for six months. Dancers of any level may apply for an intensive six-month training internship to receive twelve classes a week for $3.00 each (regularly $12.50) in exchange for twelve hours of work at the studio. There is a $200 nonrefundable fee once you're accepted into the internship program. They also run an extensive work-study program that's open to dancers at any level. Students work in various positions around the studio (front desk, cafe, office, boutique, or cleaning crew). For each work-study hour and a half worked, you earn one discounted class ($3.00).

JOSÉ LIMÓN DANCE FOUNDATION
611 Broadway, ninth floor (just north of Houston)
(212) 777-3353
www.limon.org
This warm and welcoming studio offers classes in the Limón modern dance technique. Students can work as class monitors (open up the studio, sign students in, troubleshoot, and close up the studio after class), cleaning monitors, or office assistants in exchange for taking classes. They keep a list of those interested in work-study positions and generally use students who regularly attend classes, but no specific audition is required. The math is: Cleanup monitors work three shifts (about one hour each) in exchange for four free classes per week; class monitors work four shifts in exchange for a full scholarship (all the classes they want to take); one hour of office work exchanges for one class for $3.00 (regularly $12.00).

MOVEMENT RESEARCH
648 Broadway, Room 806 (between Bleecker and Bond Streets)
(212) 598-0551
(212) 539-2611 (hot line)

www.movementresearch.org
Movement Research classes are more likely to win you a chance to work on an Off Off Broadway performance art piece than a part in a Broadway musical. If that's your type of dance, this is absolutely the place for you. They offer a full schedule of classes and workshops in contact improvisation, modern and postmodern techniques, as well as other classes that defy simple definition but combine all kinds of movement influences from around the world. Work-study students are expected to work about ten hours a week in exchange for unlimited free classes. Hours and assignments are flexible and could include registering students for morning or weekend classes, working on the tech crew during performances, running light errands, or distributing flyers.

PERIDANCE
132 Fourth Avenue, second floor (between 12th and 13th Streets)
(212) 505–0886
www.peridance.com
Offers classes in ballet, jazz, tap, yoga, hip-hop, and an emphasis on all forms of modern. They have cleaning work-study positions. Clean a studio (8:30 to 9:30 P.M. any Monday through Friday) and get two classes free. Stop by to fill out an application; no audition required.

STEPS ON BROADWAY
2121 Broadway (between 74th and 75th Streets)
(212) 874–2410
www.stepsnyc.com
Classes in all styles for all levels. They have auditions once a month for scholarships. You need to be a competent dancer to pass the audition, as well as being willing to work ten hours a week for all the free classes you want.

THE WEST SIDE DANCE PROJECT
357 West 36th Street (between Eighth and Ninth Avenues)
(212) 563–6781
This small dance studio offers classes in jazz, ballet, and tap. They have auditions a couple of times a year for their scholarship program. You don't necessarily need to be a "dancer" to win one of these positions. They look for people who are pursuing careers in the musical theater and are hoping to improve their dance skills. Scholarship winners are required to work one three-hour shift at the front desk a week and must take at least five hours of dance classes a week.

"Money disappears like magic."

—Arabic Proverb

MAGIC: CHEAP TRICKS

YOU MIGHT THINK THE closest you can get to seeing a free magic show in New York is watching how quickly people's money disappears when they play three-card monty, but you'd be wrong. There is a thriving world of magic in this city, and even with nothing up your sleeve, you can be entertained by many of the finest magicians in the world without spending a single quarter (not even that one you have hidden behind your ear). Just stop into any of the handful of magician supply shops around the city to be dazzled at the magic counter, or during some of their weekly free performances.

ABRACADABRA SUPERSTORE

19 West 21st Street (between Fifth and Sixth Avenues)
(212) 627–5194
www.abracadabrasuperstore.com
Saturday at 2:00 and 5:00 P.M., Sunday at 3:00 P.M.
As you walk into this wonderland of magic, gags, costumes and masks, you're sure to be greeted by Nyrobi, the loudmouth parrot. Stop by any weekend to enjoy the free magic shows performed by professional magicians on staff as well as talented guest performers. While the store is chock-full of an amazing assortment of fun stuff for kids and adults to spend money on, there's no pressure to buy anything. Stop in anytime for trick demonstrations at the magic counter (though they won't tell you how they're done unless you buy the kits).

HALLOWEEN ADVENTURE

104 Fourth Avenue (at 11th Street)
(212) 673–4546
www.halloweenadventure.com
Sunday at 3:00 P.M., spring through fall.
Just walking around this store, playing with all the unusual novelty items and gags, and trying on all the wild costumes, masks, and hats could be enough entertainment for a day, but bring the kids by on Sunday afternoon (spring through fall) and you even get Magic Mike's Super Sunday Spectacular. They set up a stage in front of the store and put together a fun show demonstrating about fifteen to twenty tricks you can learn— and, of course, buy—at their friendly magic department. Here, too, there's no pressure to buy. In fact, sometimes they even give it away: On selected Sundays they offer free magic lessons and tricks for kids six to sixteen. Call for schedule and details.

SOCIETY OF AMERICAN MAGICIANS (SAM) AND INTERNATIONAL BROTHERHOOD OF MAGICIANS (IBM)

Soldiers, Sailors and Airmens Club
283 Lexington Avenue (between 36th and 37th Streets)
www.magicsam.com or www.geocities.com/ibmring26/home
(SAM) First Friday of the month at 8:00 P.M.
(IBM) Last Friday of the month at 8:30 P.M. (except July, August, and December).
These two magicians' associations hold monthly meetings that bring together an array of talent, from those trying to break into the business

Old Dogs and New Tricks

How do you make a Burrito disappear? Stop by the downstairs dining room at Maui Tacos (330 Fifth Avenue, between 32nd and 33rd Streets, 212–868–9722) any Saturday afternoon, from 1:00 to 4:30 P.M. Since 1938 a group of professional and amateur magicians have been gathering (only recently at Maui Tacos) to perfect new tricks, exchange ideas, sample some exotic salsas, take full advantage of the free refills on the sodas, and try to slip something past their hardest audience—each other. There is no formal show here, just a chance to see some amazing artists working on their craft in an informal, one-on-one setting. And the tacos are pretty tasty too. Over the years, the group has migrated to various eateries. If you don't find them at Maui Tacos, call the folks at Tannen's or Abracadabra. They should know where to find them.

to masters of the art. And where there are magicians, there is magic. Most meetings offer a full evening of free performances. Almost all IBM meeting are open to the public, but only some SAM meetings are open for all. Check the Web sites for schedule and information.

TANNEN'S MAGIC STUDIO

24 West 25th Street, second floor (between Broadway and Sixth Avenue)
(212) 929–4500
www.tannensmagic.com
Well, they won't tell you how they're done, but everyone behind the counter at Tannen's is a bona fide magician and can show you any trick in the house. And there are thousands of tricks in the place. Of course, the only way to find out the secrets behind the magic is to buy the tricks, but they will demonstrate any one of them for free. There are no shows at this store, but just spend some time around the counter and you're sure to catch a trick or two.

Section 2:

LIVING IN NEW YORK

"The remarkable thing about my mother is that for thirty years she served us nothing but leftovers. The original meal has never been found."

—Calvin Trillin

FOOD: ON THE HOUSE

AST FOOD, GOURMET FOOD, exotic food, health food, breads, cakes, wings, hors d'oeuvres, hot dogs, canapés, sushi, Italian, Mexican, Chinese, food, food, food. Anything you desire, it's in New York, and it's better than anywhere else in the world. But for free? Yes indeed. Wander through the many gourmet markets and selected specialty stores around the city and you'll find a delightful (and filling) selection of samples to chow down on. Make your way to any number of bars and restaurants that set out some grand and some not-so-grand spreads during happy hours. And if you must spend money, you can shop at some fancy joints for pennies, if you know when to go.

HAPPY HOURS

Many bars, pubs, and restaurants around the city offer some kind of free food during happy hours. What you'll find at these places runs the gamut from basic bar food to sumptuous buffets. For the most part you are expected to buy a drink to partake of the eats, but there are usually all kinds of discounts on the drinks as well during happy hours. And hey, if you don't drink or don't feel like footing the bill for a martini, no one says you can't just order a club soda. Be sure to leave the bartender a nice tip though. Yes, in New York, even Cheap Bastards should remember to tip. While I have included here only those places that have a long history of offering free eats, policies do change from time to time.

EAST SIDE

ABBEY TAVERN
354 Third Avenue (at 26th Street)
(212) 532–1978
Free chips and appetizers on the bar and a small buffet of fries, wings, or onion rings between 4:00 and 6:00 P.M.

ASHTON'S
208 East 50th Street (at Third Avenue)
(212) 688–8625
There's always something substantial to chow down during happy hour at this friendly Irish pub. Monday through Friday, 5:00 to 7:00 P.M.

JAMESON'S
975 Second Avenue (between 51st and 52nd Streets)
(212) 980–4465
You can stop in any Monday, Tuesday, or Wednesday night from 4:00 to 7:00 and find a small selection of bar munchies set out at this quiet neighborhood bar.

MCCORMACK'S PUBLIC HOUSE
365 Third Avenue (between 26th and 27th Streets)
(212) 683–0911
An Irish pub with free food available from 5:00 to 7:00 P.M. Monday through Friday, usually appetizers like skins or wings (though one night

they put out some kind of black sausage thing—mmm-mm). Also, they broadcast international rugby games.

METROPOLITAN HOTEL LOBBY BAR
569 Lexington Avenue (at 51st Street)
(212) 752-7000
Wings and cheese available at the bar from 5:00 to 7:00 P.M.. While you're in the lobby, be sure to grab an apple at the end of the reception desk.

THE OLD STAND
914 Third Avenue (at 55th Street)
(212) 759-4836
This comfortable and quiet neighborhood bar/restaurant serves up a generous spread of four or five selections on their happy hour buffet. The menu could include pasta, barbecued chicken, sausage and onions, and cheese and crackers. Monday through Friday, 5:00 to 7:00 P.M.

PIG 'N WHISTLE ON 3RD
922 Third Avenue (between 55th and 56th Streets)
(212) 688-4646
This low-key Irish pub sets out a small buffet of a couple of tasty selections like chicken fingers, mini pizzas, poppers, or wings. Monday through Friday, 5:30 P.M. to 7:30 P.M.

POOLBEG STREET PUB
304 Third Avenue (at 23rd Street)
(212) 253-6848
An Irish pub that serves wings during their happy hour Monday through Friday. They usually put them out about 5:30; once they're gone, they're gone. Get 'em while they last.

RODEO BAR
375 Third Avenue (at 27th Street)
(212) 683-6500
www.rodeobar.com
A fun and casual Tex-Mex bar/restaurant with barrels full of freshly roasted peanuts all around. At happy hours (Monday through Friday, 4:00 to 7:00 P.M.) they supply a small buffet of munchies (wings, nachos, potato skins, and the like). On Monday nights kids eat free, and every night they have live rockabilly or country music and never charge a cover. Yee-ha!

ROLF'S
281 Third Avenue (at 22nd Street)
(212) 477-4750
This German restaurant sets out free finger sandwiches at the bar 6:00 P.M. until they're gone seven nights a week. Be sure to check out the over-the-top Christmas decorations.

T. G. WHITNEY'S
244 East 53rd Street (between Second and Third Avenues)
(212) 888-5772
Free wings, vegetables and dip, Monday through Friday, 5:00 to 7:00 P.M.

WEST SIDE

D. J. REYNOLDS
351 West 57th Street (between Eighth and Ninth Avenues)
(212) 245-2912
Try your luck at this quiet and friendly Irish pub. Every Monday through Friday from 5:00 to 8:00 P.M. they set out something different. One night it might be a hearty snack of wings or chicken nuggets; another night you could end up with a substantial meal of steak or chicken marsala over pasta.

FIDDLER'S GREEN
58 West 48th Street (between Fifth and Sixth Avenues)
(212) 819-0095
This popular Irish pub sets out some wings or pasta.

FLASH DANCERS N.Y.C.
1674 Broadway (between 52nd and 53rd Streets)
(212) 315-5107

 Expensive drinks.

This strip joint offers a free hot buffet for lunch and dinner with an expensive, strictly enforced one-drink minimum (nothing less than $8.00), While you're taking in the topless "dishes" walking around this "Gentleman's Club," you can dine on the other dishes at the buffet. They put out a spread (excuse me) of about four entrees for lunch (noon to 2:00 P.M.) and dinner (5:00 to 7:00 P.M.). They start charging to get in at 5:00 P.M. Monday through Friday. So, besides the pricey drink, there's never a charge for lunch, but if you want dinner, you need to slip in before 5:00 P.M. to avoid the steep admission charge.

KENNEDY'S
327 West 57th Street (between Eighth and Ninth Avenues)
(212) 759–4242
This Irish pub puts out a bit of bar food wings or meatballs. Monday through Friday, 4:30 to 7:00 P.M. or until it's gone. Good for a nibble, but it probably won't fill you up.

KOYOTE'S CAFE
307 West 47th Street (between Eighth and Ninth Avenues)
(212) 956–1091
This lively neighborhood bar with pool tables and a fun jukebox offers up a couple of selections on the buffet Monday through Friday, 4:00 to 7:00 P.M. You'll always find some kind of pasta; the other choice could be hot dogs, wings, egg rolls, chicken nuggets, or who knows.

LANGAN'S
150 West 47th Street (between Sixth and Seventh Avenues)
(212) 869–5482
This makes a great pretheater stop. Monday through Friday, 5:00 to 8:00 P.M., you'll find chips and salsa at the bar and a small buffet of bar food, which could include wings, mozzarella sticks, meatballs, or other tasty munchies.

NINTH AVENUE SALOON
656 Ninth Avenue (between 45th and 46th Streets)
(212) 307–1503
This quiet gay bar for Hell's Kitchen locals and theatergoers serves up a free dinner every Sunday evening from 6:00 to 9:00 P.M. During the summer it's a barbecue dinner of burgers, hot dogs, potato salad, and fixin's; in the colder months it's heartier fare.

O'FLAHERTY'S ALE HOUSE
334 West 46th Street (between Eighth and Ninth Avenues)
(212) 581–9366 or (212) 246–8928
A theater district Irish pub that sets out some free Murphy's stew or shepherd's pie for Actor's Night every Wednesday at about 10:30 P.M. Don't worry—you don't have to recite any Shakespeare to partake. Also,

free live music seven nights a week (acoustic, rock, and Irish).

O'REILLY'S TOWNHOUSE
21 West 35th Street (between Fifth and Sixth Avenues)
(212) 502–5246
This lively Irish pub with a busy after-work crowd sets out a free buffet of shepherd's pie, pasta, or wings Monday through Friday from 5:00 P.M. "till it's gone."

PIG 'N WHISTLE
165 West 47th Street (between Sixth and Seventh Avenues)
(212) 302–0112
Just down the block from Langan's, this makes a great pretheater stop as well. Monday through Friday, 5:00 to 8:00 P.M., chow down on chips and salsa at the bar, and a buffet of appetizers.

RED LIGHT BISTRO
50 Ninth Avenue (between 14th and 15th Streets)
(212) 675–2400
A comfortable and hip lounge that sets out a variety of hors d'oeuvres during happy hour Monday through Friday, 5:00 to 8:00 P.M.

RUDY'S BAR AND GRILL
627 Ninth Avenue (at West 44th Street)
(212) 974–9169
Look for the Big Pig outside to find the place and "pig out" on the free hot dogs. This is a real neighborhood joint. The franks are always available (1:00 to 10:00 P.M.), but don't try asking for one without ordering a drink first.

DOWNTOWN, EAST AND WEST VILLAGE

CUCINA DI PESCE
87 East 4th Street (between Second and Third Avenues)
(212) 260–6800
This Italian restaurant sets out free mussels at the bar every day beginning at about 5:00 P.M.

Sing for Your Supper

Here are a few places to stop by and lend a hand or join in on some chanting and get yourself a full meal.

FOOD NOT BOMBS NYC, *Tompkins Square Park; (212) 254–3697, ext. 395. The artists collective/punk rock club ABC No Rio serves up free vegetarian meals in Tompkins Square Park every Friday, Sunday and Monday at about 3:30 P.M. This meal is generally meant for the homeless, but they always need volunteers to help in food preparation—and of course they'll feed you, too. Stop by ABC No Rio at about 1:00 to help cook (156 Rivington Street, between Clinton and Suffolk Streets).*

HARE KRISHNA COMMUNITY HOUSE, *48 Avenue B (between 3rd and 4th Streets); (212) 674–0698 or (888) HUNGRY–5. Stop by for the Sunday-evening Love Feast. The chanting begins at 6:00 P.M. and the eating begins at about 8:15 P.M. This is a very small and welcoming temple, and the vegetarian meals are delicious. They also serve a vegetarian meal every day for the homeless in Tompkins Square Park and they always need volunteers to help out (and get a free meal as well).*

SRI SRI RADHA GOVINDA MANIR, *305 Schermerhorn Street (between Nevins and Bond Streets), Brooklyn; (718) 855–6714; www.radhagovinda.net. This is the main New York Hare Krishna temple; it's very large and well attended. They offer free vegetarian feasts on Wednesday and Sunday night at about 8:00. All are welcome, and there's no need to shave your head.*

11TH STREET BAR
510 East 11th Street (between Avenues A and B)
(212) 982–3929
Free wings on Friday, 4:00 to 7:00 P.M.

JIM BRADY'S
75 Maiden Lane (between William and Gold Streets)
(212) 425–1300
Free buffet Monday through Friday, 5:00 to 7:00 P.M.

NATHAN HALES
6 Murray Street (between Broadway and Church Street)
(212) 571–0776
Free buffet (tacos, wings, and the like) on Monday night from 5:00 to
7:00 P.M.

NEW YORK DOLLS
59 Murray Street (between Church Street and West Broadway)
(212) 227–6912

THE CATCH   An expensive one-drink minimum.

If seeing topless women parade around in front of you makes you think,
Man, I could really go for a chicken Parmesan right now, this is the place
for you. This strip joint offers a free catered lunch and dinner, as long as
you buy at least one expensive drink. You will not get away without
spending at least eight bucks. They serve lunch at noon and dinner at 5:00
P.M. No admission charge to get in at these times.

THE THIRSTY SCHOLAR
155 Second Avenue (between 9th and 10th Streets)
(212) 777–6514
They set out a free a load of wings, rings, shepherd's pie, or whatever the
kitchen happens to have available from about 6:00 P.M. until whenever it's
gone. Monday through Friday, 6:00 to 8:00-ish P.M.

TY'S BAR
114 Christopher Street (between Bleecker and Hudson Streets)
(212) 741–9641
On the second Tuesday of every month, get yourself a hearty meal and shake
the hand of some of New York's bravest (and gayest) as this gay saloon plays
host to the monthly gathering of the gay firemen and EMS organization,
Fire-FLAG/EMS. All are welcome. The buffet opens at about 8:30 P.M.

BROOKLYN

HANK'S SALOON
46 Third Avenue (at Atlantic Avenue)
Brooklyn
(718) 625–8003
www.hankstavern.com

Free live country/rock/rockabilly music Wednesday through Sunday night at this hardcore Brooklyn dive. On Sunday night don't miss the free barbecue. You never know what they'll be serving up; some weeks it could be a mighty fine spread, others it might be hockey-puck hamburgers and shriveled hot dogs. No cover, no minimum.

THE POURHOUSE
790 Metropolitan Avenue (at Humboldt Street)
Williamsburg, Brooklyn
(718) 599–0697
www.thepourhouse.com
This cozy neighborhood bar that strives to be a "community center with alcohol" sets out free bagels every Sunday from 2:00 to 9:00 P.M. They also host a film night once a month in the comforts of the back room, with free popcorn.

FREE SAMPLES: A SAMPLING

New York City is overrun with gourmet markets, farmer's markets, and specialty stores that charge an arm and a leg for anything from a leg of lamb to overpriced olives from around the world. These markets, however, are also gold mines of free samples. You can get a taste of almost anything, from gourmet breads, cakes, and cookies to olive oils, cheeses, and exotic fruits.

AJI ICHIBAN
37 Mott Street (between Pell and Mosco Streets);
(212) 233–7650

157 Hester Street (between Mott and Elizabeth Streets);
(212) 925–1133

41–51A Main Street (between 41st Road and Sanford Avenue,
Queens); (718) 460–6663

This Chinese candy store offers some truly unusual, intensely flavorful delicacies. You'll find signs all over the store encouraging you to try such unusual fare as the dried curry squid, mini roasted crabs, and preserved chili olives. There are tamer selections of chocolates, biscuits, and gummy candies as well.

BAKERY SOUTINE
104 West 70th Street (between Columbus Avenue and Broadway)
(212) 496–1450
www.soutine.com
A lovely neighborhood bakery that always sets out something sweet to nibble on.

BALTHAZAR BOULANGERIE
80 Spring Street (between Crosby Street and Broadway)
(212) 965–1785

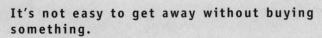

THE CATCH It's not easy to get away without buying something.

Considered one of the best bakeries in the city (and one of the most expensive), Balthazar always offers something to snack on at the register. It's a very small place, so it isn't easy to get away without buying something so you don't look like a Cheap Bastard. If you're willing to brave the stares from behind the counter and from those on line, dive right in— their treats are delicious.

CHANNEL VIDEO
427 Columbus Avenue (between 82nd and 83rd Streets)
(212) 496–2759
www.channelvideo.com
Yes, a video store. One of the few remaining independent video stores in the city offers a great selection of videos, knowledgeable service, and . . . free freshly popped popcorn while you select your movies. Also, check out the 99-cent video section for everything from documentaries to soft-core porn.

CHELSEA MARKET
75 Ninth Avenue (between 15th and 16th Streets)
(212) 243–6005
The former home of the Nabisco Company and the birthplace of the Oreo cookie has been transformed into a sumptuous marketplace of gourmet shops. Sample breads, brownies, gourmet butters, cookies, and fruit. Selections are particularly abundant on weekends, when you can also sample some fine wines (Friday and Saturday) and even dance a tango (on Saturday).

COUNTRY CORNER
196 Columbus Avenue (at 69th Street)
(212) 874–0095
www.americanFOLKart.com

This delightful store of American folk art, books, dolls, and other bits of fun always sets out a box of freshly baked star cookies to match the ceiling. The cookies come from the nearby Bakery Soutine, where you can also get a bit to nibble on (see listing above).

GARDEN OF EDEN FARMERS MARKET
310 Third Avenue (between 23rd and 24th Streets);
(212) 228–4681
162 West 23rd Street (between Sixth and Seventh Avenues);
(212) 675–6300
7 East 14th Street (between Fifth Avenue and University Place);
(212) 255–4200
www.gardenofedengourmet.com

Always a great selection of samples including cheeses, breads, deli meats, a full olive bar, desserts, and exotic fruits.

GODIVA CHOCOLATIER
www.godiva.com

DOWNTOWN LOCATIONS
33 Maiden Lane (at Nassau Street); 212 809–8990
21 Fulton Street (at Front Street, South Street Seaport);
(212) 571–6965

MIDTOWN LOCATIONS
Grand Central Station; (212) 808–0276
52 West 50th Street (between Fifth and Sixth Avenues);
(212) 399–1875
701 Fifth Avenue (between 54th and 55th Streets); (212) 593–2845
560 Lexington Avenue (at 50th Street); (212) 980–9810
200 Park Avenue (at 42nd Street); (212) 697–9150
1460 Broadway (at 41st Street); (212) 840–6758

UPTOWN LOCATIONS
2325 Broadway (at 84th Street); (212) 579–3197
245 Columbus Avenue (between 71st and 72nd Streets);
(212) 787–5804
793 Madison Avenue (at 67th Street); (212) 249–9444

Gourmet chocolates at gourmet prices, but on selected days they have some sweets out for sampling, as well as offering free cups of their high-class coffee or hot chocolate. Stop into any location and pick up a copy of their catalog, where they publish what and when they'll be giving away every month.

GOURMET GARAGE
453 Broome Street (at Mercer Street); (212) 941–5850
117 Seventh Avenue South (at Christopher Street);
(212) 414–5910
2567 Broadway (between 96th and 97th Streets);
(212) 663–0656
301 East 64th Street (between First and Second Avenues);
(212) 535–6271
Sample from the olive bar, cheeses, and other gourmet treats from time to time.

GREENMARKET FARMER'S MARKET
Union Square, 17th Street and Broadway
(212) 477–3220
www.cenyc.org
New York has many official farmer's markets (twenty-seven throughout the five boroughs), which attract a wide variety of upstate and Long Island farmers into the city to sell their wares. The hands-down best market to get samples of everything from heirloom tomatoes and organic apples, beans, and peppers to fresh bread, cakes, and jams is the Union Square market, held every Monday, Wednesday, Friday, and Saturday. Call or check the Web site for information on other markets around the city.

JEFFERSON MARKET
450 Sixth Avenue (between 10th and 11th Streets)
(212) 533–3377
Good bakery, cheese, and deli samples.

POMMES FRITES
123 Second Avenue (between 7th and 8th Streets)
(212) 674–1234
Specializing in "Authentic Belgian Fries," they offer free samples that consist of about six large fries and your choice of two gourmet dipping sauces. No pressure to buy. A great little snack.

RENAISSANCE NEW YORK HOTEL
714 Seventh Avenue (between 48th and 49th Streets)
(212) 765–7676
www.renaissancehotels.com

Bowls of apples are available in the second-floor lobby, along with some nice comfy chairs. A good place to duck into when you have some time to kill.

TODARO BROS.
555 Second Avenue (between 30th and 31st Streets)
(212) 532–0633
A gourmet market with samples of cheeses, olive oils, bread, and more.

TURQUACINO FINE FOOD MARKETPLACE
252 Bleecker Street (between Sixth and Seventh Avenues)
(212) 937–9504
Samples of olive oils, desserts, cheeses, and a full olive bar.

VINTAGE NEW YORK
482 Broome Street (at Wooster Street)
(212) 226–9463
You might expect to find this listing in the wine tasting section, but they charge for tastes of their New York wines (five one-ounce tastes for $1.00). Don't let that stop you from stopping in the store. Go for the delicious cheese and sinful chocolate truffles they always have out for the taking. Also, because of some loophole in the law—they sell only New York wines—this is the only wine shop in New York City open on Sunday.

WHOLE FOODS MARKET
250 Seventh Avenue (at 24th Street)
(212) 924–5969
This health food supermarket is good for sampling on weekends. Be sure to taste the teas and check out the bakery.

W HOTELS
201 Park Avenue (Union Square at 17th Street); (212) 253–9119

541 Lexington Avenue (at 49th Street); (212) 755–1200

130 East 39th Street (between Lexington and Park Avenues); (212) 685–1100

120 East 39th Street (between Lexington and Park Avenues); (212) 686–1600

1567 Broadway (at 47th Street); (212) 930–7400

These elegant and funky hotels have amazing lobbies with board games, books, couches, comfy chairs, and overflowing bowls of delicious green apples for you to munch away on.

EAT LATE, EAT CHEAP!

Hey, eating late may not be very good for the size of your waist, but it can do wonders of the size of your wallet. If you must spend money—and of course I generally do frown on that—then drop by one of these places to eat for half price (after the specified times). These shops, restaurants, gourmet markets, and health food stores all have a policy of cutting their prices at the end of the day to get rid of that day's fresh sandwiches, salads, and other assorted taste delights.

AMISH MARKET

731 Ninth Avenue (between 49th and 50th Streets);
(212) 245-2360

240 East 45th Street (between Second and Third Avenues);
(212) 370-1761

59 Maiden Lane (between William and John Streets);
(212) 742-2436

www.amishmarkets.com

All three cut prices on gourmet sandwiches at 6:00 P.M. All stores close at 10:00 P.M. They don't exactly advertise this, so make sure they don't try to charge you the full price when you get to the register. They also have great olive bars for sampling and occasionally cheeses and desserts for you to taste.

DAIKICHI SUSHI

122 East 42nd Street (between Park and Lexington Avenues); (212) 661-3299; half price 8:00-9:00 P.M.

176 West 72nd Street (at Broadway); (212) 873-0243; half price 9:00-10:00 P.M.

7 West 33rd Street (between Fifth and Sixth Avenues);
(212) 465-2214; half price 5:00-7:00 P.M.

469 Seventh Avenue (between 35th and 36th Streets);
(212) 741-9325; half price 6:00-7:00 P.M.

This chain of sushi take-out shops offers half-price prepacked combinations at the end of the day at some of their many locations around the city. Check above for specific locations and times.

FAIRWAY

2127 Broadway (between 74th and 75th Streets); (212) 595–1888
2328 Twelfth Ave (at 133rd Street); (212) 234–3883

This popular Upper West Side market offers half price on gourmet sandwiches, sushi, and bakery goods at about 11:00 P.M. every night (they
close at 1:00 A.M.). The sandwiches are overstuffed and at half price will
run you about $2.00 each. This is a great way to stock up on lunches for
the week. The Harlem store cuts at the bakery prices at about 9:30 or
10:00 P.M. (they close at 11:00 P.M. every night).

FASHION SOUP

124 West 41st Street (between Sixth Avenue and Broadway)
(212) 704–0909

As the Campbell's soup commercial goes, "Soup is good food." But
these soups are nothing like those watered-down cans of cream of
mushroom your mom used to stockpile. These are hearty, tasty, thick,
and chunky bowls of soups that fill you up like a meal. Every day
there's a new selection of soups and stews with delicious twists on
favorites (tomato soup with fennel and artichoke, corn chowder with
chicken) or ingenious blends (cream of carrot with ginger, vegetarian
mulligatawny). Half-price soups are offered from 3:30 P.M. to closing
(about 5:30).

INTEGRAL YOGA NATURAL FOODS

229 West 13th Street (between Seventh and Eighth Avenues)
(212) 243–2642
www.iynaturalfoods.com

A natural food store with an extensive salad bar including all kinds of
beans, vegetables, tofu creations, and other green and brown edibles.
They sell off generous platters of leftovers from the day at greatly
reduced prices ($1.99 for a small and $3.99 for a large) starting at 6:30
P.M. Monday to Friday, and at 5:30 on weekends.

ISOBEL'S KITCHEN

130 Church Street (at Murray Street)
(212) 566–5407

This small gourmet sandwich shop sells its sandwiches and wraps at half
price from 4:00 to 5:00 P.M. Monday through Friday.

NEWS CAFE
107 University Place (between 12th and 13th Streets)
(212) 353-1246
A newsstand/sandwich shop that cuts prices in half on sandwiches and salads at 7:00 P.M.; and on muffins, croissants, and danish at 8:00 P.M. Feel free to sit and read the newspapers and magazines from around the world while eating your cheap dinner (try not to get any dressing on the papers, though). Closes at 10:00 P.M. every night.

NEW WING WAH
90 Chambers Street (between Church Street and Broadway)
(212) 732-9881
This fast-food Chinese and Japanese joint offers its large buffet (including sushi) for half price after 2:30 P.M. Monday through Saturday; it closes at 10:00 P.M.

SOHO NATURAL DELI
127 Spring Street (at Greene Street)
(212) 226-8237
A typical New York corner deli salad bar with a selection including Chinese dishes, sushi, cold salads, fresh fruit, and more. The salad bar is half price from 7:00 P.M. until it's all gone.

TODARO BROS.
(see page 91 for information)
At this gourmet market they sell off their leftover fresh sandwiches for half price from 8:00 to 10:00 P.M. every night.

TURQUACINO FINE FOOD MARKETPLACE
(see page 91 for information)
This gourmet market with lots of great samples along the aisles also offers half-price sandwiches and wraps after 8:00 P.M. every night; closes at midnight.

WILD OATS COMMUNITY MARKET
2421 Broadway (corner of 89th Street)
(212) 874-4000
www.wildoats.com
A health food store that offers 50 percent off at the salad bar after 9:00 P.M.; they close down the salad bar at about 10:00 or 10:30 P.M.

ZABAR'S

2245 Broadway (between 80th and 81st Streets)
(212) 496–1234 or (800) 697–6301
www.zabars.com

At this world-famous marketplace for gourmet cheeses, deli, coffee, bakery and more, they cut the prices on prepared sandwiches at about 6:00 P.M. Monday through Saturday. They close at 7:30 P.M. Monday through Friday and 8:00 P.M. on Saturday.

"I like best the wine drunk at the cost of others."

—Bergen Evans

WINE TASTINGS: CHEAP DRUNK

NOT ONLY DO THE WINE shops of New York offer you a chance to try some of the finest wines and spirits from around the world, but you can also end up learning a heck of a lot about the fruits of the vine. You'll find two types of wine tasting situations at stores around the city. One is the local shop that uncorks a bottle or two for customers to try (and hopes you'll buy). The other, more desirable situation is when a vintner or wine distributor brings out an entire line of wines for the public to sample. You get to try more wines, the staff are usually very knowledgeable and eager to teach you about the wines without pushing you to buy anything, and you can usually depend on them bringing something tasty along "to cleanse the palate" between wines. All this can be true about the local shop, but you're just as likely to find a guy with a bottle saying, "Here, try some of this stuff, I hear it's good." Most shops offer a discount on whatever is being tasted that day, so if you're inspired to lay down some cash, this will lighten the blow.

WINE TASTINGS BY THE WEEK

SHOP	MONDAY	TUESDAY	WEDNESDAY	THURSDAY	FRIDAY	SATURDAY
Acker Merrall & Condit Co.						2:00–5:00 P.M.
Ambassador Wine & Spirits		4:00–8:00 P.M.		4:00–8:00 P.M.	4:00–8:00 P.M.	
Astor Wines & Spirits				5:00–8:00 P.M.	5:00–8:00 P.M.	3:00–6:00 P.M.
Bacchus	5:00–8:00 P.M.	5:00–8:00 P.M.	5:00–8:00 P.M.	5:00–8:00 P.M.	5:00–8:00 P.M.	5:00–8:00 P.M.
Beekman Liquors					4:00–7:00 P.M.	
Best Cellars	5:00–8:00 P.M.	5:00–8:00 P.M.	5:00–8:00 P.M.	5:00–8:00 P.M.	5:00–8:00 P.M.	2:00–4:00 P.M.
Burgundy Wine Co.						11:00 A.M.–7:00 P.M.
Candlelight Wines						1:00–5:00 P.M.
Chelsea Wine Vault					4:00–7:00 P.M.	1:00–5:00 P.M.
Cork & Bottle					5:00–7:00 P.M.	
86th Street Corner Wine					4:00–8:00 P.M.	
86th Street Wine & Liquor						5:00–8:00 P.M.
Elizabeth & Vine						5:00–8:00 P.M.
Gramercy Park					5:00–8:00 P.M.	
Grand Harvest	5:00–8:00 P.M.	5:00–8:00 P.M.	5:00–8:00 P.M.	5:00–8:00 P.M.	5:00–8:00 P.M.	
International Wine & Spirits				4:00–7:00 P.M.		4:00–7:00 P.M.
Italian Wine Merchants						1:00–4:00 P.M. (SELECTED SATURDAYS)
Morell & Company						2:00–5:00 P.M.
Mister Wright Liquors					4:00–7:00 P.M.	4:00–7:00 P.M.
New Erlich Wine & Spirits			5:00–8:00 P.M.	5:00–8:00 P.M.	5:00–8:00 P.M.	1:00–4:00 P.M.
Ninth Avenue Vintner						4:00–8:00 P.M.
Park East Wine & Spirits						4:00–7:00 P.M.
Sea Grape Wine & Spirits				5:30–8:30 P.M.		
67 Wine & Spirits		4:00–7:00 P.M.	4:00–7:00 P.M.	4:00–7:00 P.M.	4:00–7:00 P.M.	4:00–7:00 P.M.
Spirits of Columbus				4:00–7:00 P.M.	4:00–7:00 P.M.	4:00–7:00 P.M.
Union Square			4:00–7:00 P.M.	4:00–7:00 P.M.	4:00–7:00 P.M.	2:00–7:00 P.M.
Washington Square Wines						4:00–7:00 P.M.
Windsor Court				5:00–7:00 P.M.	5:00–7:00 P.M.	

EAST SIDE

AMBASSADOR WINES & SPIRITS
1020 Second Avenue (at 54th Street)
(212) 421–5078
This local shop holds tastings Tuesday, Thursday, and Friday, 4:00 to 8:00 P.M.

BACCHUS
2056 Broadway (at 71st Street)
(212) 875–1200
www.bacchuswineoneline.com
A warm and welcoming shop uncorks a bottle every evening for you to sample on Monday through Saturday, from 5:00 to 8:00 P.M. This shop offers a hand-picked selection of moderate priced and fine wines, including my personal favorite vintage, "Fat Bastard" wine. Occasionally, the daily tastings turn into full evening events that highlight wines from around the world accompanied by music and dancing from these regions.

BEEKMAN LIQUORS
500 Lexington Avenue (between 47th and 48th Streets)
(212) 759–5857
Sophisticated local shop. Friday, 4:00 to 7:00 P.M.

BEST CELLARS
1291 Lexington Avenue (between 86th and 87th Streets)
(212) 426–4200
www.bestcellars.com
This is a great no-nonsense, yet know-it-all place to go to check out some great-tasting wines. The very knowledgeable staff serve up some delightful inexpensive wines on weekday evenings (5:00 to 8:00); on Saturday (2:00 to 4:00 P.M.) they usually pair the wine with food prepared by local chefs.

CORK & BOTTLE
1158 First Avenue (between 63rd and 64th Streets)
(212) 838–5300
Local shop. Friday, 5:00 to 7:00 P.M.

86TH STREET WINE & LIQUOR
306 East 86th Street (at Second Avenue)
(212) 396–3535
Local shop. Saturday, 5:00 to 8:00 P.M.

GRAMERCY PARK

121 East 23rd Street (between Park and Lexington Avenues)
(212) 505–0550
Local shop. Friday, 5:00 to 8:00 P.M.

GRAND HARVEST WINES

Grand Central Station (across from Track 17)
107 East 42nd Street (at Lexington Avenue)
(212) 682–5855
This small up-scale shop opens up a few bottles for tasting every afternoon. The knowledgeable staff can talk your ear off about the wines you're
sampling, but they definitely steer the conversation toward selling you a
bottle. Monday through Friday after 5:00 P.M.

ITALIAN WINE MERCHANTS

108 East 16th Street (between Union Square East and Irving Place)
(212) 473–2323
www.italianwinemerchant.com
This elegant wine shop specializing in (you guessed it) wines from Italy
hosts complimentary walk-around tastings on selected Saturdays from
1:00 to 4:00 P.M., with at least ten bottles to sample, along with green
market antipasti.

MISTER WRIGHT LIQUORS

1593 Third Avenue (between 89th and 90th Streets)
(212) 722–4564
This large store cracks open a few bottles for tasting on Friday and
Saturday from 4:00 P.M. to 7:00 P.M. It could be anything from cheap (or
shall I say *inexpensive?*) to fine wines.

PARK EAST WINES & SPIRITS

1657 York Avenue (at 87th Street)
(212) 534–2093
Local shop. Saturday, 4:00 to 7:00 P.M.

UNION SQUARE

33 Union Square West (between 16th and 17th Streets)
(212) 675–8100
www.unionsquarewines.com
This posh shop is always pouring something wonderful and unusual for
you to try. Every week (Wednesday through Friday, 4:00 to 7:00 P.M.;

Saturday, 2:00 to 7:00 P.M.) they play host to a number of distributors, vintners, and sommeliers from around the city and the world who pour their selections for you to sample in the lavish upstairs salon. From time to time they also collaborate with local restaurants to provide food to match the wines.

WINDSOR COURT WINE SHOP
474 Third Avenue (between 32nd and 33rd Streets)
(212) 779-4422
Local shop. Thursday and Friday, 5:00 to 7:00 P.M.

WEST SIDE

ACKER MERRALL & CONDIT CO.
160 West 72nd Street (between Columbus Avenue and Broadway)
(212) 787-1700
This cozy local shop opens a couple of bottles every Saturday from 2:00 to 5:00 P.M.

CANDLELIGHT WINES
2315 Broadway (between 83rd and 84th Streets)
(212) 877-7085
A small local store that opens up a couple of bottles and sets out some cheese and crackers on Saturday, 1:00 to 5:00 P.M.

CHELSEA WINE VAULT
75 Ninth Avenue (between 15th and 16th Streets)
(212) 462-4244
www.chelseawinevault.com
A great wine find located in the Chelsea Market. They offer two days of tastings every week. Stop by any Friday from 4:00 to 7:00 P.M. for a free evening of wine and food tastings. This is a very social, cocktail-hour type of atmosphere. On Saturday afternoon from 1:00 to 5:00 P.M., they crack open a few bottles for a much less formal take-a-swig-as-you-buy-a-bottle ambience. Don't miss their once-a-year Open House Anniversary celebration. This is a wonderful event that happens on a Saturday in early November: You'll find more than fifty wines for sampling, free catered hor d'oeuvres, and free introductory wine classes. They also run the Chelsea Wine Institute, which offers introductory and advanced classes in wine

education. You can attend these classes for free by volunteering to be a teaching assistant or a wine pourer (see page 145 for information).

86TH STREET CORNER WINE & LIQUOR COMPANY
536 Columbus Avenue (at 86th Street)
(212) 496–1769
Local shop. Friday, 4:00 to 8:00 P.M.

INTERNATIONAL WINES & SPIRITS
2903 Broadway (at 113th Street)
(212) 280–1850
Local shop. Thursday and Saturday, 4:00 to 7:00 P.M.

MORRELL & COMPANY WINE & SPIRITS MERCHANTS
1 Rockefeller Plaza (at 49th Street, between Fifth and Sixth Avenues)
(212) 688–9370
www.morrellwine.com
This fancy (and expensive) wine store brings in distributors to hawk their line of wines every Saturday, 2:00 to 5:00 P.M.

NEW ERLICH WINES & SPIRITS
222 Amsterdam Avenue (at 70th Street)
(212) 877–6090
A small corner shop that opens one or two bottles for sampling, Wednesday through Friday after 5:00 P.M., and Saturday 1:00 to 4:00 P.M.

NINTH AVENUE VINTNER
669 Ninth Avenue (between 46th and 47th Streets)
(212) 664–WINE (9463) or (877) 664–9463
A friendly community shop that brings in vintners to show off their wines most Saturdays, 4:00 to 8:00 P.M.

67 WINES & SPIRITS
179 Columbus Avenue (at 68th Street)
(212) 724–6767
www.67wine.com
A fine store for fine wines and every bit of wine paraphernalia you could ever imagine. Make your way up to the second-floor kitchen area and get an education in wines by sampling vintages of different countries, regions,

types, and styles Tuesday through Saturday, 4:00 to 7:00 P.M. They often have cooking demonstrations or at least something tasty to nibble along with the wines. Check their Web site for a listing of weekly events.

SPIRITS OF COLUMBUS

730 Columbus Avenue (between 95th and 96th Streets)
(212) 865–7070
This local shop offers tastes from a few inexpensive bottles Thursday through Saturday, 4:00 to 7:00 P.M. Most Fridays they sample a selection of kosher wines.

DOWNTOWN EAST

ASTOR WINES & SPIRITS

12 Astor Place (8th Street, between Lafayette Street and Broadway)
(212) 674–7500
www.astoruncorked.com
New York's largest wine store offers tastings grouped by region or type, giving you the opportunity to try everything from Dom Perignon to the wines of New Zealand and South Africa; from moderately priced to fine wines. The friendly staff offer samples in a no-pressure-to-buy atmosphere. Be sure to cleanse your palate with the gourmet breads and cheeses that often accompany the wines. Thursday and Friday, 5:00 to 8:00 P.M.; Saturday, 3:00 to 6:00 P.M. Check the Web site for a calendar of events.

ELIZABETH & VINE

253 Elizabeth Street (between Houston and Prince Streets)
(212) 941–7943
This tiny shop offers samples from a few bottles along with cheese and crackers. Saturday, 5:00 to 8:00 P.M.

DOWNTOWN WEST

BURGUNDY WINE COMPANY

323 West 11th Street (between Greenwich and Washington Streets)
(212) 691–9092
www.burgundywinecompany.com
Stepping inside this store may feel more like walking into someone's office (someone who happens to be a bit of a wino), but rest assured it is a full-

Corkscrew U

Don't know your Asti Spumonti from your elderberry wine? Take a class. There are many courses offered throughout the city that will let you expand you choice of wines beyond twist-off or cork. Most of these are one-day seminars on wines from specific regions of the world, but some are in-depth courses exploring every aspect of the wine, from seeds to sipping. And you can take the classes for free by volunteering to be a "pourer" for these classes. Basically all that's involved is showing up for the class an hour or so early, setting out the glasses and class materials for the paying students, pouring the wines that are used in the classes, and staying a little while after the class ends to load the glasses in the dishwasher. While the class is on, you're able to fully participate and taste all the wines used. See the chapter titled Education: Cents-less Smarts for more details on classes at the Chelsea Wine Institute, the International Wine Center, and the New School Culinary Arts Program.

fledged wine store. Their small collection of wines focuses exclusively on fine Burgundies and Rhônes. Every Saturday from 11:00 A.M. to 7:00 P.M., they select a couple of their favorites for you to taste.

SEA GRAPE WINE & SPIRITS
512 Hudson Street (between Christopher and West 10th Streets)
(212) 463–7688
Local shop. Thursday, 5:30 to 8:30 P.M.

WASHINGTON SQUARE WINES
545 LaGuardia Place (between Bleecker and West 3rd Streets)
(212) 477–4395
A local shop that holds a tasting every Saturday, 4:00 to 7:00 P.M.

"You'd be surprised how much it costs to look this cheap."

—Dolly Parton

HAIR, BEAUTY, AND MASSAGE: FREE-STYLE

JUST BECAUSE YOUR BANK account is running low doesn't mean you can't look and feel like a million bucks. In fact, looking good and feeling good can look and feel a whole lot better the less you pay to get that way. And in New York anything you need or want done can be had for nothing or very little: haircuts, coloring, highlights, facials, makeovers, manicures, and massage. The most common places to look for free or cheap services are salons with training programs, beauty and barbering schools, and manufacturers testing new products.

PRODUCT TESTING CENTERS

Here's your chance to be the first on your block to try out the newest products that some of the leading hair care manufacturers are developing. These companies are in the final stages of testing these items and want your opinion. Fear not: These creams, colors, mousses, and gels have all gone through a battery of tests already and are safe for you to use. In other words, you won't end up with a head full of green hair (unless, of course, that's what you want). You should know, though, that they won't be able to customize colors for your hair. You will be able to choose your colors, but they must be selected from the standard set of colors prepared for the shelves of any local store.

CLAIROL PRODUCT EVALUATION SALON
345 Park Avenue, lobby (between 51st and 52nd Streets)
(212) 546–2701
The services they offer and the products they test include hair coloring, perms, relaxers, conditioners, styling mousses, and gels. All services are free and performed by licensed and skilled stylists. You must stop by first to apply—Monday through Friday from 9:30 to 11:00 A.M. or 1:30 to 4:00 P.M. All men and women eighteen or over may participate. The services they provide at any given time depend on the products being tested. The most common and consistent service offered is hair coloring. Once you're accepted onto the models' panel, you're welcome to come back in once a month for treatments.

L'ORÉAL TECHNICAL CENTER
575 Fifth Avenue (at 47th Street)
(212) 984–4147
www.loreal.com

> **THE CATCH** **Women must have shoulder-length or shorter hair (but not too short).**

This is the product evaluation salon for all L'Oréal coloring and hair care products. Stop by Monday through Thursday 10:00 A.M. to 4:00 P.M. for an evaluation and patch test. If they accept you into the program, they will color your hair every four weeks. They occasionally use men as well (long hair not necessary), but primarily seek women.

HAIR SALONS

These are some of the most exclusive (and expensive) salons in the city, and they all have training programs for fully licensed hairstylists who are receiving further instruction in specific styles or techniques. This makes it a low-risk situation: You can feel reasonably confident you won't end up with an accidental Mohawk at these salons. The only catch is that you are sometimes required to spend two to three hours at the salon when you are modeling for a class. Many of the salons that offer free services can be picky about whom they use as models; women are generally used more than men, and longer hair gets you an appointment quicker than shorter hair. All the salons listed below offer free cuts and/or colorings.

BUMBLE & BUMBLE
146 East 56th Street (between Lexington and Madison Avenues)
(888) 528-6253

 For free cuts and styling, models must have long enough hair to have at least 2 to 3 inches cut off.

This salon has a large training program. To get a free cut or style, you'll need to be chosen as a model for one of their seminars (they hold about twenty-five a year). Modeling calls are held on Monday evening at 6:00 P.M. the week before a seminar. If you're chosen as a cut model, you sign up for a slot at 11:00 A.M. or 2:00 P.M. If you're chosen as a styling model, you'll need to be available the entire day, but you'll receive a $100 gift certificate toward any products or services in the salon. Call to find out when they are holding their next interviews. If you aren't chosen as a model, you can still schedule a low-price cut or color from a staff apprentice for $10 to $20 on Monday from 10:00 A.M. to 4:00 P.M.

DEVACHAN HAIR & DEPARTURE LOUNGE
560 Broadway, basement (between Prince and Spring Streets)
(212) 274-8686
www.devachansalon.com
Call to book a time with one of the talented assistants at this cavernous, space-age Soho salon. Appointments are usually on Tuesday.

Don't Be THAT Cheap!

While these may be students, and you may be getting your hair done for free or at a very low price, this is still New York, so don't forget to tip! The fact is, as students these stylists probably aren't being paid. They may even be paying to do this work for you. A Cheap Bastard can still be a nice bastard.

FACE STATION
855 Lexington Avenue (between 64th and 65th Streets)
(212) 249–8866 or (877) 815–FACE (3223)
www.facestation.com
They set up appointments throughout the week. Call or stop by to put your name on the list.

JEAN LOUIS DAVID TRAINING CENTER
10 East 41st Street (between Fifth and Madison Avenues)
(212) 779–3555
This trendy version of Supercuts has locations all over the city and gives New Yorkers moderately priced cuts and styles. But if you book a slot at their training center, it's all free. They train licensed stylists to work in the Jean Louis David style (basically, using a clipper for much of the work). They also offer free coloring services. You can call to set up an appointment, but a more effective strategy is stopping by in person a few days before you'd like an appointment. They make appointments for Monday, Tuesday, and Wednesday, morning and afternoon. Men and women are welcome.

JEFFREY STEIN SALON
685 Third Avenue (at 43rd Street); (212) 557–0005

1336 Third Avenue (at 76th Street); (212) 772–7717

Jeffrey Stein has seven salons around the city, but these two offer free cuts for hair models on Wednesday morning (43rd Street) and on Tuesday (77th Street). They offer cuts to men and women, depending on what skills and styles they're working on. Call one to two weeks in advance to set up an appointment.

LEN MILO SALON
341 Amsterdam Avenue (at 76th Street)
(212) 580–4657
www.teammilo.com
This is a relaxed neighborhood salon with a friendly staff. The senior staff give lots of supervision and hands-on assistance to the stylists in training, so you can feel confident that you'll walk out of there looking good. They're always looking for models for a free cut or color. Call a few days to a week in advance for an appointment anytime on Monday, Tuesday, or Wednesday.

Fancy Places at Not-so-Fancy Prices

These salons all run training programs and charge reduced rates for stylish cuts given by their students. These appointments are generally easier to get than the free ones:

AEREA, 18 East 17th Street (between Fifth Avenue and Broadway); (212) 308–3838; Tuesday and Wednesday; $10 cut, $15 color.

ARROJO CUTLER SALON, 115 East 57th Street (between Park and Lexington Avenues); (212) 308–3906; Tuesday, Wednesday, and Thursday; $8.00.

JACQUES DESSANGE, 505 Park Avenue (at 59th Street); (212) 308–1400; Sunday and Monday daytime, and Tuesday and Wednesday evening; $15 cut, $20 color, women only.

NARDA SALON, 111 East 56th Street (at Park Avenue); (212) 421–4810; Tuesday and Thursday; $20.

PAUL LABRECQUE SALON, 171 East 65th Street (at Third Avenue); (212) 595–0099; Monday; $20.

PRIVE, 310 West Broadway (between Grand and Canal Streets); (212) 274–8888; Tuesday and Wednesday; $20.

SHIGE KOSUDA SALON, 141 East 55th Street (between Lexington and Third Avenues); (212) 759–2397; Tuesday and Wednesday; $10.

VIDAL SASSON DOWNTOWN, 90 Fifth Avenue (between 14th and 15th Streets); (212) 229–2200; Wednesday; $18.

VIDAL SASSON UPTOWN, 730 Fifth Avenue (at 56th Street); (212) 535–9200; Wednesday; $18–$25.

MIANO VIEL SALON AND SPA

16 East 52nd Street, second floor (between Fifth and Madison Avenues)
(212) 980–3222
www.mianoviel.com

This very hotsy-totsy, hoity-toity salon holds classes on Wednesday night. Free cuts for class models; call or stop by to put your name on their list, and they will call you when they need someone.

MICHAEL GIOVAN SALON
229 East 53rd Street (between Second and Third Avenues)
(212) 308-3150
www.cropsforgirls.com

 To get a free cut, you have to go from long hair to very short or let Michael do whatever he wants with your hair.

This salon specializes in short haircuts for women. It may be funky, it may be conservative; you never know what it may end up being. But you know it will be very short and Michael will cut it himself. Call to make an appointment. Women only.

OSCAR BOND SALON SPA
42 Wooster Street (between Grand and Broome Streets)
(212) 334-3777
www.oscarbondsalon.com
Slick Soho style is served up at this salon. Call or stop by to let them know you're interested in being a hair model, and one of the assistants will call you back to talk about your needs and schedule a free cut.

PARLOR
102 Avenue B (between 6th and 7th Streets)
(212) 673-5520
www.parlorNYC.com
A funky and low-key East Village salon that holds classes on Wednesday morning and Thursday evening. Free cuts and colors for hair models, but you must be willing to stay for the whole class (two to three hours). Call or stop by to give them your name for an appointment.

RICARDO MAGGIORE SALON
18 West 56th Street, second floor (between Fifth and Sixth Avenues)
(212) 586-6482
www.ricardomaggiore.com
Class models get free cuts and/or coloring during the Tuesday classes. Call to put your name on the list.

SALON ZIBA
200 West 57th Street (between Broadway and Seventh Avenue)
(212) 767-0577
www.salonziba.com

You need to pay $10 for the coloring products used.

They need class models for their Wednesday-night hair coloring class. Call for an appointment.

SCOTT J. SALONS & SPAS
257 Columbus Avenue (at 72nd Street)
(212) 769–0107
www.scottj.com
Call or stop by to put your name on the list for the Wednesday-morning class for a free cut and/or coloring.

SUITE 303
The Chelsea Hotel
222 West 23rd Street, third floor (between Seventh and Eighth Avenues)
(212) 633–1011
www.suite303.com
This small salon in the artsy Chelsea Hotel uses models on occasion, depending on how many assistants are training at the time. Call for details.

YVES DURIF
130 East 65th Street (between Park and Lexington Avenues)
(212) 452–0954
This very welcoming salon in a beautiful Upper East side brownstone uses models on Wednesday night for color and cuts at no charge. Stop in some-time during the week to take a Polaroid; they'll call you to make an appointment when they have an opening.

BEAUTY SCHOOLS

These schools are training folks to sit for their state licensing exams, so the amount of experience and skill fluctuates greatly from student to student. You do take on some risk of a coif catastrophe when you put your head in their hands. In fact, they usually have you sign a release to this effect before you get your haircut. The students are supervised, but the level of supervision varies from place to place. The better you describe what you'd like done, the happier you'll be with your results.

AMERICAN BARBER SCHOOL
252 West 29th Street (between Seventh and Eighth Avenues)
(212) 290–2289

A low fee is charged for work done by students.

They offer haircuts for $4.00, but you might get lucky and find their "flyer guy" handing out flyers for free cuts at 29th Street and Eighth Avenue. Check around noon Monday through Friday.

ATLAS BARBER SCHOOL
32 Third Avenue (between 9th and 10th Streets);
(212) 475–1360

80 East 10th Street (between Third and Fourth Avenues);
(212) 475–5699

They charge a fee for services performed by students.

This must be the minor-league farm system for Astor Place Haircutters (world renowned for their quick clipper cuts at $11 a snip). If you're in the market for one of those maybe neat, maybe funky, anything-you-can-do-with-a-clipper-in-ten-minutes-cuts, this is the place for you. It's $5.00 at the Third Avenue location, but if you walk around the block to 10th Street it's only $4.00. Why is it cheaper around the corner? Cheaper rent.

AVEDA INSTITUTE
233 Spring Street (between Sixth Avenue and Varick Street)
(212) 807–1492

They charge a fee for services performed by students.

This upscale beauty school offers hair, facial, and spa services by students using Aveda's organic products. Prices are a bit steeper than at other beauty schools, but still pretty cheap by New York standards (a forty-five-minute facial costs $35; haircut $15; coloring $30 to $60). You can also be a model for Aveda classes and receive services for free. Call (212) 367–0339 for details.

CHRISTIAN NAIL SCHOOL

27 West 34th Street, third floor (between Fifth and Sixth Avenues)
(212) 643–1022
www.nailschool.com

 They charge a low fee for services provided by students.

Manicures are $5.00 for women and $6.00 for men. Pedicures are $10. Nail and pedicure kits are $5.00 each.

JON LOUIS SCHOOL OF BEAUTY

91–14 Merrick Boulevard (between 91st Street and Jamaica Avenue), Jamaica, Queens; (718) 658–6240

210 East 188th Street (between Valentine Street and Grand Concourse), the Bronx; (718) 733–2828

 They charge a low fee for services performed by students.

Haircuts $1.50 to $5.00, facials $6.00, lip waxing $2.50. The Bronx School also occasionally needs models for classes, in which case you get work performed by instructors, and for free. Call for details.

LEARNING INSTITUTE FOR BEAUTY SCIENCE

22 West 34th Street (between Fifth and Sixth Avenues);
(212) 967–1717

38–15 Broadway (at Steinway Street), Astoria, Queens;
(718) 726–8383

2384 86th Street (at Twenty-fourth Avenue), Bay Ridge, Brooklyn;
(718) 373–2400
www.libsbeautyschool.com

 They charge a low fee for services performed by students.

Okay, this place isn't too swanky, and the cuts won't be cutting edge, but if you're in the market for a basic cut, style, color, or facial, it certainly is cheap (especially on Wednesday). Their most consistent clientele are old ladies and recently released convicts, which makes for a very interesting waiting room! The fees are $5.00 for a shampoo and cut, facials $7.00, manicure $4.00, and lip, chin, or eyebrow wax $2.00. They also have reduced price specials on Tuesday, Wednesday, and Thursday for specific services (Tuesday: $7.00 hair color; Wednesday: $2.00 off all nonchemical treatments; Thursday: $14.95 perms). All work is performed by students.

MASSAGE

LOVING TOUCH CENTER INTERNATIONAL SCHOOL OF TRADITIONAL REIKI
59 West 19th Street (between Fifth and Sixth Avenues)
(212) 570–1623
www.reiki-ltc.org
This is not your Uncle Ike's idea of a massage. Reiki works with the energy of the universe (rei) and the body's energy (chi); the practitioners only lightly touch you during a session. The results can be surprisingly relaxing, calming, and healing. They hold free "Healing Circles" on Monday and Wednesday evening, which consists of a guided meditation, fifteen-minute hands-on sessions, and a question-and-answer discussion about the practice. Work is performed by Reiki masters and students. Call ahead to confirm time and location.

THE SWEDISH INSTITUTE FOR MASSAGE THERAPY
226 West 26th Street (between Seventh and Eighth Avenues)
(212) 924–5900
www.swedishinstitute.com

THE CATCH They charge low fees for massage therapy performed by students.

If you want a free massage, you'll have to start dating a massage therapist, and even then it's not a sure thing (we've all seen the *Seinfeld* episode). So when you need some good cheap hands-on massage, check out the P. H. Ling Clinic at the Swedish Institute. They have two options for low-cost massage. The Stress Reduction Clinic is open to all (but slots fill up quickly) and offers a package of six relaxing and refreshing massages for $125. You register for a series of six one-hour massages, and each week you will receive either a Swedish or Shiatsu session (based on therapist availability). No preferences for modality are taken; you take what you're given from week to week. The Therapeutic Massage Clinic is available to those who have a prescription from a doctor or chiropractor for treatment on a specific injury or condition. You must register for a package of twelve one-hour massages for $225. This series consists of twelve consecutive weekly sessions. Each patient will receive both Eastern (Shiatsu) and Western (Swedish, sports massage, or the like) treatments throughout the twelve weeks. The work is performed by students in their final semester and supervised by faculty. Both clinics are offered three times a year and very popular, applying for a slot as early as possible is advised.

MAKEUP

FACE STATION
855 Lexington Avenue (between 64th and 65th Streets)
(212) 249–8866 or (877) 815–FACE (3223)
www.facestation.com
Call to put your name on the list to model in one of their Sunday classes for free services, and you may learn a thing or two as well.

IL MAKIAGE MAKE-UP CLUB
Professional Division
107 East 60th Street (between Madison and Park Avenues)
(212) 371–0551
Be a model for one of their afternoon makeup classes and you not only get a makeover for nothing, but also get $25 worth of makeup for free. The classes are held Sunday through Wednesday.

NYBS CREATIVE ARTS
944 Eighth Avenue, second floor (between 55th and 56th Streets)
(212) 245–6371
www.nybsca.com
This makeup school with a primarily Japanese student body is always looking for models for class (of any ethnicity). You can even get paid for your time. Call to set up an interview. Classes held in the afternoon, Monday through Friday.

SHISEIDO STUDIO
155 Spring Street (between Wooster and West Broadway)
(212) 625–8820
www.shiseidostudio.com

Each client is limited to one free private makeover and facial a year, but classes are unlimited.

It's hard to believe that this place exists, but it's true. This "store" does not sell a single item—they give it all away. Free makeovers, free facials, free classes, free product samples. Obviously they won't argue with you if you want to buy some of their products from another location, but your money is no good here. Stop by anytime for makeover assistance and mini facials. Call or check the Web site to schedule an appointment for a full forty-five-minute facial, facial massage, and complete makeover or for a slot in one of their many classes. They are also happy to let you bring by a crowd of friends for a makeup or facial party (bridal or baby showers, sweet-sixteens, birthdays, corporate events, and so on). Talk about your low-stress event planning!

Rugs, a Blender, and a Makeover

Whenever you're in need of some professional beauty assistance, stop by any makeup counter at the finer department stores and have a pro do the work for you. Try the counters at the following stores:

MACY'S, *151 West 34th Street (at Sixth Avenue); (212) 695–4400.*

BERGDORF GOODMAN, *754 Fifth Avenue (at 58th Street); (212) 753–7300.*

SAKS FIFTH AVENUE, *611 Fifth Avenue (at 50th Street); (212) 753–4000.*

LORD & TAYLOR, *424 Fifth Avenue (at 38th Street); (212) 391–3344.*

BLOOMINGDALE'S, *1000 Third Avenue (between 59th and 60th Streets); (212) 705–2000.*

All the above offer free makeovers using their oh-so-pricey prod-ucts. Of course the hope is that you will then buy a load of $43 mascara, $59 lipsticks, and $94 skin cleansing citrus retonifier—but that's up to you.

REAL ESTATE: THIS LAND IS YOUR LAND

YES, APARTMENTS IN NEW YORK are just as ridiculously expensive as you've heard they are. With studio apartments the size of a closet going for more than $1,000 a month considered to be a steal—if you can find one—the price of four walls and a bed has really made living in Manhattan almost impossible. But even while the rents were continuing to skyrocket, I managed to find myself a spacious studio apartment in a desirable neighborhood for the unbelievable rent of $521 a month (and it just went up from $508). You might think I'm lucky, but I contend that all it takes for anyone to get such a deal is lots of patience and perseverance. There are thousands of apartments like this all around the five boroughs (and, yes, plenty in Manhattan) through the Mitchell-Lama and 80/20 programs. And these places can be yours without any exorbitant broker's fee, "key fee," or huge deposit.

116

All that's generally required to move in is the first month's rent and one month's rent as security. The secret is getting your name on as many waiting lists as you can for older buildings, and putting in as many applications as you can for new developments. This won't solve your apartment needs in the short term, though. Unfortunately, it can take between one and ten years for your name to come up (I waited three years), but don't let that stop you from putting your name on lists. Even if you're going through the I-don't-even-know-if-I'll-still-be-in-New-York-in-three-years syndrome, put your name on the lists. If you're still here, and you probably will be, you'll be happy you did. If you aren't, they'll just call the next lucky Cheap Bastard.

LOW-RENT, NO-FEE APARTMENTS

THE 80/20 PROGRAM
New York City Housing Development Corporation
110 William Street (between John and Fulton Streets)
(212) 227–5500
www.nychdc.org

THE CATCH Each building has various maximum income eligibility limitations.

Almost every luxury building that goes up in New York these days is a part of the 80/20 Program. The idea is that the building gets certain tax breaks if they make 20 percent of their new apartments available to low- or moderate-income tenants (and, of course, charge them low to moderate rents). If you qualify for an apartment, you could end up living in a luxury doorman building at a glamorous address while paying about a third to a quarter of what your hoity-toity neighbors are shelling out. To qualify, though, you do have to do some work. Each building has its own income requirements (some up to as much as about $44,000 a year), and there are heaps of paperwork and interviews you then need to go through. The good news is, once you're in, you're in; you don't need to maintain a low income to remain in the apartment. Rent is based on 30

At Your Service

Can't afford any New York City rents? Can't afford to raise a family in New York? Well then, how about raising a family and living in a penthouse duplex on Central Park West? Yes, it can be done. Get a position as a live-in nanny, butler, cook, or personal assistant to the upper crust of New York society and live way beyond your means.

The most common live-in job (particularly for women) is as a nanny. Besides room and board, nannies are paid between $400 and $800 a week for their child care duties and some light housekeeping responsibilities (though some families try to push that part of the job description to the limit). Agencies and families are looking for at least a one-year commitment and some experience. The best way to look for a nanny position is through word of mouth, but there's no shortage of agencies to place you as well. Any reputable agency will not charge you a fee; any fees are paid by the families. Here are a few good places to start your search:

PROFESSIONAL NANNIES INSTITUTE, 501 Fifth Avenue, Suite 908; (212) 692–9510; www.profnannies.com.

A CHOICE NANNY, 850 Seventh Avenue, Suite 305; (212) 246–5437; www.achoicenanny.com.

NANNIES PLUS, (973) 752–5100 or (800) 752–0078; www.nanniesplus.com.

THE NANNY AUTHORITY, (973) 466–2669 or (877) 466–2669; www.nannyauthority.com.

NY NANNY CENTER, (516) 767–5136 or (516) 373–5136; www.nynanny.com.

FAMILY EXTENSIONS, (203) 966–9944 or (800) 932–2736; www.familyextensions.com.

WWW.NANNYJOBS.COM.

If taking care of somebody else's kids isn't your idea of a good time, there are many other live-in positions you can apply for. The rich and famous need you to do everything from cook for them to clean for them, teach their children, keep track of their personal calendars, and attend to their private aircraft. If your calling is to be a major domo, valet, chauffeur, or housekeeper, try these agencies:

STERLING DOMESTICS, 633 Third Avenue (between 40th and 41st Streets); (212) 661–5813; www.sterlingny.com.

DOMESTIC PLACEMENT NETWORK, (805) 640–3608, or (877) 206–5262; www.dpnonline.com.

BEST DOMESTIC SERVICES OF NEW YORK CITY, 10 East 39th Street, Suite 909, (212) 683–3070; www.bestdomestic.com.

percent of your annual income. Call and ask them to send you the listing of the current buildings in the program. The competition can be stiff for these apartments, so be prepared to apply to a number of buildings. The time between application and move-in date can be anywhere from a few months to a few years.

MITCHELL-LAMA HOUSING COMPANIES

CITY-SPONSORED DEVELOPMENTS

Department of Housing Preservation and Development
100 Gold Street (between Frankfurt and Spruce Streets, near the Brooklyn Bridge)
(212) 863–8000 (administrative office)
(212) 863–6500 (city-sponsored Mitchell-Lama)
(212) 863–5610 (affordable housing hot line)
www.ci.nyc.ny.us/html/hpd/html/housing/mitchell-lama.html

STATE-SPONSORED DEVELOPMENTS

NYS Department of Housing and Community Renewal (DHCR)
25 Beaver Street (between Broad and New Streets)
(212) 480–7343
www.dhcr.state.ny.us/ohm/ohm.htm

**Applicants must meet income require-
ments, and waiting lists can be long.**

There are 141 city-sponsored buildings and 269 state-sponsored buildings in the Mitchell-Lama program (many in the five boroughs), with a total of more than 160,000 units throughout the system. This program was created in the 1950s to provide affordable housing for low- and moderate-income families. The apartments in these buildings are larger than the average shoe boxes most New Yorkers call home, there are no broker's fees, and the rents are amazingly low. Get the lists of buildings with open waiting lists through the Web sites or call. You must apply to each building separately; there is no centralized waiting list. The waits could be anywhere from one to ten years, so apply early and to many buildings. The income requirements vary, depending on the building and the size of your household. Once you have an apartment, though, you are not required to maintain a low income level. You will need to submit your income tax forms to the building management each year, which adjusts your rent yearly according to state-mandated levels. Once you have exceeded a certain prescribed level of income, you'll be required to pay "market value"—still ridiculously cheap. Market value rents (the maximum you will pay) range from studio apartments for $521 to three-bedroom apartments with a terrace for $997 (these do vary somewhat from building to building).

NEW YORK CITY PARTNERSHIP (NYCP)
1 Battery Park Plaza, fifth floor
(212) 493–7500 (administrative office)
(212) 493–7420 (new homes hot line)
www.nycp.org

THE CATCH Houshold income must not exceed $70,950 to be eligible.

This is a chance to own a new home or condo in neighborhoods around the city with small down payments (as low as 5 percent) and many tax exemptions and incentives—and maybe even no closing costs. The mission of the NYCP's New Homes/Neighborhood Builders program is to increase homeownership opportunities for moderate-income families who are priced out of the conventional real estate market. If you qualify, you can become the owner of a brand-new condo, single-family, or multifamily home. These homes or buildings are built from the ground up by reputable architects and contractors, come complete with many amenities, and are heavily subsidized by the city. There are developments in all five boroughs in such neighborhoods as Fort Green, Harlem, Coney Island, Bedford Stuyvesant, Williamsburg, Crown Heights, Hunts Point, and others. Check out the Web site for a list of current projects.

"Children are poor man's riches."

—English proverb

CHILDREN AND TEENS: OLLI OLLI OXEN FREE

NEW YORK IS AN AMAZING place for kids, and not just for those who can afford to go to the Manhattan Day School. Yes, at times it may seem like there are so many places to go, sights to see, things to do — and ways to drop a load of cash — that New York doesn't feel very kid-friendly for a parent's wallet. Fear not. There are classes, movies, fun and games, readings, even health insurance and tons of other fun and useful things for kids without Mom and Dad having to stop at the ATM. During the week, you can fill out any day's schedule with the endless free after-school programs. And on weekends, there is never a shortage of creative fun for the whole family in the major parks, museums, and other institutions throughout the city.

Dial-a-Teacher

Can't find the capital of Uzbekistan? Stumped by the square root of hypotenuse? Or just want to check that you spelled Crispus Attucks correctly? Then call up a teacher and get some help. The Dial-a-Teacher program, run by the United Federation of Teachers, has been helping out baffled students and parents for more than twenty years by fielding over 2,000 calls a week. A staff of forty-five teachers fluent in Spanish, French, Haitian Creole, Italian, Greek, Hebrew, Chinese, and, yes, English stand at the ready to help you with your homework in any subject Monday through Thursday, 4:00 to 7:00 P.M., throughout the school year.

These folks won't just give you the answers to your questions; since these are all qualified teachers you're talking to, they will strive to reteach the ideas behind the questions, making sure you understand the answers. And if you have already finished your homework, they will be happy to check your work with you. Dial-a-Teacher also offers a battery of workshops for parents during the day or in the evening designed to make parents more aware of what their children are learning and teach them how to help their children more effectively at home.

Dial-a-Teacher can arrange to hold workshops at local schools or at their Manhattan headquarters. If you attend workshops at the Dial-a-Teacher offices, they will send a bus to pick you up, take you home, and even serve you breakfast and lunch! And yes, all help and workshops are free of charge. For homework assistance, call (212) 777–3380. To find out more about workshops, call (212) 598–9205 or click on "Sevices" at the Web site www.uft.org.

AFTER-SCHOOL PROGRAMS

BEACON SCHOOLS

80 locations throughout the five boroughs
(See Appendix C for locations)
The NYC Department of Youth and Community Development
156 William Street (between Ann and Beekman Streets)
(212) 676–8255
www.nyc.gov/html/dycd/html/beacons.html

The Beacon programs are school-based community centers located in every school district in the city. The eighty programs vary somewhat, but all generally include homework help, tutoring, arts and crafts activities, sports, drama, music and cultural activities, computer classes, and Internet access. The programs also strive to provide community services from vocational training to health education. Registration is required to participate in these free programs. Most provide evening activities for teens and adults as well. See Appendix C for the complete listing of program locations. For schedules of activities, call the local centers. For more general information on the Beacon program and to find up-to-date location information, check the Web site.

NEW YORK CITY RECREATION CENTERS
42 locations throughout the five Boroughs
(See Appendix D for locations)
(212) 360–8222 or (718) 699–4219 (general information)
www.nycparks.com
At every one of New York City's Public Recreation Centers, you will find a variety of after-school programs (Monday through Friday, 3:00 to 6:00 P.M.) for children ages six to fourteen. The programs at each location vary depending on the center's facilities and staffing, but could include swim programs, sports instruction, computer classes, Internet access, homework help, arts and crafts, and classes in literacy, performing arts, visual arts, and much more. For schedules and more information, check with the local recreation centers.

ARTS AND CRAFTS

THE ART SHACK
Pier 25 (Hudson River and North Moore Street)
(212) 732–7467
www.hudsonriverpark.org
Spend a great afternoon on the pier creating all types of projects (painting, drawing, sculpting . . .) with fun teachers and fresh air. All materials are supplied. Weather permitting, Saturday and Sunday, noon to 5:00 P.M., June through August.

COOPER-HEWITT, NATIONAL DESIGN MUSEUM
2 East 91st Street (at Fifth Avenue)
(212) 849–8390
www.si.edu/ndm

You must be a New York City high school student.

Through a program called Design Directions, high school students interested in any aspect of design (fashion, industrial, graphic, media, film, interior, architecture, urban planning, and so forth) connect with the vast professional resources in New York City. Programs include daylong workshops, after-school programs, design studio visits, and precollege preparation (college visits; application and portfolio workshops). All classes are free and open to all on a first-come, first-served basis.

FOOLS CO. INC.'S NEW YORK SCHOOL FOR PERFORMING ARTS
Theater at St. Clements
423 West 46th Street (between Ninth and Tenth Avenues)
(212) 307–6000
foolsco@nyc.rr.com

 You must be between sixteen and twenty-one years old.

For almost twenty years Jill Russell has been training young adults in all aspects of the performing arts through the Artsworker Apprentice program; free weekly workshops in performance, movement, masks, puppetry, and more, open to all with the desire to learn. No audition or previous experience is needed, but preregistration is required. Call or e-mail for more information.

JAZZMOBILE
PS 197
135th Street and Fifth Avenue
(212) 866–4900 (administrative office); (212) 866–3616 (hot line)
www.jazzmobile.org

Since 1969, Jaazzmobile has been offering free Saturday music workshops and master classes for students ages seven and up at PS 197 in Harlem with such musicians as Max Roach, Branford Marsalis, and Donald Byrd. Students need to have at least some basic music knowledge to participate, and must register and have their skill evaluated to determine if they fit into the beginning, intermediate, or advanced classes. In summer they also bring a lineup of world-class musicians to the parks, libraries, schools, and street corners of New York City and the surrounding areas. Check the Web site for details.

Little Green Thumbs

Every Tuesday afternoon from April through October, the Battery Park City Parks Conservancy gives your kids a good reason to play in the dirt. They offer children in the second, third, and fourth grades a chance to learn about every aspect of gardening and plants, from planting seeds to pressing flowers. The children get dirty tending and harvesting the Battery Park City Parks children's plots. No experience is necessary, but space is limited and registration is required. For more information, call (212) 267–9700 or check the Web site www.bpcparks.org.

THE KITCHEN

512 West 19th Street (between Tenth and Eleventh Avenues)
(212) 255–5793, ext. 15
www.thekitchen.org

Once a month the stage of this downtown dance/theater/performance space is taken over by children twelve and over who want to bring their own poetic thoughts to life. With the guidance of guest artists and the Kitchen staff, this workshop takes their words from the page to the stage by exploring the elements of performance poetry (sound, music, improvisation, space, movement, and so on). No audition or registration is required. Saturday, noon to 2:00 P.M., but call to confirm dates and times.

THE MUSEUM OF MODERN ART (MoMA)

Education Department
11 West 53rd Street (between Fifth and Sixth Avenues)
(212) 708–9828
www.moma.org

High school students meet guides from MoMA for walks through some of the major galleries and museums around the city to talk about all things art. The programs are free and open to all, and no preregistration is required. Thursday, at 4:00 to 5:30 P.M.; call for details on where to meet.

NEW YORK UNIVERSITY PROGRAM IN EDUCATIONAL THEATRE

Pless Annex, 82 Washington Square East, Room 23 (at Washington Place)
(212) 998–5869
www.nyu.edu/education/music/edtheatre

$110 materials fee.

Twelve- to eighteen-year-old budding thespians take part in a free five-week intensive summer program called "Looking for Shakespeare." Throughout the session, students will work with a host of theater professionals to shape an original play based on the Bard's themes, but taken directly from the participants' own lives. While working on the play, the performers receive coaching in playwrighting, improvisation, acting, voice, and movement, culminating in a fully staged production for the public. Participants must interview and audition for the program, but no experience is necessary, just enthusiasm and energy.

THE WOOSTER GROUP
The Performing Garage
33 Wooster Street (between Broome and Grand Streets)
(212) 966–9796
www.thewoostergroup.org

 You must be a twelve- to seventeen-year-old New York City student.

This edgy, experimental theater company offers a free three-week summer institute every August. Students get experience working alongside professional artists like company members Willem Dafoe and Spalding Gray, as well as developing performance skills and creating original work. No prior experience is required; call for an application.

FILM

MUSEUM OF MODERN ART (MoMA)
11 West 53rd Street (between Fifth and Sixth Avenues)
(212) 708–9828 (Friday Night at the Movies
for High School Students)
(212) 708–9805 (family films on Saturday morning
for four- to ten-year-olds)
www.moma.org
The education department at MoMA presents Friday Night at the Movies for High School Students, a series of six classic and contemporary films in the spring and fall. Each series consist of films grouped under an

intriguing theme (for instance, The Irresistible Villain: *Dr. Jekyll and Mr. Hyde, Psycho,* and *The Usual Suspects*) and is followed by talks with the film department curators of the museum. Hey, they even throw in free pizza and soda sometimes. Saturday mornings the family events department invites you to bring the little kiddies down to the museum for a free lineup of short films. They run programs three or four Saturdays every season. The museum is undergoing a great deal of construction, and these programs have been moved around a lot; call for dates, location, and schedule.

RIVER FLICKS
Pier 25, Hudson River and North Moore Street
(212) 732–7467
www.hudsonriverpark.org
Great cult films (all rated G or PG) screen on the pier every Friday at about 8:00 P.M. (or when it gets dark) in July and August. In past seasons films have included *Mary Poppins, Little Shop of Horrors, Willy Wonka and the Chocolate Factory,* and *The Producers.* They set up some chairs on the pier for your comfort, and there's also plenty of room for you to bring a blanket and picnic under the stars while you watch. Of course, no movie is complete without the popcorn—and it's free, too.

FILMS AT PUBLIC LIBRARIES

Many public libraries throughout the city have regularly scheduled films and videos for children between the ages of three and ten every week. These programs usually run anywhere from thirty minutes to a couple of hours and consist of a few short films that could include vintage Disney cartoons, films of children's books, and rare children's classics as well as occasional feature-length films. For more details, check out the library Web sites: www.nypl.org/branch/events/ (for the Bronx, Staten Island, and Manhattan); www.brooklynpubliclibrary.org/calendar/index.htm; or www.queenslibrary.org/events/kidsprgms.asp. Below is a list of the branches with screenings for children every week. These schedules do change from time to time. Be sure to call the branch to confirm schedules.

MANHATTAN BRANCHES

96TH STREET LIBRARY, 112 East 96th Street (between Park and Lexington Avenues); (212) 289–0908; Wednesday at 4:00 P.M.

Busting Blockbuster

Forget about spending almost $5.00 to rent videos at Blockbuster or any local video store. Most local libraries have a large collection of children's videos. Disney, cartoons, educational and full-length features, classics, and new releases—you'll find plenty on the shelves to please all tastes. You can borrow tapes for a week (three days in Queens). Watch out for the late fees, though: $1.00 per day at the NYPL, $2.00 per day in Brooklyn, and a whopping $3.00 per day in Queens.

115TH STREET LIBRARY, 203 West 115th Street (between Seventh and Eighth Avenues); (212) 666–9393; Monday at 10:00 A.M.

AGUILAR LIBRARY, 174 East 110th Street (between Third and Lexington Avenues); (212) 534–2930; Thursday at 1:00 P.M.

COUNTEE CULLEN LIBRARY, 104 West 136th Street (between Lenox and Seventh Avenues); (212) 491–2070; Friday at 10:00 A.M. and 11:00 A.M.

COLUMBUS LIBRARY, 742 Tenth Avenue (between 50th and 51st Streets); (212) 586–5098; Friday at 3:30 P.M.

HUDSON PARK LIBRARY, 66 Leroy Street (between Seventh Avenue South and Hudson Street); (212) 243–6876; Wednesday at 4:00 P.M.

JEFFERSON MARKET LIBRARY, 425 Avenue of the Americas (at 10th Street); (212) 243–4334; Tuesday at 3:30 P.M.

ST. AGNES LIBRARY, 444 Amsterdam Avenue (between 81st and 82nd Streets); (212) 877–4380; Thursday at 4:00 P.M.

YORKVILLE BRANCH LIBRARY, 222 East 79th Street (between Lexington and Third Avenues); (212) 744–5824; Thursday at 4:00 P.M.

BRONX BRANCHES

ALLERTON LIBRARY, 2740 Barnes Avenue (at Allerton Avenue); (718) 881–4240; Thursday at 3:30 P.M.

FORDHAM LIBRARY CENTER, 2556 Bainbridge Avenue (at Fordham Road); (718) 579-4244; Wednesday at 3:30 P.M.

FRANCIS MARTIN LIBRARY, 2150 University Avenue (at 181st Street); (718) 295-5287; Monday at 2:00 P.M.

MORRISANIA LIBRARY, 610 East 169th Street (at Franklin Avenue); (718) 589-9268; Thursday at 3:30 P.M.

VAN NEST LIBRARY, 2147 Barnes Avenue (between Parkway South and Lydig Avenue); (718) 829-5864; Friday at 3:30 P.M.

WEST FARMS LIBRARY, 2085 Honeywell Avenue (between East 179th and East 180th Streets); (718) 367-5376; Thursday at 3:30 P.M.

BROOKLYN BRANCHES

BROOKLYN HEIGHTS, 280 Cadman Plaza West (at Tillary Street); (718) 623-7100; Friday at 4:00 P.M.

EAST FLATBUSH, 9612 Church Avenue (near Rockaway Parkway); (718) 922-0927; check for details.

NEW UTRECHT, 1743 86th Street (at Bay 17th Street); (718) 236-4086; Tuesday, 11:00 A.M. (ages five and under), Wednesday, 11:15 A.M. (ages one and two), Wednesday, 3:30 P.M. (ages six through twelve).

STONE AVENUE, 581 Mother Gaston Boulevard (at Dumont Avenue); (718) 485-8347; Friday at 3:00 P.M.

WALT WHITMAN, 93 St. Edwards Street (at Auburn Place); (718) 935-0244; Thursday at 4:00 P.M.

WILLIAMSBURG, 240 Division Avenue (at Marcy Avenue); (718) 302-3485; Thursday at 10:15 A.M.

QUEENS BRANCHES

CENTRAL LIBRARY, 89-11 Merrick Boulevard (between Eighty-ninth and Ninetieth Avenues); (718) 990-0700; call for schedule.

CORONA, 38-23 104th Street (between Thirty-eighth and Thirty-ninth Avenues); (718) 426-2844; Friday at 3:30 P.M.

SPORTS AND GAMES

BATTERY PARK CITY PARKS
Rockefeller Park House (Hudson River and Chambers Street)
(212) 267–9700
www.bpcparks.org or www.hudsonriverfestival.com
Teens ages twelve to eighteen are all welcome to drop by to take part in any or all of the ongoing activities here from June through October. There's teen art on Tuesday, 3:30 to 5:30; teen soccer on Tuesday, 2:30 to 5:30; teen chess on Thursday, 5:00 to 6:30; and backgammon Monday, 3:30 to 5:30.

BIG CITY FISHING
Pier 25 (Hudson River and North Moore Street)
Pier 40 (Hudson River and Houston Street)
(212) 533–PARK (7275)
www.hudsonriverpark.org
New York City and fishing? Not two things you would think go together well. Well, the Hudson River is the cleanest it has been for almost a hundred years and the fish are abundant, so come on down and cast a line. The fishing is open to all, but mostly it's children that do the casting. If you're big enough to hold a rod, you're welcome to participate in this catch-and-release fishing. All equipment, bait, and instructions are provided free of charge. Wednesday through Sunday, 10:00 A.M. to 6:00 P.M., June through September.

THE CENTER FOR ANTI-VIOLENCE EDUCATION
421 Fifth Avenue, second floor (between 7th and 8th Streets)
Park Slope, Brooklyn
(718) 788–1775
www.cae-bklyn.org

Free for fourteen- to eighteen-year-old girls only.

Sign up for a free self-defense course or an after-school karate class for teen girls. The self-defense course lasts for five weeks and is offered five times a year; the karate class is taught throughout the school year. The form of karate they teach (Goju) uses a lot of spiritual and meditative exercises (along with the usual kicks, chops, and hii-yaas!) to build the girls' inner strength as well as outer. They also offer low-cost/sliding-scale classes for younger children (girls and boys), and adults.

THE CHARLES A. DANA DISCOVERY CENTER
Central Park at 110th Street and Lenox Avenue
(212) 860–1370
www.centralparknyc.org
Sitting majestically on the Harlem Meer at the north end of the park, the
Dana Discovery Centers offers a variety of free family programs and hands-
on exhibits throughout the year. From April through October stop by any
Tuesday through Sunday from 10:00 A.M. to 4:00 P.M., and the center will
provide you with poles, unbarbed hooks, bait, and instruction booklets for
you to while away the hours with some catch-and-release fishing. The
Dana Center also offers a variety of educational programs, nature exhibits,
jazz concerts (see page 39) and swing dancing on the plaza (see page 70).

CITY PARKS YOUTH TENNIS
Locations throughout the five boroughs
(718) 699–4200
www.nycparkstennis.org
Join in the largest youth tennis program anywhere in the world. During
the summer (July and August), children ages six through eighteen receive
free lessons twice a week in city parks throughout the city. Racquets are
provided for children who need them. In August kids can also take part in
a citywide tournament and the Tennis with Pros program, where they get
lessons from tennis greats like Andre Agassi and Venus Williams.

CULLMAN AFTER SCHOOL LIBRARY CHESS PROGRAM
Libraries throughout the city
(212) 643–0225
www.chessintheschools.org
This program offers children of all ages the chance to learn the intricacies
of chess as well as the opportunity to play against each other and take
part in citywide tournaments. Hey, they even give everyone a free sub-
scription to the chess magazine *School Mates*. The clubs meet weekly;
check the Web site for library locations and schedules.

LASKER RINK
Central Park (110th Street and Lenox Avenue)
(212) 348–4867
www.centralparknyc.org

Registration is required.

Free after-school ice skating lessons are available for all children eight to
seventeen years old, January through March, Tuesday from 4:00 to 6:00 P.M.

To take part you must register at the North Meadow Recreation Center at 97th Street, midpark. All those registered for the lessons also get free entry to any public skating session at the rink during the rest of the week. Skate rentals are available free of charge for the Tuesday after-school lessons, but you'll have to pay for them the rest of the week ($3.50).

LEARN TO PLAY . . . SOCCER, BASEBALL, FIELD HOCKEY, LACROSSE, BASKETBALL, ROLLER SKATE
City recreation centers and parks throughout the five boroughs
(212) 360–8212
www.nycparks.org
These separate programs run by the City Parks Department offer girls and boys thirteen and under (and sometimes fourteen-year-olds) the chance not only to learn the basics of any of these sports, but also to play and compete with other children throughout the city. Free and open to all, these leagues go on at different times of year and provide children with all the skills and equipment they need to enjoy these games. Call for schedules and locations.

LEARN TO SWIM PROGRAM
City pools and recreation centers throughout the five boroughs
(718) 699–4219
www.cityparksfoundation.org or www.nycparks.org
Everybody in the pool! Free swimming instructions for children ages three through fourteen are available during the summer at all thirty-three city-run outdoor pools, and lessons continue throughout the year at city-run indoor pools and recreation centers. Recreation center memberships for children under thirteen are free, for fourteen- to seventeen-year-olds it costs $5.00 to $10.00. (For more information on other city recreation center offerings, see the chapter titled Fitness, Fun, and Games: Cheap Thrills. For complete listings of recreation center locations see Appendix D.)

NORTH MEADOW RECREATION CENTER
Central Park, 97th Street, midpark
(212) 348–4867
www.centralparknyc.org
This is a gold mine of free activities for kids and adults. They offer free classes in everything from dance (African, jazz, modern, and more) to martial arts (kung fu, tai chi, et cetera). Free climbing wall and classes for kids, athletic clinics in all sports, and a computer fitness learning center. They even have a small (very small) gym available for you to work out on your own.

HEALTH INSURANCE

HEALTHSTAT
Mayor's Office for Health Insurance Access
Human Resources Administration
330 West 34th Street (between Ninth and Tenth Avenues)
(888) NYC–6116 or (866) 692–9900 (TTY)
www.nyc.gov/healthstat
This is free or low-cost health insurance available to New York City residents up to age eighteen. The cost of enrolling depends on your income and the size of your family. It's free for anyone whose income is below a certain level; if your income is higher, you may have to pay $9.00 or $15.00 per month per child. This is comprehensive coverage (including medical, vision, and dental) and a pretty amazing deal even if you aren't qualified to receive it for free.

MUSEUMS

BELVEDERE CASTLE/HENRY LUCE NATURE OBSERVATORY
Central Park (enter at West 81st or East 79th Streets)
(212) 772–0210
www.centralparknyc.org
Hours: Tuesday through Sunday, 10:00 A.M.–5:00 P.M.
Besides being a castle built high on a hill (a pretty desirable destination for any kid or adult), this is also the home of a nature observatory complete with your fair share of frogs, turtles, birds, and lots of hands-on exhibits. The urban park rangers who run the observatory also run guided tours (free!) on weekends. And if you prefer to explore the wilds of the park on your own, you can borrow a free Birding Kit from them. The kit is filled with useful stuff like a pair of binoculars, a field guide, a sketch pad, and colored pencils. Check out the Web site for tour schedule and details.

BROOKLYN CHILDREN'S MUSEUM
145 Brooklyn Avenue (between St. Marks and Prospect Streets)
(718) 735–4400
www.brooklynkids.org

Free hours: Friday during the summer 5:00–7:00 P.M.
(suggested donation $4.00 all other times)
For more than a hundred years, the world's first children's museum has been entertaining and enlightening kids with a mixture of hands-on exhibits, performances, and an extensive collection of cultural objects and natural history specimens. They're a bit stingy with the free hours (two hours on Friday during the summer), but when they do it, they do it right. In addition to full access to the museum, Free Fridays always have fun musical performances for young and old alike on the rooftop.

FIRE ZONE/NEW YORK FIRE DEPARTMENT FIREHOUSES

34 West 51st Street (between Fifth and Sixth Avenues)
Firehouses throughout the five boroughs
(212) 698–4520
www.fdny.org
Free hours: Monday 4:00–7:00 P.M. ($5.00 all other times).
Think of this as the Universal Studios Tour for fire safety. This totally interactive exhibit gives kids (over five-years-old) a chance to explore a re-created firehouse, and then come along and help put out a "real" fire. Reservations are required all times except the Monday-night free hours, where people are let in on a first-come, first-served basis. But if you can't make it here during the free hours, why not stop by any local firehouse for a tour? It's a little known fact that when New York's Bravest are between calls, they love to show off their houses, the truck, and of course the "fire pole" to any young firefighters-to-be. But be aware that the show could end at a moment's notice: If the big bell rings, then it's off they go.

LEFFERT'S HOMESTEAD

Prospect Park (near Flatbush Avenue and Empire Boulevard)
(718) 789–2822
www.prospectpark.org
Hours: Friday through Sunday, 1:00–4:00 P.M.; extended hours during the summer months.
This is one of the few surviving Dutch Colonial farmhouses in Brooklyn, and possibly the only children's historic house museum in the country. The house gives children a chance to explore American history and experience everyday life as it was in the little farming village of Flatbush through hand-on exhibits, storytelling, and seasonal celebrations and crafts workshops. All activities are free and open to all.

SONY WONDER TECHNOLOGY LAB
550 Madison Avenue (at 56th Street)
(212) 833–8100
www.sonywondertechlab.com
Hours: Tuesday, Wednesday, Friday, and Saturday, 10:00 A.M.–6:00 P.M.;
Thursday, 10:00 A.M.–8:00 P.M.; Sunday, noon–6:00 P.M.
Start your visit off by meeting B. B. Wonderbot, the talking, all-knowing robot, and wind your way through four floors of interactive fun. Then walk out with your very own "Certificate of Achievement in the Advanced Program in Communication Technology." This is a very popular site; you're advised to make reservations by calling the above number at least a week in advance. They accept reservations only on Monday, Wednesday, and Friday from 10:00 A.M. to 2:00 P.M. You can get in without a reservation, but it could be a long wait in line.

STORES FOR THE FUN OF IT

There are a few stores around the city that are too amazingly fun to miss. Of course, the danger here is that you'll be tempted, pressured, or whined into spending some actual money. If you can think of these as incredible interactive museums (without gift shops!), then you'll have a great time playing with their "exhibits."

F.A.O. SCHWARZ
767 Fifth Avenue (at 58th Street)
(212) 644–9400
www.fao.com
They have crowned themselves "The Ultimate Toy Store"—and they live up to the billing. Three huge floors of the newest, biggest, best, most state-of-the-art (and most expensive!) toys and games to be found anywhere in the world, and almost all of them are available for you to play with. Plenty of costumed characters, roving magicians, and ridiculously friendly staff make any visit a fun and memorable one.

HALLOWEEN ADVENTURE
104 Fourth Avenue (at 11th Street)
(212) 673–4546
www.halloweenadventure.com
Just walking around this store, playing with all the unusual novelty items and gags, and trying on all the wild costumes, masks, and hats could be

enough entertainment for a day, but bring the kids by on Sunday after-noon at 3:00 (spring through fall) and you even get Magic Mike's Super Sunday Spectacular. They set up a stage in front of the store and put together a fun show demonstrating about fifteen to twenty tricks you can learn—and, of course, buy—at their friendly magic department. There's no pressure to buy, though. In fact, sometimes they even give it away: On selected Sundays they offer free magic lessons and tricks for kids six to sixteen. Call for schedule and details.

NBA STORE
666 Fifth Avenue (at 52nd Street)
(212) 515-6221
www.global.nba.com/nycstore
If you're a basketball fan, this place is a slam dunk. Of course, you'll find every piece of NBA and WNBA paraphernalia you could imagine, but you don't need to buy a thing to have a great time. Lots of free video games, basketball carnival games, and even a full-sized cushioned basketball court make the spot worth a visit. They also host a full schedule of spe-cial events, including in-store appearances and workshops by basketball greats, concerts, and the daily broadcast of the Web show *NBA Beat* (Monday through Friday, 5:00 to 7:00 P.M.). Check the Web site for a sched-ule of special events.

NEW YORK DOLL HOSPITAL
787 Lexington Avenue (between 61st and 62nd Streets)
(212) 838-7527
This trauma center for teddy bears and other cuddlies in critical condition is unlike any shop you've been in before. If you're prepared for piles of decapitated dolls, unstuffed animals, and just some of the oddest, rarest, and most unique-looking dolls anywhere, then stop by to see who has checked in recently. The doctor on call is sure to be the third-generation owner Irving Chase, a seemingly curmudgeonly fellow who turns kind-hearted when kids come by to visit his patients.

ZANY BRAINY
2407 Broadway (between 88th and 89th Streets); (917) 441-2066
112 East 86th Street (between Park and Lexington Avenues);
(212) 427-6611
2530 Hylan Boulevard (at New Dorp Lane), Staten Island;
(718) 980-4282
www.zanybrainy.com

This is a toy store with one great extra-added attraction: every day they offer free fun activities for kids. On weekdays they generally have play-times for toddlers and preschoolers; on weekends they bring out more crafts and costumed characters for kids up to age twelve. All the projects you make at these events are yours to take home (free of charge!). Stop in for a schedule or check the Web site.

STORYTELLING

BANK STREET BOOKSTORE
610 West 112th Street (at Broadway)
(212) 678–1654
www.bnkst.edu/html/bookstore
Wednesday at 10:30 A.M. and other times throughout the week.
Considered one of the best bookstores for and about children in the city. Every week you'll find many author readings, musical performances, and costumed characters for children, as well as discussions and presentations for parents. There's a regularly scheduled story time every Wednesday at 10:30 A.M. for toddlers, and other events are scheduled throughout the week. Check the Web site or call for details. Almost all events are free, though some require reservations.

Playtime!

From the countries that brought you Lego and Biro comes a chance to bring your children (five and under) for an informal playtime every Tuesday and Thursday, 11:00 A.M. to 1:00 P.M., in the Heimbolt Family Children's Learning Center at the Scandinavia House. Lots of toys to play with (coincidentally, Lego and Biro), Scandinavian costumes, storybooks in the Scandinavian languages (and English), and even a stage. Children, parents, and caregivers from all backgrounds are welcome. The Scandinavia House is located at 58 Park Avenue (between 37th and 38th Streets). For more information, call (212) 879–9779 or check the Web site www.scandinaviahouse.org.

BARNES & NOBLE BOOKSELLERS

www.bn.com

At every Barnes & Noble superstore springing up all over the city you'll find lots of free readings every week for kids and adults. At these locations you'll find story times where B&N staff, authors, costumed characters, and other guest readers gather children around to hear a book or a story. Of course, the kind folks at Barnes and Noble wouldn't mind if you decided to buy the book, but that's up to you. Call stores to confirm dates and times.

EAST SIDE

240 EAST 86TH STREET (between Second and Third Avenues); (212) 794–1962; Saturday (once a month).

CITICORP BUILDING, 160 East 54th Street (at Third Avenue); (212) 750–8033; Wednesday at 10:00 A.M.

UNION SQUARE, 33 East 17th Street (between Park Avenue and Broadway); (212) 253–0810; Saturday at 2:00 P.M.

WEST SIDE

2289 BROADWAY (at 82nd Street); (212) 362–8835; Sunday at 10:00 A.M. (once a month).

LINCOLN CENTER, 1972 Broadway (at 66th Street); (212) 595–6859; Sunday at noon.

BROOKLYN

PARK SLOPE, 267 Seventh Avenue (at 6th Street); (718) 832–9066; Tuesday at 10:30 A.M., and Thursday at 3:30 P.M.

QUEENS

BAYSIDE, 23–80 Bell Boulevard (at Northern Boulevard); (718) 224–1083; Monday at 12:30 P.M., and Wednesday at 10:30 A.M.

FOREST HILLS, 70–00 Austin Street (between 69th Road and Continental Avenue); (718) 793–1395; Tuesday at 10:30 A.M., and Thursday at 6:30 P.M.

THE BRONX

BAY PLAZA, 290 Baychester Avenue; (718) 862–3945; Monday at 10:30 A.M., Thursday at 5:30 P.M., and Saturday at 11:00 A.M.

2245 RICHMOND AVENUE (between Nome and Travis Streets); (718) 982–6983; Tuesday and Saturday at 10:30 A.M., and Thursday at 7:00 P.M.

BOOKS OF WONDER
16 West 18th Street (between Fifth and Sixth Avenues)
(212) 989–3270
www.booksofwonder.com
Every Sunday at 11:45 A.M.
This is a literary wonderland for kids, and one of the few remaining independent bookstores in the city devoted solely to children's books. Join them every Sunday for story time: Staff members read their favorite classic and contemporary children's stories.

HANS CHRISTIAN ANDERSEN STATUE
Central Park
Enter at 72nd Street and Fifth Avenue
Saturday, 11:00 A.M.–noon, June through September
(rain or shine).
This is storytelling at its purest: No reading, just master storytellers recounting tales from around the world (and of course featuring many by Mr. H. C. Andersen himself). Once the weather turns cooler, the storytelling moves to the comfortable confines of the Scandinavia House (58 Park Avenue between 37th and 38th Streets) on the second Saturday of each month at 11:00 A.M. (from October through May). For more information on the Scandinavia House schedule, call (212) 879–9779 or check the Web site www.scandinaviahouse.org. The stories are appropriate for children five years and up.

IMAGINATION PLAYGROUND
Prospect Park
Ocean Avenue, south of Lincoln Road (across from the Wolman Rink)
Brooklyn
(718) 965–8943
Every Thursday at 3:00 P.M., May through October.
Librarians and guest readers present works by popular children's authors.

NEW YORK PUBLIC LIBRARY
www.nypl.org/branch/events/
Almost every branch of the NYPL has a children's section with regularly scheduled readings for kids at least once a week. Many—such as the

Donnell Library (20 West 53rd Street, between Fifth and Sixth Avenues; 212–621–0618)—have lots of special classes and workshops in everything from poetry to cat's cradles. For more details, pick up a copy of the monthly *Events for Children and Young Adults* catalogs at any branch or check out the library's Web site. (For branch locations, see Appendix B.)

NYU PROGRAM IN EDUCATIONAL THEATER
Provincetown Playhouse
133 MacDougal Street (between West 3rd Street and Washington Square South)
(212) 998–5868
www.nyu.edu/education/music/edtheatre
Sunday at 3:00 P.M.
A popular series of professional storytellers from around the country and around the world. The program also presents a couple of free theater productions for children and young adults each year in the Black Box Theater. Call for schedule and details.

READINGS IN THE PARKS
Various parks throughout the five boroughs
(212) 360–8290
www.cityparksfoundation.org or www.nycparks.org
May through August.
This early-literacy program for five- to nine-year-olds gives kids the chance to hear stories in the comfort of their own neighborhood parks. Children, their families, storytellers, librarians, and volunteers gather to read aloud and talk about books. Call for more information, locations, and schedule.

THE SCHOLASTIC STORE
557 Broadway (between Prince and Spring Streets)
(212) 343–6166
www.scholastic.com/sohostore
Drop by this colorful, energetic store almost anytime and you'll find something going on for you to enjoy. Every month the people who brought you Clifford the Big Red Dog and Harry Potter put together a full schedule of special events and hands-on activities, including author signings, celebrity appearances, crafts workshops, and, of course, regular story times (Tuesday and Thursday at 11:00 A.M.). Check the Web site or drop by the store for the schedule of events.

"We haven't the money, so we've got to think."

—Lord Rutherford

EDUCATION: CENTS-LESS SMARTS

F ROM THE IVY LEAGUE to technical schools, from GED to Ph.D., from continuing education to just-for-fun classes, if you can think of it (and even if you can't), you can learn it in New York. Many classes are offered completely free of charge and with no catch, while others can be had for nothing (or next to nothing) if you're willing to volunteer your time instead of paying. When volunteering, you're put to work in administrative offices, studios, or classrooms and your work hours are exchanged for classroom hours. You will find the math for these exchanges spelled out in each listing, but always check with the school to confirm these details. The economics of these work-study programs can change over time.

ARTS

BATTERY PARK CITY PARK CONSERVANCY
South Cove
(212) 267–9700
www.bpcparks.org

 Registration is recommended; space is limited.

Drawing classes are offered Saturday and Wednesday morning and Tuesday afternoon twice a year: June through July, and September through October. All materials provided free of charge. Call for class locations and times.

CHAMBERS POTTERY
153 Chambers Street, second floor (between Church Street and West Broadway)
(212) 619–7302

 Work-study in exchange for free classes. The math: 3 hours of work = 1 hour of free class time.

This small Tribeca pottery studio offers classes for children and adults. A limited amount of space is available for work-study students.

CRAFT STUDENTS LEAGUE
610 Lexington Avenue (at 53rd Street)
(212) 735–9731
www.ywcanyc.org

 Work-exchange assistants can work in the studios or the offices. A limited number of assistants is needed. The math: 1 hour of work = 1 hour of class time.

Since 1932, they have been offering classes in all aspects of fine arts and crafts, including book arts, decorative arts, wearable art, ceramics, drawing, painting, mixed media, jewelry, metalsmithing, beading, decorative finishes, and woodworking.

DIEU DONNE PAPERMILL
433 Broome Street (between Broadway and Crosby Street)
(212) 226–0573
or (877) DD–PAPER (toll-free outside New York only)
www.papermaking.org

 Internship and work-exchange programs. The math: 5 days of work = 1 day of studio time; 8 days of work = 1 class.

A studio, gallery, and mill in Soho dedicated to advancing the art of hand papermaking.

DOWNTOWN COMMUNITY TV CENTER
87 Lafayette Street (between White and Walker Streets)
(212) 966–4510
www.dctvny.org

 Interns work sixteen hours a week in exchange for free classes and equipment and facilities rental.

Learn the creative and technical skills you need to produce your own television programs. DCTV offers interns the use of top-of-the-line equipment and studios, and classes in every aspect of television production, in exchange for time spent working in their offices or on their cable TV productions.

FILM/VIDEO ARTS
462 Broadway, Suite 520 (at Grand Street)
(212) 941–8787
www.fva.com

 Interns work sixteen hours a week in exchange for free classes and equipment and facilities rental.

Michael Moore, the producer and director of the documentaries *Roger and Me* and *The Awful Truth* on Bravo—and an F/VA alumus—says this about F/VA: "Film/Video Arts puts this art form in the hands of people who really aren't supposed to be doing it because it is really such an expensive process. What Film/Video Arts has done is to say, 'Money should not be in the way of getting these resources in the hands of people whose stories we should hear.'" F/VA provides state-of-the-art facilities, equipment, and a full schedule of classes for film and video production to all for low rates, but for interns it's all free.

GREENWICH HOUSE POTTERY

16 Jones Street (between Bleecker and West 4th Streets)
(212) 242–4106
www.greenwichhousepottery.com

 Work-study assistants work in the office, gallery, library, studio, or classes in exchange for free or reduced-rate pottery classes.

A full schedule of pottery classes for children, teens, and adults. Greenwich House also has a very fluid and somewhat negotiable work-study program. Students can work in a variety of positions for one to eight hours a week to be a part of the program. Depending on what skills you have and the job you take on, you can get anywhere from $100 off tuition to full tuition plus free firing time and twenty-four-hour access to the studio.

MANHATTAN NEIGHBORHOOD NETWORK

537 West 59th Street (between Tenth and Eleventh Avenues)
(212) 757–2670
www.mnn.org

QUEENS PUBLIC TELEVISION (QPTV)

41-61 Kissena Boulevard, Suite 2077 (in Flushing Plaza), Flushing;
(718) 886–8160

94–50 159th Street (on the campus of York College), Jamaica;
(718) 523–7700

(718) 886–4880 (information hot line)

www.qptv.org

 You must be a resident of Manhattan or Queens, and agree to produce a program for public access TV.

These organizations administer public access for cable TV services in Manhattan and Queens. The federally mandated obligation of cable TV is that they must provide a channel for all residents to exercise their First Amendment right of freedom of expression. They provide training on production equipment (video production, studio production, editing, audio, basic lighting, digital video and editing, and so on) as well as equipment for programs aired on public access TV. Training and equipment are available in the other boroughs, but classes are not free. (Contact Brooklyn Community Access Television (BCAT), (718) 935–1122, www.brooklynx.org/bcat; Staten Island Community Television, (718) 727–1414, www.sictv.org; or BronxNet, (718) 960–1180, www.bronxnet.org.

URBAN GLASS
647 Fulton Street (entrance on Rockwell, between DeKalb and Fulton Streets)
Brooklyn
(718) 625–3685
www.urbanglass.com

 Studio and office volunteers are "paid" at a rate of $7.00 an hour. This amount is applied to the cost of any class.

This is New York's only glass art studio open to the general public. They offer classes in glassblowing, neon, lamp working, casting, and anything else that has to do with glass. The classes can be very expensive ($600 for beginning glassblowing), so it can take a while to gain enough hours to work off the class. The good news is, many of your volunteer hours can be spent in the studio. So you can get a lot of useful hands-on experience while you work (and you may even pick up a few great bits of discarded glass art while tooling around). The bad news is, it gets awfully hot in the studio; dress appropriately.

FOOD AND WINE

CHELSEA WINE INSTITUTE
75 Ninth Avenue (between 15th and 16th Streets)
(212) 255–4221
www.chelseawinevaultnyc.com

 Work as a teacher's assistant or wine pourer to attend classes for free.

The institute is located in the beautiful brick cellars under the Chelsea Wine Vault. The wine education center offers tasting courses and wine-maker dinners for everyone from the novice to the connoisseur. They also organize the extensive Windows on the World wine classes, which are eight weeks long. As a volunteer, you'll show up about two hours before the class begins, set up the tables, pour wine during the class, and clean up afterward. You can participate fully and taste the wines during the lectures.

INTERNATIONAL WINE CENTER
1133 Broadway, Suite 520 (between 25th and 26th Streets, just west of Fifth Avenue)
(212) 627–7170
www.learnwine.com

 Serve as a pourer in exchange for free classes.

The Wine Center offers classes to members of the wine trade and others who seriously want to learn more about wines. They offer three levels of courses, with certificates and diplomas from the prestigious Wine & Spirit Education Trust (WSET) in London. The courses range from eight weeks to a two-year advanced program and can be quite expensive, but you can take them for free by being a pourer for the classes. You'll need to show up about an hour before each class to set up, pour wines during the class tastings, and clean up afterward. They use three pourers per class and slots do fill up quickly; call far in advance to reserve a spot.

THE NATURAL GOURMET INSTITUTE
FOR FOOD AND HEALTH
48 West 21st Street, second floor (between Fifth and Sixth Avenues)
(212) 645–5170
www.naturalgourmetschool.com

 Work as a kitchen assistant or in their office to audit classes.

Slice and dice, scrub the pots, and *Bam!* you can become the next Emeril (but healthier—the school offers classes in "Health Supportive Cooking"). They have a full schedule of classes to satisfy everyone from the novice cook to the most experienced chef. All classes are vegetarian and have a holistic healing bent. The classes range from basic cooking how-tos like "Knife Skills," "Snack Attack: Healthier 'Junk' Food," and "Choosing Safe Foods" to healthful vegetarian and ethnic specialties like "Dazzling Vegan Desserts," "The Miracle of Miso," and "Authentic Indian Buffet." Kitchen assistants begin working an hour before the class, preparing ingredients and the kitchen; participate in and nibble their way through the classes; and clean up the kitchen after the class is over.

NEW SCHOOL CULINARY ARTS PROGRAM
131 West 23rd Street (between Sixth and Seventh Avenues)
(212) 255–4141
NSCulArts@aol.com

 Work as a kitchen assistant to audit classes or as a work-study office assistant in exchange for classes. Office assistant math: 3 hours of work = 1 hour of class.

The kitchen assistant program is similar to the one at the Natural Gourmet Institute, except the classes are not limited to vegetarian subjects and can be much more indulgent. The schedule includes classes in basic techniques ("How to Boil Water," "Introduction to French Cooking," and "Creative Hors d'Oeuvres"), light and vegetarian cooking ("Low-Fat Sauces," "Light Italian Cooking," and "Cooking for the Way We Eat Today"), holiday cooking and baking ("The Hanukkah Feast," "For Pumpkin Lovers Only," and "Czech Christmas Cookies"), desserts ("Introduction to Cake Decorating," "Strudel Workshop," and "New Chocolate Desserts"). Kitchen assistants do not participate in the classes they work; they only observe. Work-study students are able to take part in classes. Everyone gets to feast on the results of the class work.

MIND

BROOKLYN PUBLIC LIBRARY'S BUSINESS LIBRARY
280 Cadman Plaza West (between Tillary and Pierrepont Streets)
(718) 623–7000
www.brooklynpubliclibrary.org

"You should only be successful and make us proud."

An abundance of classes and workshops are offered throughout the year targeted toward entrepreneurs, small-business owners, students, small investors, and anyone interested in Brooklyn business. Some highlights include an entrepreneur series; a business fair in May and June; and the "Made in Brooklyn" breakfast series (Yes! Including a free continental breakfast) highlighting specific industries in Brooklyn, from music and film to Key lime pies and Caribbean beef patties. They also play host to the SCORE program, in which small business start-ups get personalized mentoring from established and retired business owners. Free Internet access is available as well.

THE COOPER UNION FOR THE ADVANCEMENT OF SCIENCE AND ART
Cooper Square (8th Street between Bowery and Third Avenues)
(212) 353–4120
www.cooper.edu

 Brains, brains, talent, and brains, plus a $50 application fee.

Every one of the 900 students at this top college of art, architecture, and engineering attends completely tuition-free. They do have to cover their own room, board, books, and a $600 student fee per year, but the $25,000 tuition bill is on the house. It shouldn't surprise you that the competition to get into this premier school is pretty stiff. Each year about 2,400 men and women from around the world apply for Cooper Union, and only about 300 are accepted. Gentlemen, start your slide rulers.

EGLISE FRANÇAIS DU ST-ESPRIT
109 East 60th Street (between Madison and Park Avenues)
(212) 838–5680
www.stespritnyc.net
Free beginning and intermediate French classes are taught every Sunday from 10:00 to 11:00 A.M. These are very small and intimate classes (they have room for no more than ten students per class). They run from September through December and January through June.

ENGLISH CLASSES FOR SPEAKERS OF OTHER LANGUAGES
New York Public Library
Various branches in Manhattan, the Bronx, and Staten Island
(212) 340–0918
www.nypl.org
Beginner and intermediate English classes are offered three times a year (fall, winter, and spring). Space is limited, and registration is required. Check the Web site for branch locations and class schedules.

Libraries with Class!

At branches of the New York Public Library (www.nypl.org), Brooklyn Public Library (www.brooklynpubliclibrary.org), and Queens Public Library (www.queenslibrary.org), you will find literally thousands of free classes, lectures, and workshops in everything imaginable offered throughout the year. Here is just a sampling of classes. For details and schedules, stop into any branch or check the Web sites.

401(k) Rollover
How to Do a Term Paper
Fashion Design for Teens
Arts and Crafts
Ballroom Dancing
Basic and Intermediate Internet
Basic Mouse Skills
Bead Making Workshop
Jewelry Making
Become a Stamp Collector
Breaking the Rules Again: Teens Writing Poetry
Career Exploration Inventory
Citizenship Preparation Workshop in Manadarin
College and You
Computers for Seniors
Conserving Home Energy
Create a Quilt
Create Your Own Photo Album
Create Your Own Shadow Puppet
Crocheting Class
Dance with a Mexican Touch
Doing Business in Taiwan
Drum Clinic
E-mail Basics
ESOL Class
Estate Planning
GED Class

Get Connected to Consumer Health Information
Book Discussions
Health Information on the Internet
Health on the Internet
How to Read the NYC Subway Map
Illustrated Bookmaking
Internet Search Strategies
Introduction to Computers
Introduction to Excel
Introduction to PowerPoint
Introduction to Word
Investing: How to Research Companies and Industries
Job and Résumé Resources Online
Knitting Classes for Beginners
Knitting Club
Learning about the Rights of Immigrants
Makeup Tips and Techniques
Making Your Assets Last
Open Mike Night
Origami
Picture Book Hour
Poetry Writing Workshop
Polish Your Résumé!
So You Want to Be a Songwriter
Sorting through the Life Insurance Maze

Stay C.O.O.L. Under Fire: Dealing with Difficult People
Staywell Exercise for Older Adults
Success in Math
Great Ideas Forum
Checking and Credit 101 Workshop
Cantonese Program for Parents
Bridge Club
Tai Chi for Seniors
Telescope Moon Watching
The Art of Breathing and Relaxation
The Art of Public Speaking
The Big Apple on the Big Screen
The History of Greenwich Village
The Write Stuff: A Writing Workshop for Adults
Toddler Time
Understanding the 2001 Tax Relief Act
Using MS Word for Your Newsletter
Using Music in Literacy and ESOL
Voice-Over Workshop: How to Break into the Lucrative World of Voice-Overs
Watercolor Class
Work for the U.S. Postal Service

Get a Job, Get a Degree

New York is home to two top ranked universities and countless other colleges and technical schools throughout the five boroughs. Like any business, these schools need a large support staff to keep the doors open and the students happy—and that's where you come in. From office assistants and administrative staff to maintenance and mailroom clerks, almost all of these jobs include the fringe benefit of free or seriously reduced tuition for classes at these and affiliated schools. So instead of paying as much as $30,000 a year for that graduate degree, why not have them pay you for your time? Forget about paying $10,000 to become a computer systems analyst; you can take advantage of the system to get it for nothing. Salaries at the schools vary, but you probably won't be making the kind of money you can retire on. Still, this extra benefit can make it a very profitable position. Here are some places to start your search:

> **COLUMBIA UNIVERSITY,** *475 Riverside Drive, Room 1901 (between 119th and 120th Streets); (212) 870–2425; www.hr.columbia.edu/hr.*

> **NEW YORK UNIVERSITY,** *7 East 12th Street, first floor (at Fifth Avenue); (212) 998–1250; www.nyu.edu/hr.*

HENRY GEORGE SCHOOL OF SOCIAL SCIENCE

**121 East 30th Street (between Park and Lexington Avenues)
(212) 889–8020
www.henrygeorgeschool.org**

Free adult education classes that deal with the hidden factors at work in the economy. Classes include "Progress and Poverty" and "Applied Economics and Economic Science." The classes meet once a week for ten weeks; preregistration is required. They also offer free film forums and upper-level courses such as "Current Events," "The Genesis of Modern Economics," and "Money and Banking." All courses and forums are offered in Spanish as well.

HOUSING EDUCATION PROGRAM

NYC Department of Housing Preservation and Development
100 Gold Street, Room 6C
(212) 863-8830
www.nyclink.org/hpd

 You must be a New York City resident or property owner.

This city-run program offers a comprehensive set of courses to help home-owners learn how to keep their properties in good fiscal and physical health. Classes include "Basic and Advanced Building Management," "Building Finances," "Tenant Relations," "Building Maintenance," and others. Courses are generally offered three to five times a year, but many fill up quickly; early registration is recommended.

BODY

BATTERY PARK CITY PARK

Esplanade Plaza (Hudson River and Liberty Street)
(212) 267-9701
www.bpcparks.org
A free tai chi class is taught every Friday at 8:30 A.M. from May through October.

DIAS Y FLORES

520-522 East 13th Street (between Avenues A and B)
(212) 254-1744
This community garden offers free yoga, tai chi, and drawing classes during the summer months. All supplies for the drawing classes are provided free, but bring your own yoga mats and towel for the others. Call for schedules and details.

GUARDIAN ANGELS TRAINING ACADEMY

763 Eighth Avenues (between 46th and 47th Streets)
(212) 397-7822
www.guardianangels.org

You have to volunteer for at least one four-hour patrol a week.

They offer free self-defense training, Capoeira, and Thai boxing classes to volunteers. The Guardian Angels are those (in)famous red-bereted folks who patrol the subways, streets, and public events to "offer assistance and protection to any member of the public and will not hesitate to physically protect victims of crime." Since they were founded by Curtis Sliwa in 1979, they have been called vigilantes by some and by others . . . Guardian Angels.

HIGH VIBE HEALTH & HEALING
85 East 3rd Street (between First and Second Avenues)
(212) 777–6645
www.highvibe.com
This "Living Food" and heath supplements store offers free classes on such subjects as fasting, family nutrition, essential oil treatments, and gallbladder and liver detox. They also hold raw food preparation workshops, but they charge for those.

HIMALAYAN INSTITUTE
East West Books
78 Fifth Avenues (between 13th and 14th Streets)
(212) 243–5995
www.himalayaninstitute.org/hinyc/

 Work-study students exchange classes for office work. The math: 1 hour of work = 1 hour of class.

Offers a full schedule of classes, seminars, and workshops on yoga, meditation, and vegetarian cooking.

NORTH MEADOW RECREATION CENTER
Central Park
97th Street, midpark
(212) 348–4867
www.centralparknyc.org
This is a gold mine of free activities for kids and adults. They offer free classes in everything from dance (African, jazz, modern, and more) to martial arts (kung fu, tai chi, et cetera), and they also have a small (very small) gym available for you to work out on your own.

THE OHASHI INSTITUTE
147 West 25th Street, eighth floor
(646) 486–1187 or (800) 810–4190
www.ohashiatsu.org

 Work-study students may work in the office, on the cleaning crew, or on special projects in exchange for credit toward classes. The math: 1 hour of work = $10 credit toward class for the first year, $12 thereafter.

Ohashi offers a six-level curriculum on its own style of Shiatsu massage (Ohashiatsu) that can be taken by both professionals and laypeople. Ohashiatsu is a stretching, relaxing, and energizing acupressure type of massage that works with the Eastern healing philosophies of chi (energy) and the meridians (energy channels) of the body.

SPIRIT

THE ASIAN CLASSICS INSTITUTE/THREE JEWELS COMMUNITY CENTER
211 East 5th Street (between Second and Third Avenues)
(212) 475–7752 or (212) 475–6650
www.world-view.org
The institute offers general-interest and teacher-training courses in Tibetan Buddhism, meditation, and Tibetan language, all free of charge. The general-interest courses are drop-in classes open to all, and the formal study teacher-training courses are open to those "willing to make a serious commitment to their studies." These courses have attendance requirements, homework assignments, and tests. The Three Jewels Community Center offers free meditation classes, free coffee and tea, free Internet access, and a free lending library. They are also associated with Godstow Retreat Center, where you can get away from the city for a free retreat in exchange for household chores (see page 217 for more information on Godstow).

FALUN DAFA
Central Park (81st Street and Central Park West) and many other sites throughout the city.
(212) 978–9511 or (877) FALUN–99
www.falundafa.org (general information)
www.falun-nyc.net (New York locations and schedules)

None (as long as you aren't in China)

From the folks who brought you tai chi comes a new, very old traditional Chinese exercise, Falun Dafa (or Falun Gong). It's a practice that aims to improve mental and physical well-being through a series of easy-to-learn exercises, meditation, and development of "one's Heart/Mind Nature." And from the folks who brought you Tiananmen Square comes a whole new wave of oppression. This is the group that has gained a lot of attention recently by being banned in China and has seen brutal suppression of its practitioners by the Chinese government. So there must be something to it. They offer free introductory classes as well as weekly group practices.

MANHATTAN JEWISH EXPERIENCE (MJE)
131 West 86th Street (between Columbus and Amsterdam Avenues)
(212) 787–9533
www.jewishexperience.org
If you're like me and all you remember about Hebrew school as a kid was falling asleep, then here's your chance to try it again. The big difference is, this time you'll stay awake and maybe even enjoy it. MJE offers a full schedule of basic courses for free, including "A Crash Course in Basic Judaism," "Hebrew Reading Crash Course I, II, and III," and "Ask the Rabbi." Classes are fun, unintimidating, interactive, and geared for all Jews, particularly those with little or no background in Judaism. These classes are not meant to recruit Jews into a particular sect, but to help you gain a deeper understanding of the age-old traditions and how they fit into modern life. Plus, it's not a bad place to meet a nice Jewish girl or guy and make your mother happy. They also have a full program of intermediate and advanced courses and lectures for which they do charge a small fee ($5.00 per class or $30.00 per semester). Hey, they even set out some free soft drinks and noshes every week.

JUMPSTART MEDITATION
Washington Square Church
135 West 4th Street (between Sixth Avenue and Washington Square West)
(212) 330–7646
Every Wednesday evening at 6:45 the folks of Jumpstart Meditation invite you to join them for an ongoing meditation class in the church kitchen, rec room, or whatever space happens to be available that night. A small informal group comes together to "Om" and share thoughts and questions on Tibetan Buddhist meditation. They also provide you with some great

free books and CDs for you to continue your meditation on your own. Call to confirm days and times.

NEW YORK SHAMBHALA CENTER
118 West 22nd Street, sixth floor (between Sixth and Seventh Avenues)
(212) 675-6544
www.ny.shambhala.org

 Work-study exchange for free classes. The math: 1 hour of work = $10 credit toward classes.

The center offers all forms of meditation classes and lectures from absolute beginner to advanced. All are welcome to the beginning meditation Dharma Gathering every Tuesday night for a free class and discussion.

THE OPEN CENTER
83 Spring Street (between Broadway and Lafayette Streets)
(212) 219-2527, ext. 117
www.opencenter.org

 Volunteer four hours a week for unlimited free classes (depending on availability).

They offer a huge array of classes and workshops in holistic learning and living. There are classes in everything from feng shui, reflexology, belly dancing, and salsa aerobics to Taoism, Kabbalah, tantric sex, and herbalism. You can also find ongoing yoga and meditation classes here, as well as a number of certification programs. They treat their volunteers with great respect and support. If you're interested in alternative learning, this is the place for you.

THE SRI CHINMOY CENTRE
(718) 297-6456
www.srichinmoy.org

 They invite you to become a "seeker"— a follower of Sri Chinmoy—but it's not a high-pressure situation.

Four-day learn-to-meditate classes at various locations throughout the city (most consistently in Queens and Manhattan). On the first Friday of each month, there's a chance to meet and meditate with Sri himself. Call for schedules and details.

HEALTH AND MEDICAL:
LIVE FREE OR DIE

NEW YORK SURELY RANKS among the most expensive places to stay healthy. From ordinary checkups to health insurance, getting sick here will cost you. The good news is, New York is also one of the major centers for medical schools and clinical studies, which provide many opportunities for free and low-cost care, often with cutting-edge treatments (excuse the pun). New York is also a center for bleeding-heart liberals, so in this town big government still plays some role in providing services to those in need of low-cost health care through the extensive Health & Hospitals Corporation system, and at some community clinics.

WHATEVER AILS YOU: CLINICAL STUDIES

Medical centers throughout New York run clinical trials for almost any condition imaginable, from cancer to acne, from athlete's foot to weight loss. People are always needed to participate in these studies, and all medication and care are provided free of charge—in fact, you can even get paid for participating in many of these studies.

NEW YORK HEADACHE CENTER
30 East 76th Street, second floor (at Madison Avenue)
(212) 794–3550 or (718) 935–9666
Conducts clinical trials on different medication and treatments for migraines and other types of headaches. All research-related examinations and treatments are free, and financial compensation is often provided.

COLUMBIA-PRESBYTERIAN MEDICAL CENTER
Department of Dermatology
161 Fort Washington Avenue, Room 750 (between 165th and 168th Streets)
(212) 305–6953
cpmcnet.columbia.edu
Constantly organizing new trials for medication and treatment of various skin conditions including acne, toe fungus, wounds, and more. Treatment and medication are free, and compensation is provided.

RESEARCH TESTING LABORATORIES
255 Great Neck Road
Great Neck, Long Island
(516) 773–7788
www.rtlab.com
Runs studies in everything from weight loss to hair loss. Compensation is provided.

HHC TO THE RESCUE

New York City Health & Hospitals Corporation (HHC) was created to provide comprehensive medical care to all people "regardless of their ability" to pay. The corporation consists of eleven acute-care hospitals, six diagnostic and treatment centers, four long-term care facilities, seven communicare centers, forty-six child health clinics, six oral health clinics, and a home health care agency. HHC also operates MetroPlus Health Plan, a health maintenance organization (HMO) for Medicaid recipients. You can expect waits to be a bit longer for all appointments and at emergency rooms at these facilities than at private hospitals, but sit tight and they'll get to you. For more information, check the Web site www.nyc.gov/hhc or call (212) 788-3321.

MANHATTAN

BELLEVUE HOSPITAL CENTER, 462 First Avenue (at 27th Street); (212) 562-4141.

COLER-GOLDWATER MEMORIAL HOSPITAL,
1 Main Street (Coler); (212) 848-6000.
900 Main Street (Goldwater); (212) 318-8000.
Roosevelt Island

GOUVERNEUR NURSING FACILITY & DIAGNOSTIC AND TREATMENT CENTER, 227 Madison Street (between Jefferson and Clinton Streets); (212) 238-7000.

HARLEM HOSPITAL CENTER, 506 Lenox Avenue (at 135th Street); (212) 939-1000.

METROPOLITAN HOSPITAL CENTER, 1901 First Avenue (97th Street, between First and Second Avenues); (212) 423-6262.

RENAISSANCE DIAGNOSTIC & TREATMENT CENTER, 215 West 125th Street (between Seventh and Eighth Avenues); (212) 932-6500.

THE BRONX

JACOBI MEDICAL CENTER, 1400 Pelham Parkway South (at Eastchester Road); (718) 918-5000.

LINCOLN MEDICAL AND MENTAL HEALTH CENTER, 234 East 149th Street (between Park and Morris Avenues, near the Grand Concourse); (718) 579-5000.

Pick a Study, Any Study

To find a study for a particular condition, check out these Web sites:

NATIONAL DATABASES

CENTER WATCH, *a friendly consolidated listing by category;* *www.centerwatch.com.*

NATIONAL INSTITUTE FOR HEALTH, *a searchable database of conditions and studies; www.cancer.gov/clinical_trials.*

AIDS CLINICAL TRIAL INFORMATION SERVICE, *(800) 874-2572; www.actis.org.*

NATIONAL CANCER INSTITUTE, *www.cancertrials.nci.nih.gov.*

VERITAS MEDICINE, *a database of clinical studies by condition; www.veritasmedicine.com.*

NATIONAL LIBRARY OF MEDICINE, *a database of trials by condition, location, and category; www.aegis.com/pubs/trials.*

NEW YORK MEDICAL CENTERS

BETH ISRAEL MEDICAL CENTER, *www.wehealny.org/studies.*

NYU MEDICAL CENTER, *(212) 252-7170.*

NYU AIDS CLINICAL TRIALS UNIT, *(212) 263-6565; www.med.nyu.edu.actu.*

COLUMBIA-PRESBYTERIAN, *cpmcnet.columbia.edu/dept/ctrials/ active.*

MORRISANIA DIAGNOSTIC & TREATMENT CENTER, 1225 Gerard Avenue (between East 167th and East 168th Streets); (718) 960-2777.

NORTH CENTRAL BRONX HOSPITAL, 3424 Kossuth Avenue (210th Street, between Gunhill and Jerome Avenues); (718) 519-5000.

SEGUNDO RUIZ BELVIS DIAGNOSTIC & TREATMENT CENTER, 545 East 142nd Street (between Brock and St. Anns Avenues); (718) 579-4000.

BROOKLYN

CONEY ISLAND HOSPITAL, 2601 Ocean Parkway (between Avenue Z and Shore Parkway); (718) 616-3000.

CUMBERLAND DIAGNOSTIC & TREATMENT CENTER, 100 North Portland Avenue (between Park and Myrtle Avenues); (718) 260-7500.

DR. SUSAN SMITH MCKINNEY NURSING AND REHABILITATION CENTER, 594 Albany Avenue (at Rutland Road); (718) 245-7000.

EAST NEW YORK DIAGNOSTIC & TREATMENT CENTER, 2094 Pitkin Avenue (between Pennsylvania and New Jersey Avenues); (718) 240-0400.

KINGS COUNTY HOSPITAL CENTER, 451 Clarkson Avenue (between Albany and New York Avenues); (718) 245-3131.

WOODHULL MEDICAL AND MENTAL HEALTH CENTER, 760 Broadway (at Flushing Avenue); (718) 963-8000.

QUEENS

ELMHURST HOSPITAL CENTER, 79-01 Broadway (at 79th Street); (718) 334-4000.

QUEENS HOSPITAL CENTER, 82-68 164th Street (at the Grand Central Parkway); (718) 883-3000.

STATEN ISLAND

SEA VIEW HOSPITAL REHABILITATION CENTER AND HOME, 460 Brielle Avenue (Bradley and Rockland Avenues); (718) 317-3000.

DEPRESSION/MENTAL HEALTH STUDIES AND CLINICAL TRIALS

A number of hospitals and research centers throughout New York conduct ongoing clinical studies of depression and medications for mental illnesses such as Prozac, Zoloft, Wellbutrin, and others. If you qualify for a study, they can provide you with up to one year of free medication and medical care. All studies are supervised and monitored by doctors and psychiatrists adhering to strict clinical testing protocols, some of which could involve the use of a placebo.

MOUNT SINAI MEDICAL CENTER, Compulsive, Impulsive and Anxiety Disorders Clinic, 99th Street and Madison Avenue; (212) 659-8732.

NEUROPSYCH RESEARCH ASSOCIATES, 1236 Park Avenue (at 96th Street); (212) 722-6604.

NEW YORK PRESBYTERIAN/CORNELL MEDICAL CENTER, Depression Treatment Study Program, 525 East 68th Street (at York Avenue); (212) 746-5705.

NEW YORK PSYCHIATRIC INSTITUTE, Depression Evaluation Service, 1051 Riverside Drive, Suite 3300; (212) 543-5734.

ST. LUKE'S/ROOSEVELT HOSPITAL, Mood Disorders Research Program, 910 Ninth Avenue (at 58th Street); (212) 523-7666.

STD CLINICS

There are fifteen city-run STD (sexually transmitted diseases) Clinics located throughout the five boroughs that provide free testing and treatment for all common STDs. They also provide anonymous and confidential HIV testing and counseling. Of course, you can also get free condoms at all locations. These clinics all operate on a take-a-number-and-wait-on-line basis, so you can never predict how long the wait will be. Always call to check hours and services before heading down to one of these clinics. For more information, call the hot line at (212) 427-5120 or check the Web site www.ci.nyc.ny.us/html/doh/html/std/stdfree.html.

MANHATTAN

CENTRAL HARLEM STD CLINIC, 2238 Fifth Avenue (at 137th Street); (212) 690-1760.
Monday through Friday, 8:30 A.M.–4:30 P.M.

EAST HARLEM STD CLINIC, 158 East 115th Street (off Lexington Avenue); (212) 360-5962.
Monday through Friday, 8:30 A.M.–4:30 P.M.

WEST HARLEM STD CLINIC, 21 Old Broadway, Room 204 (at 126th Street); (212) 678-6691 or (212) 678-6697.
Monday through Friday, 8:30 A.M.–4:30 P.M. Only HIV and syphilis testing.

CHELSEA STD CLINIC, 303 Ninth Avenue (at 28th Street);
(212) 239-1725.
Monday through Friday, 8:30 A.M.–4:30 P.M.; Saturday, 9:00 A.M.–
2:00 P.M.

RIVERSIDE STD CLINIC, 160 West 100th Street (between
Columbus and Amsterdam Avenues); (212) 865-7757 or
(212) 865-7758.
Monday through Friday, 8:30 A.M.–4:30 P.M.

THE BRONX

MORRISANIA STD CLINIC, 1309 Fulton Avenue (at East 169th
Street, off Third Avenue); (718) 901-6564.
Monday through Friday, 8:30 A.M.–4:30 P.M.; Saturday, 8:30 A.M.–
1:30 P.M.

BROOKLYN

CROWN HEIGHTS STD CLINIC, 1218 Prospect Place, second floor
(at Troy Avenue); (718) 735-0580.
Monday through Friday, 8:30 A.M.– 4:30 P.M.

FORT GREENE STD CLINIC, 295 Flatbush Avenue Extension, fifth
floor (at Willoughby Street); (718) 643-4133.
Monday through Friday, 8:30 A.M.–4:30 P.M.; Saturday,
8:30 A.M.– 1:30 P.M.

BEDFORD-STUYVESANT STD CLINIC, 485 Throop Avenue first
floor (between Putnam and Madison Streets); (718) 574-2482.
Monday through Friday, 8:30 A.M.–4:30 P.M.

WILLIAMSBURG STD CLINIC, 151 Maujer Street, basement
(between Graham and Manhattan Avenues); (718) 782-3606.
Tuesday and Thursday, 8:30 A.M.–4:30 P.M. HIV counseling and
testing only.

BROWNSVILLE STD CLINIC, 259 Bristol Street, Room 79
(between Blake and Dumont Avenues); (718) 495-7277.
Monday, Wednesday, and Friday, 8:30 A.M.–4:30 P.M. HIV counsel-
ing and testing only.

QUEENS

CORONA STD CLINIC, 34-33 Junction Boulevard (between Roosevelt
and Northern Avenues); (718) 476-7627 or (718) 476-7815.
Monday through Friday, 8:30 A.M.–4:30 P.M.

Safety First: Free Condoms

A Cheap Bastard can be a Sexy Bastard, but there's no reason you can't also be a Safe Bastard. Here is a list of places to pick up your free condoms.

THE BIG CUP, *228 Eighth Avenue (between 21st and 22nd Streets); (212) 206–0059. Mixed in among the piles of postcards and flyers for clubs and upcoming events at this gay coffeehouse, you'll find a jar filled with packages of condoms (sometimes flavored!). These are from Positive Health Project (212–465–8304), a needle exchange and harm reduction agency.*

GAY MEN'S HEALTH CRISIS (GMHC), *119 West 24th Street (between Sixth and Seventh Avenues). Provides a huge amount of free services for people with AIDS and everything you need for AIDS prevention, including condoms-a-plenty. Check out the front desk on the fourth and seventh floors. For more information on other services they provide, call (212) 807–6655 or (800) AIDS–NYC, or check the Web site www.gmhc.org.*

LESBIAN & GAY COMMUNITY CENTER, *208 West 13th Street (between Seventh and Eighth Avenues). The newly renovated center is home to a full schedule of weekly meetings, support groups, workshops, and social activities, many of which are free. You'll also find the free Pat Parker/Vito Russo Library, and there's always free condoms available at the front desk. For more information on schedule and activities, call (212) 620–7310, or check the Web site www.gaycenter.org.*

JAMAICA STD CLINIC, 90–37 Parsons Boulevard, first floor (off Jamaica Avenue); (718) 262–5570.
Monday through Friday, 8:30 A.M.–4:30 P.M.; Saturday, 9:00 A.M.–1:30 P.M.

ROCKAWAY STD CLINIC, 67–10 Rockaway Beach Boulevard (at Beach 67th Street); (718) 945–7150.
Monday through Friday, 8:30 A.M.–4:30 P.M.

STATEN ISLAND

RICHMOND STD CLINIC, 51 Stuyvesant Place (at Wall Street); (718) 983–4515.
Monday through Friday, 8:30 A.M.–4:30 P.M.

"I cannot afford to waste my time making money."

—Jean Louis Agassiz

FITNESS, FUN, AND GAMES: CHEAP THRILLS

REE TIME IS A PRECIOUS commodity in New York, whether you're visiting or you live here. And no place offers more extravagant ways to drop a load of cash when you're able to break away from the hustle and bustle of life in the big city. But wait! There are also tons of things to do and places to go to wind down without breaking the bank. Here are some suggestions for great destinations, recreational activities, and other ways to take it easy for free in New York City. From early morning tai chi classes in Battery Park City Park and kayaking along the Hudson to in-line skating lessons in Central Park and a refreshing dip in any of the many public pools throughout the city, New York City really gives you a chance to enjoy your *free* time. The schedules change from time to time, so be sure to call and confirm all information before showing up.

PARK IT HERE! PARKS OFFERING
A VARIETY OF ACTIVITIES

BATTERY PARK CITY PARKS CONSERVANCY
Hudson River (from Chambers to Vesey Streets)
(212) 267–9700
www.bpcparks.org
This is the mother lode of free fun and games offerings. The free activities they present on a weekly basis from May through October include: aggressive in-line skating lessons (Saturday and Sunday), volleyball (Wednesday at 6:30 P.M.), chess (Thursday at noon), backgammon (Monday at noon), tai chi (Friday at 8:30 A.M.), and drawing classes (Tuesday at 3:00 P.M. and Wednesday at 11:30 A.M.). You can also borrow a wide variety of recreational supplies like Frisbees, basketballs, jump ropes, board games, and more from the Park House at Rockefeller Park (at Chambers Street; bring a photo ID). They even have a couple of free pool tables available near the Park House. Other programs they run throughout the season include a drumming circle, fishing, bird-watching, family dances, lots of children's programs, walking tours, concerts, and on and on. Check out the Web site for more information, or get a copy of their most recent calendar; they add new activities every season.

CENTRAL PARK
59th Street to 110th Street
(between Fifth Avenue and Central Park West)
(212) 310–6600
www.centralparknyc.org
Whole books have been written about this oasis of natural splendor amid the concrete jungle, and there are many entries in this one about specific destinations for free goings-on. Here's a quick rundown of some of the park's free delights: walking tours; in-line skating lessons; tango, salsa, and swing dance; nature exhibits; the Conservatory Gardens; fishing and birding; borrowed sports equipment from the North Meadow Recreation Center; art galleries; theater; concerts, and much more. To get information about anything going on in the park, check the Web site or stop by one of the park's three visitor centers: Belvedere Castle (midpark at 79th Street; 212–772–0210), the Dairy (midpark at 65th Street; 212–794–6564), and Charles A. Dana Discovery Center (inside the Park at 110th Street and Lenox Avenue; 212–860–1370).

Pentanque

BRYANT PARK, *Sixth Avenue (between 40th and 42nd Streets); www.bryantpark.org; (212) 768–4242 or (201) 457–0844. Monday and Friday noon to 2:00 p.m., April through October. Pentanque (pronounced pay-*Tonk*) is the French version of bocci, which is the Italian version of lawn bowling, which is the English version of shuffleboard (kind of). The game is played every week at Bryant Park and free lessons are given every Monday and Friday afternoon. You can stop by for a game or take part in a tournament along the picturesque gravel paths of Bryant Park.*

HUDSON RIVER PARK
Pier 25 (Hudson River at North Moore Street)
(212) 627–2020 or (212) 414–9384
www.hudsonriverpark.org

May through October, Pier 25 is a haven for freebies and cheapies. Their Ping-Pong table is available free of charge on a first-come, first-served basis. The table stands at the ready, complete with paddles and balls anytime the weather permits (replacement balls or racquets are available at the snack bar or Art Shack). Other free activities at the pier include films, fishing, children's Art Shack, swing and salsa dance events with live bands, and kayaking at the nearby Downtown Boathouse (Pier 26). They also have miniature golf and beach volleyball available for a low fee.

RECREATION CENTERS

New York City Department of Parks and Recreation runs forty-two recreation centers throughout the five boroughs, and for the price of $25 a year (yes, a year!) you have access to every single one of them. Now, to be totally honest, some of these are not exactly state-of-the-art facilities, but they do have much of the same equipment you'd find at the high-price gyms around town (Nautilus machines, Lifecycles, free weights, dumbbells, et cetera). Some also offer a full schedule of classes (aerobics, yoga, tai chi, boxing, and more), and some even have indoor and outdoor pools (you won't find that at many of the more expensive clubs around town!). Many of the centers also have extensive programs for children and seniors, and all have free after-school programs for kids eight through thirteen. The computer resource centers at many of the centers offer classes and instruction on the Internet and computer programs.

 Some of the adult classes charge a small fee in addition to the membership.

For information check the Web site www.nycparks.com and click on "Things to Do," or call the chief of recreation's office in each borough (see Appendix D for recreation center locations).

CHIEF OF RECREATION'S OFFICE

(212) 408–0243 (Manhattan)

(718) 965–8941 (Brooklyn)

(718) 430–1858 (the Bronx)

(718) 520–5936 (Queens)

(718) 390–8020 (Staten Island)

Meet the Mets!

Besides being the best, most exciting baseball team in New York City (that's my opinion and I'm sticking to it), the New York Mets were made for Cheap Bastard baseball fans. There are two great ways to see a Mets game free, and legally, too.

1. *Any Wednesday night they're playing at Shea, just be one of the first 800 people to bring a Pepsi can or bottle to the picnic area in center field and get in free. Get there early!*

2. *During any home game, join the hardiest of the Mets faithful watching the game from the walkway of the subway station for the 7 train looking out over right field.*

For schedule and information, call (718) 507–8499 or check the Web site www.mets.com.

Get In-Line:
Central Park Skate Patrol

Not too steady on those skates? Don't let that stop you from getting out there and hitting the road, but make your first stop (or crash!) at the Free Braking and Safety Clinic in Central Park, taught by certified volunteers. Stationed at the East and West Side 72nd Street entrances to the park every Saturday and Sunday from 12:30 to 5:30 P.M. (mid-April to mid-October), these kind and patient volunteers will hold your hand while you master the art of staying in an upright position with blades on your feet. Be sure to pick up a copy of their free **Central Park Pocket Guide for Skaters,** *which offers a great map and lots of useful information for the beginning skater. They also offer advanced group classes and lessons (but they charge for those). For more information, call (212) 439–1234 or check out the Web site www.skatepatrol.org.*

GROUP SKATES

Organized group skates have become quite popular in the city. Each one has a slightly different attitude, ethos, and skill level, but all demand that you be prepared to skate through the streets and that you hone your flirting-while-blading skills. There are groups skating almost every night of the week, spring through fall. All require you to wear helmets and wrist guards.

EMPIRE SKATE CLUB OF NEW YORK
(212) 774–1774
www.empireskate.org
This is a membership organization that welcomes all skaters to join in a number of group skates every week. The Tuesday Night Skate (meets at Krispy Kreme, 141 72nd Street, between Columbus and Amsterdam, at 8:00 P.M.) is for all levels. The Thursday Evening Roll (convenes at the Columbus Circle entrance to Central Park at 59th Street at 6:30 P.M.) is for intermediate to advanced skaters. The Sunday Morning Skate (also meets at the Columbus Circle entrance to Central Park at 59th Street, at 11:00 A.M.) is open to all levels. All skates are canceled in the case of rain or wet streets; call to confirm.

TIME'S UP
(212) 802–8222
www.times-up.org
An environmental activist organization puts together bike and skate rides throughout the year with a point: Get rid of the cars! Critical Mass is an "organized coincidence" that aims to exercise the rights of skaters and cyclists as road users. Meet at Union Square (14th Street and University Place) at 7:00 P.M. on the last Friday of every month, year-round. The Moonlight Ride/Roll through Central Park happens on the first Friday of every month at 10:00 P.M. The group meets at the Columbus Circle entrance to Central Park at 59th Street. The Prospect Park Moonlight Ride/Roll is the first Saturday of every month at 9:00 P.M. and starts at Grand Army Plaza (Flatbush Avenue and Eastern Parkway). Both are relaxing and easygoing tours through these parks. They also run many other rides throughout the five boroughs; check their Web site for details.

WEDNESDAY EVENING SKATE
North end of Union Square (17th Street, between Broadway and Park Avenue)
(212) 696–7247
www.weskateny.org
This very popular skate tours different sections of the city each week and meets between 7:30 and 8:00 P.M. The group rides for about two hours. Open to all levels.

BOATING

THE DOWNTOWN BOATHOUSE
Pier 26 (Hudson River, between Canal and Chambers Streets); Saturday and Sunday, 9:00 A.M.–6:00 P.M.; some weekdays, 5:00–7:00 P.M. (call the status line).

Pier 64 (Hudson River and 24th Street); Saturday and Sunday, 10:00 A.M.–5:00 P.M.

(212) 385–2790 (daily status line)
www.downtownboathouse.org
May through October.
These two locations offer free kayaking on a first-come, first-served basis. They provide the boats, safety equipment, and brief instructions, and you provide the muscle. You can take a leisurely ride in the local embayment, and once you have some experience you can join them on their free three-

hour rides to the Statue of Liberty or the Intrepid Museum. The long rides leave from Pier 26 at 8:00 A.M. every Saturday and Sunday; get there earlier to put your name in the lottery for a slot. The Boathouse is entirely volunteer run. Volunteer and get yourself some advanced lessons and extra access to the boats.

THE GOWANUS DREDGERS CANOE CLUB
Red Hook, Brooklyn
(718) 243–0849
www.waterfrontmuseum.org/dredgers
Weekday evenings and weekends by appointment, spring through fall.
Question: What do Venice and Brooklyn have in common? Answer: Great Italian food, pigeons, and canals. Yes, canals—but you can take a ride through Brooklyn's canals for free! (though the "O Solo Mio" may not be quite as good). E-mail a member of the club through the Web site, and they will be happy to take you on for a canoe trip down this undiscovered trail.

EVERYBODY IN! PUBLIC POOLS

In addition to the pools at the recreation centers (see Appendix D), there are a number of city-run outdoor pools to cool yourself off in during those steamy summer months. These pools are all free and are open from Memorial Day through Labor Day. Daily hours are generally 11:00 A.M. to 7:00 P.M. You can get more information by clicking on "Things to Do" at the Web site www.nycparks.com or by calling the pools.

MANHATTAN

DRY DOCK (EAST VILLAGE), East 10th Street between Avenues C and D; (212) 677–4481.

JOHN JAY (UPPER EAST SIDE), East 77th Street east of York Avenue; (212) 794–6566.

LASKER (CENTRAL PARK), 110th Street and Lenox Avenue; (212) 534–7639 (Olympic-sized pool).

MARCUS GARVEY (CENTRAL HARLEM), 124th Street and Fifth Avenue; (212) 410–2818.

SHELTERING ARMS (EAST HARLEM), East 112th Street and First Avenue; (212) 860–1372.

WAGNER (EAST HARLEM), East 124th Street between First and Second Avenues; (212) 534–4238.

THE BRONX

CLAREMONT, 170th Street and Clay Avenue; (718) 901–4792. Haffen, Ely and Burke Avenues; (718) 379–2908.

MAPES, East 180th Street (between Mapes and Prospect Avenues); (718) 364–8876.

VAN CORTLANDT, West 242nd Street and Broadway; (718) 548–2415.

BROOKLYN

BUSHWICK HOUSES, Flushing Avenue and Humboldt Street; (718) 452–2116.

COMMODORE BARRY, Flushing and Park Avenues (between Navy and North Elliot Streets); (718) 243–2593.

DOUGLAS AND DEGRAW, Third Avenue and Nevins Street; (718) 625–3268.

HOWARD GLENMORE AND MOTHER GASTON BOULEVARD (at East New York Avenue); (718) 385–1023.

KOSCIUSKO (between Marcy and Dekalb Avenues); (718) 622–5271.

SUNSET PARK, Seventh Avenue (between 41st and 44th Streets); (718) 965–6578.

QUEENS

ASTORIA, 19th Street and 23rd Drive; (718) 626–8620.

FISHER, 99th Street and Thirty-second Avenue; (718) 779–8356.

LIBERTY, 173rd Street and 106th Avenue; (718) 657–4995.

STATEN ISLAND

FABER, Faber Street and Richmond Terrace; (718) 816–5259.

LYONS, Pier 6 and Victory Boulevard; (718) 816–9571.

TOTTENVILLE, Hylan Boulevard and Joline Avenue; (718) 356–8242.

WEST BRIGHTON, Henderson Avenue (between Broadway and Chappel Street); (718) 816–5019.

BEACHES

While no one would confuse New York City with Maui, it does have its fair share of sandy beaches within city limits. The city parks department maintains 14 miles of public beaches, all of which are open from Memorial Day through Labor Day. And you know, New York has a much better subway system than Maui. In fact, all city beaches are accessible by public transportation, though some more easily than others. For more information, go to www.nycparks.com and click on "Things to Do."

BRIGHTON BEACH AND CONEY ISLAND
Brighton 1st Street to West 37th Street
Brooklyn
(718) 946–1350
These two beaches are really one long stretch of shoreline that's a very popular destination because of its legendary reputation and easy accessibility. It's located at the end of the F, B, W, and Q subway lines. The throngs also show up because the area offers so much more then just sand and sun. A trip to Coney Island isn't complete with out a walk through Astroland (what remains of the famous amusement park) and a ride on the oh-so-rickety and oh-so-thrilling roller coaster the Cyclone (a kick worth paying $4.00 a ride; 718–372–0275, www.astroland.com). Astroland also has a fireworks display every Friday night at 9:30 during the summer. Don't miss the stalls of antiques/junk/whatever being hawked along Surf Avenue. Farther down the boardwalk is Brighton Beach. Known as "Odessa by the Sea," Brighton has become the home of New York's thriving Russian immigrant community, and a walk along Brighton Avenue certainly makes you feel like you've been transported to the heart of Mother Russia. There are also some amazing deals to be found on fresh fruits and vegetables along the avenue.

MANHATTAN BEACH
Oriental Boulevard (from Ocean Avenue to Mackenzie Street)
Brooklyn
(718) 946–1373
Located just a bit farther down the shore from Brighton Beach, this more secluded beach isn't quite as populated as the big guys next door and also offers areas for you to fire up the barbeque and picnic. The buses B1 and B49 will take you to the beach.

Everything and Anything

Be sure to get yourself one of the invaluable New York City Department of Parks and Recreation Special Events Calendars for the year. It lists the vast numbers of activities going on in parks throughout the five boroughs from April through October. Many of these are one-day events that you don't want to miss—the urban park rangers' Falcon Olympics, Haunted Halloween Walks, ethnic celebrations from every corner of the world in every corner of the city, opera, symphony, and philharmonic performances, sports tournaments, and much more. Call (212) 360–1480 to get a copy, call the hot line at (212) 360–3456 for an up-to-date schedule, or check the Web site www.nycparks.org. And fear not: The schedule is free, and all the activities are gratis as well.

ORCHARD BEACH
Pelham Bay Park
The Bronx
(718) 885–2275
Looking out on Long Island Sound, this is the beach of choice for Bronx residents. The waters are generally calm and the promenade is quite lively, especially on weekends. They offer free Latin music concerts on the beach every Sunday in the summer. Take the 12 bus from the Pelham Bay subway station (6 train).

ROCKAWAY BEACH
Beach 1st Street in Far Rockaway to Beach 149th Street
Neponsit, Queens
(718) 318–4000
Popular with Brooklyn and Queens residents, this long stretch of beach (7 miles) runs almost the entire length of Rockaway. Take the A train toward Far Rockaway; many beach stops along the way.

JACOB RIIS PARK
Fort Tilden, Gateway National Park
Rockaway, Queens
(718) 763–2202
www.nps.gov/gate

Open the Gate: Gateway National Recreation Area

Administered by the National Park Service, Gateway is made up of 26,000 acres of parkland that runs through Brooklyn, Queens, Staten Island, and into northern New Jersey. There's a huge array of activities for kids and adults, from nature walks, concerts, and campfire sing-alongs to sailing lessons, gardening classes, and yoga on the beach. All activities run by the NPS are free and open to all. For a guide to their programs, locations, and activities, call (718) 354–4606 or check their Web site, www.nps.gov/gate.

Run by the National Park Service, this small strip of sand located just a short hop from Brooklyn is a very popular destination, particularly on the weekends. When the public beach is overrun, venture onto the private beaches of Rockaway, just a short walk along the dunes. From Brooklyn take the Q35 bus, and from Queens take the Q35 or the Q22 bus.

SOUTH AND MIDLAND BEACHES
Fort Wadsworth to Miller Field
Staten Island
(718) 987–0709
Staten Island's own secret beach that's hardly ever crowded.

"No entertainment is so cheap
as reading, nor any pleasure
so lasting."
—Lady Mary Wortley Montague

LIBRARIES: FREE ACCESS

LIBRARIES ARE THE ULTIMATE resource for anyone who wants it all, but doesn't want to spend anything to get it. After all, the libraries were established by Mr. "A Penny Saved Is a Penny Earned" himself, Benjamin Franklin. New York has three public library systems: the New York Public Library (in Manhattan, the Bronx, and Staten Island), the Brooklyn Public Library, and the Queens Borough Public Library. The three systems have a network of research libraries and local branches with more than 200 locations throughout the five boroughs (see Appendix B for a complete list of branch locations). At each of these branches, you'll find not only bookshelves full of reading material, but also a wide selection of videos and CDs of every kind of music conceivable. Some locations, like the Mid-Manhattan and Donnell Libraries, can rival Blockbuster and Tower Records in their video and CD selections.

You also have access to computers and the Internet as well as computer classes. In fact, you can find free classes in everything from origami and quilting to job placement and starting a small business. Many branches also have a regular schedule of music, films, theater, and readings. There are many private libraries in New York, too; some charge a membership fee to borrow materials, but all can be a great source for in-house research.

RESEARCH CENTERS

THE NEW YORK PUBLIC LIBRARY
HUMANITIES AND SOCIAL SCIENCES LIBRARY
Fifth Avenue and 42nd Street
(212) 930–0830
www.nypl.org/research/chss
This landmark Beaux Arts building is home to more than 1 million books, 135 miles of hidden bookshelves, and two friendly lions named Patience and Fortitude. You cannot take any books out of this library, but you are welcome to spend endless hours in their stunning reading rooms—and you will want to. The building recently underwent a multimillion-dollar renovation and the grandeur of these rooms, particularly the Rose Reading Room, guarantees you'll be thinking exceptionally intelligent thoughts. Don't miss the one-hour tours of the historic facility every Monday through Saturday at 11:00 A.M. and 2:00 P.M. Tours of changing exhibitions in Gottesman Hall begin at 12:30 and 2:30 P.M.. They also offer an array of classes at the South Court Training Center.

THE NEW YORK PUBLIC LIBRARY FOR THE
PERFORMING ARTS
40 Lincoln Center Plaza (65th Street and Amsterdam Avenue)
(212) 870–1630
www.nypl.org/research/lpa/lpa.html
Newly returned to its home at Lincoln Center after a three-year renovation, this is home to one of the world's most extensive collections of materials in the performing arts. Not limited to books, the library is particularly well known for its huge collections of historic recordings, videotapes, CDs, records, autograph manuscripts, correspondence, sheet music, stage designs, press clippings, programs, posters, and photographs. You can borrow a great deal of the materials in the library, though the archival collections are only available for reference. Being the performing arts library, you would expect they might have a performance or two every now and then—

Reference Desk

You will find mentions throughout this book of various goings-on at public libraries around the city. Here's a rundown of which chapters contain detailed information on these happenings:

For the complete list of **PUBLIC LIBRARY BRANCH LOCATIONS** in the five boroughs, see Appendix B.

For listing on branch libraries that offer **REGULARLY SCHEDULED FILMS,** see page 53.

For **FILMS FOR KIDS** at libraries, see pages 127–29.

For **STORYTELLING AND READINGS** at libraries, see pages 139–40.

For **CLASSES** at libraries, see page 149.

For **CONCERTS** at libraries, see page 35.

and they certainly don't disappoint. You'll find a full schedule of presentations by prominent actors, composers, musicians, writers, choreographers, and dancers throughout the week.

SCHOMBURG CENTER FOR RESEARCH IN BLACK CULTURE

515 Malcolm X Boulevard (at 135th Street)
(212) 491–2200
www.nypl.org/research/sc

This is a national research library devoted to collecting, preserving, and providing access to resources documenting the experiences of peoples of African descent throughout the world. Their collection is entirely noncirculation, but they make many of the historic materials available to the public through an extensive schedule of exhibitions, publications, and educational, scholarly, and cultural programs. They do charge for some performances, but many are free. Free guided tours of exhibitions are available by appointment only. For tour information, call (212) 491–2265.

SCIENCE, INDUSTRY, AND BUSINESS LIBRARY

188 Madison Avenue (at 34th Street)
(212) 592–7000
www.nypl.org/research/sibl

The nation's largest public information center devoted solely to science and business, the research center houses both a circulating library and an extensive noncirculating collection (1.4 million volumes). The library's Electronic Information Center connects users to the hundreds of internal and external electronic information resources, including Internet databases, CD-ROMs, electronic journals, and online services. The Electronic Training Center offers ongoing classes in computer programs, the Internet, research, and business and industry issues. Combined, the two centers have more than a hundred computer workstations ready for public use. Take the free one-hour tour Tuesday at 2:00 P.M. to learn more about the facilities. For tour information, call (212) 592–7000.

PRIVATE LIBRARIES

FRENCH INSTITUTE/ALLIANCE FRANÇAISE
22 East 60th Street (between Park and Madison Avenues)
(212) 355–6100
www.fiaf.org
Hours: Monday through Thursday, 11:30 A.M.–8:00 P.M.; Saturday,
10:00 A.M.–1:30 P.M.

 Nonmembers do not have borrowing privileges. Membership is $75 a year.

This is the largest collection of all-French materials in the United States. You're welcome to spend all day in the spacious library reading any of the 30,000 French books, perusing the hundred of French magazines, watching any of the 1,000 French videos, or listening to the many French CDs, French books on tape, or French cassettes. In other words, if it's French, it's here.

GOETHE INSTITUTE
1014 Fifth Avenue (between 82nd and 83rd Streets)
(212) 439–8700
www.goethe.de/uk/ney
Hours: Tuesday and Thursday noon–7:00 P.M.; Wednesday and
Friday until 5:00 P.M.

Nonmembers do not have borrowing privileges. Membership is $10 a year.

This is the German version of the French Institute. The big difference here is that they have half as many books, videos, CDs, newspapers, and magazines. (And, of course, they're in German, not French.)

"Get Ya Free Money Heeere!"

Okay, it's not as simple as that, but there is plenty of it out there in the form of grants and scholarships from private and public organizations, and the Foundation Center can help you find it (free of charge, of course). The library will help you sift through the more than 47,000 private and corporate giving programs to find the ones that are the best targets for your project. They have free training sessions on funding research, proposal writing, proposal budgeting, and even the occasional networking breakfast (with free pastries and coffee!). The Foundation Center (79 Fifth Avenue, second floor at 16th Street) is open Monday, Thursday, and Friday, 10:00 A.M. to 5:00 P.M.; and Tuesday and Wednesday until 8 P.M. For more information, call (212) 620–4230 or check the Web site www.fdncenter.org.

INSTITUTO CERVANTES LIBRARY
122 East 42nd Street, Suite 807 (at Lexington Avenue)
(212) 661–6011
www.institutocervantes.org
Hours: Tuesday through Friday, 10:00 A.M.–6:00 P.M.

 Nonmembers do not have borrowing privileges. Membership is $35 a year.

Okay, this time take the French Institute, double the size of the collection, translate everything into Spanish, and you have the Instituto Cervantes Library.

THE NEW YORK ACADEMY OF MEDICINE LIBRARY
1216 Fifth Avenue (at 103rd Street)
(212) 822–7300
www.nyam.org
Hours: Monday through Friday, 9:00 A.M.–5:00 P.M.

This noncirculating research library houses the second largest medical collection in the United States, following the National Library of Medicine in Bethesda, Maryland. Its extensive facilities include over 1 million volumes, more than 1,400 current journal subscriptions, and a variety of electronic resources. They also offer a full curriculum of free classes in various research methods and techniques to make your use of their library (and all libraries!) much more effective.

PAT PARKER/VITO RUSSO CENTER LIBRARY
The Lesbian & Gay Community Center
208 West 13th Street (between Seventh and Eighth Avenue)
(212) 620–7310
www.gaycenter.org
Hours: Monday through Thursday, 6:00–9:00 P.M.; Saturday, 1:00–4:00 P.M.
The collection of this library is geared toward everything to do with gay, lesbian, bisexual, transgender, and AIDS studies. This circulating library is open to all (a membership fee is requested, but not required). The library has a collection of about 12,000 books and more than 500 videos (documentaries and features). When you borrow videos, they ask you to leave a refundable deposit for the one-week loan.

Got a Question?
Get an Answer!

Q: Need to know the capital of Lithuania or the correct spelling for Engelbert Humperdink? Then give a call to free library reference lines. They are there to answer any question you have, from the most obscure facts to the most commonly asked question on all subjects. The New York Public Library's telephone reference line is (212) 340–0849, ext. 3 (Monday through Saturday, 9:00 A.M. to 6:00 P.M.). The Brooklyn Public Library's reference phone is (718) 230–2100, ext. 5 (Monday through Thursday, 9:00 A.M. to 8:00 P.M.; Friday and Saturday, 9:00 A.M. to 6:00 P.M.; Sunday, 1:00 P.M. to 5:00 P.M.), and the folks at the Queens Borough Public Library can help you at (718) 990–0714 or (718) 990–0728 (Monday through Friday, 10:00 A.M. to 8.45 P.M.; Saturday, 10:00 A.M. to 5:15 P.M.).

A: The capital of Lithuania is Vilnius. Answer courtesy of the Brooklyn Public Library Telephone Reference Line.

A: The correct spelling for both the 1960s nightclub singer and the nineteenth-century German composer of Hansel and Gretel is Engelbert Humperdinck. Answer courtesy of the New York Public Library Telephone Reference line.

NEWSPAPERS: THE FREE PRESS

IMES, **SHMIMES. You don't need to throw away 75 cents a day ($3.00 on Sunday!) to get your fill of information in New York City. Whatever your interest or point of view there's a free newspaper out there for you. Granted, the news you get from some of the free presses in the city might have a bit of a skewed worldview. But if you're looking for community news, local entertainment listings, and happenings around town, there are plenty of papers to pick up that you don't need to drop a quarter, a dime, a nickel, or even a penny to get. You'll find most of these papers in those ubiquitous newspaper boxes on almost any major street corner in Manhattan. Some can be found throughout the boroughs but are easiest to come by in Manhattan.**

BIG APPLE PARENT AND QUEENS PARENT
(212) 889–6400 or (718) 347–5700
www.parentsknow.com
This monthly magazine is dedicated entirely to parenting in New York City. Each month's issue has intelligent and informative articles, an extensive calendar of events, and lots and lots of advertising. Be aware that the magazine is targeted toward parents with no shortage of cash, so there's no focus on doing things on the cheap. There is, however, some very useful information for all to be found within their pages. You can find *Big Apple Parent* in street corner boxes and stores throughout Manhattan and in Brooklyn Heights, Carroll Gardens, and Park Slope. *Queens Parent* is distributed throughout Queens. Check the Web site or call for specific locations.

DOWNTOWN EXPRESS
(212) 242–6162
www.downtownexpress.com
Downtown Express is a biweekly newspaper covering all the goings-on in Tribeca, Battery Park City, the South Street Seaport, and the Wall Street area in Lower Manhattan. This slim publication manages to cover the huge amount of local news, arts, sports, and other happenings below Canal Street. The listings section includes local theater, music, and particularly good coverage of art galleries in the area. The paper is widely distributed in street corner boxes and stores below Canal Street.

HX
(212) 352–3535
www.hx.com
As you can tell from the full name of this weekly, *Homo eXtra* is a gay magazine. *HX* occasionally touches on such subjects as politics and current events, but is best relied on for its bar and club listings, reviews, gossip, and nothing-left-to-the-imagination advertising. You can find copies at every gay bar and store in the city as well as some street corner boxes in Chelsea.

JEWISH SENTINEL
(212) 244–4949
As you might imagine, this is the source for all things Jewish around New York—from articles on Israel and the Jewish perspective on New York to a selected listing of cultural events, gatherings, galleries, and performances that might be of interest to the Jewish community. You can pick up a copy at street corner boxes placed sporadically around Manhattan; call for specific locations.

Extra! Extra!

I have to confess that there are times when even I read one of the big daily newspapers, either to get better informed or, in the case of the Post, *just for laughs. Still, that's no excuse to spend money. If you have access to the Web, you have free access to the newspapers. Every one of the major dailies publishes its entire contents, along with even more information, on the Web every day. For the* **New York Times,** *check out: www.nytimes.com. The* **New York Daily News** *is at www.mostnewyork.com, and the* **New York Post's** *Web Site is www.nypost.com. If you feel the need to get some ink on your hands, you can always find a copy at any local library.*

LGNY
(646) 473–1985
www.lgny.com
The biweekly *LGNY (Lesbian Gay New York)* covers local and national news, politics, and arts as they affect the gay community. Also included with the second issue each month is *LGNY Latino,* New York's only Spanish-language gay newspaper. Copies of *LGNY* can be found in street corner boxes below 34th Street, particularly around Chelsea, the Lower East Side, and the West and East Village.

METRO SPORTS
(212) 563–7329
metrosportsny.com
The source for everything on the go in New York. Articles and listings on running, cycling, skiing, skating, marathons, triathlons, sports medicine, and new equipment. Most of all, the magazine is a vehicle for a lot of advertising, though the calendar of events is particularly thorough and useful. *Metro Sports* is published once a month and can be found in any sporting goods store around the city.

NEW YORK BLADE NEWS
(212) 268–2701
www.nyblade.com
New York's weekly gay community newspaper covers local and national issues, personalities and events affecting gay men and lesbians in the city. It's also a good source for arts listings and community events. The paper

is distributed widely on street corners and stores throughout Manhattan and at selected locations throughout the boroughs; call or check the Web site for specific locations.

NEW YORK PRESS
(212) 244–2282
www.nypress.com
New York's *alternative* alternative newspaper, the *Press* is chock-full of opinionated and often very funny articles on the politics, characters, events, and arts of the city. Its film, music, and events listings are among the best in the city. You'll find copies on almost any street corner in Manhattan and parts of Brooklyn (downtown, Park Slope, and Cobble Hill). Like the *Voice*, grab a copy early in the week; you may have a hard time finding one once the weekend rolls around.

NEW YORK RESIDENT
(212) 993–9410
www.newyorkresident.com
A weekly magazine with a focus on the culture and politics of the city. You'll find regular articles on health, fashion, travel, restaurants, as well as weekly theater, film, and music picks. The *Resident* is distributed widely in street corner boxes in Manhattan.

NEXT MAGAZINE
(212) 627–0165
www.nextmagazine.net
Almost an exact clone of *HX*.

THE ONION
(212) 627–1972
www.theonion.com
This on-target satirical news weekly takes on national issues, news figures, and "local" events all over the country. While their view on the news can be hysterically funny, their arts section, "The A.V. Club," is surprisingly serious and extensive. The section doesn't include timetables or movie locations, but they do include in-depth reviews and features on almost every film in the theaters at any given time, from Hollywood blockbusters to independents and documentaries. You'll also find good articles on videos and local music picks. You can grab a copy from their boxes located all over Manhattan (most plentifully under 23rd Street and in the Columbia University area) and in Park Slope and Williamsburg in Brooklyn.

ROLLING OUT NEW YORK
(212) 979-5400
An urban style weekly that includes weekly celebrity interviews, offers reviews of music and film, and touches on politics and world news as they affect the African American community; there's also a calendar of events around town. The paper can be found around Manhattan (particularly in Harlem), Brooklyn, and the Bronx.

VILLAGE VOICE
(212) 475-3300
www.villagevoice.com
The original and still the largest alternative news weekly. Since 1955, the *Voice* has been the place to go to get the other view on anything: politics, art, theater, film, literature, sex, and even a unique take on horoscopes. The paper is sure to annoy you with some of its articles and engage you with others, but you will almost always find them provocative. Even if you never agree with what they have to say, the *Voice* is always worth picking up for the extensive music, film, theater, dance, and art listings, and the sprawling classifieds including their no-holds-barred personals. Grab a copy out of one the red boxes on most street corners around the five boroughs or free at newsstands and stores around the city. Get your copy early in the week; by the time the weekend rolls around, the boxes are usually empty. You can always find a pile of papers outside their downtown office on Bowery between 5th and 6th Streets. Check the Web site to find a place to pick up a copy near you.

WEST SIDE SPIRIT AND OUR TOWN
(212) 268-8600
www.ourtownnyc.com
Both put out by the same publisher and editorial staff, these two weekly papers are basically mirror images of each other, with *Our Town* covering the East Side and *The West Side Spirit* covering (you guessed it) the West Side. Both cover the local politics, crime, and events of their areas and share a good citywide listing of arts and community events, with a strong focus on free activities. Both can be found in corner boxes and stores on their respective sides of town between 59th and 110th Streets.

"There are many things that we would throw away, if we were not afraid that others might pick them up."

—Oscar Wilde

FURNITURE AND HOUSEHOLD GOODS: ONE MAN'S TRASH . . .

ALL AROUND THE CITY you'll spot them every other day of the week. Some people call them piles of trash, but the trained eye clearly recognizes them as mountains of treasures. Furnishing New York apartments by "recycling" is not only good for the environment, it's great for the bank account. It's a long-held tradition and a way of life for students, artists, collectors, and anyone with an open mind and a creative eye. You will be shocked at the high caliber of items some people consider garbage, but it makes sense. Consider the fact that New Yorkers on average earn a great deal of money, but are forced to live in some of the smallest apartments this side of a shoe box. The result is, folks end up throwing away some mighty fine used stuff to make room for some newer finer stuff.

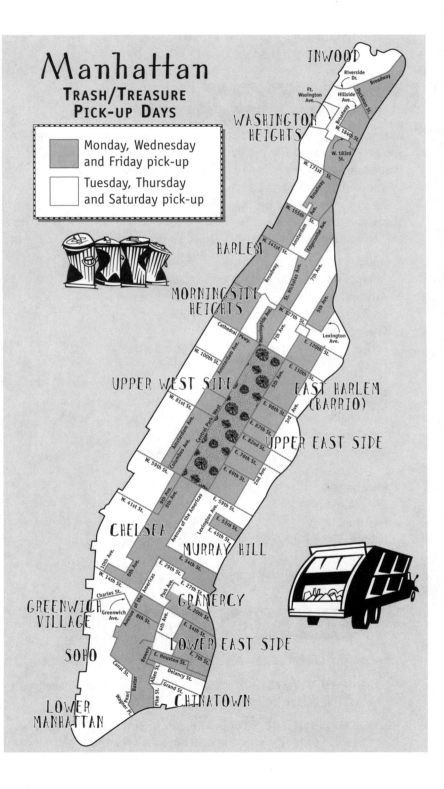

FAVORITE FINDS

Almost anything you need or want can be found on the street. I can't tell you how many times I have said "I need" this or that, only to come across that exact "this or that" a few days later on the street. You are limited only by your willingness to forage and schlep. Obviously, the smaller the item you're in the market for, the more effort you'll have to put into your search. If you're interested in larger furnishings, however, the sky's the limit. Here are some of my favorite items I've picked up from the street over the years:

Antique trunks
Antique wooden milk crate
Artwork
Bookcases
Chest of drawers
Coffee table
Couch
Decorative window flower box
Desk
Desk chairs
Director's chairs
Doctor's office scale
End tables
Exercise mat
File cabinets
Footstool
Halogen torch lamp

Ironing board
Luggage
Leather easy chair
Microwave oven
Mirrors
Oriental rugs
Ottoman
Plates, bowls, silverware
Power Mac computer, monitor,
    and printer
Spice rack
Storage boxes
Telephone
Toaster oven
Vacuum cleaner
Wicker basket
Window screens

Who knows what *you* might find!

CURBSIDE SHOPPING TIPS

Here are some helpful rules to live by when you are on the prowl:

1. **SHOP IN THE BEST NEIGHBORHOODS:** The better off the neighbors, the better the garbage.

2. **KNOW WHEN THE SHOPS ARE OPEN FOR BUSINESS:** Consult the accompanying map to see what days the Department of Sanitation

Schools Out!

For a few short weeks from late May to early June, the pickings are prime down in the Village around NYU and up in Morningside Heights around Columbia University. As the students of these hoity-toity schools close up their apartments for the year, one of the lesser-known traditions of graduation season begins: the Dumping of the Dorms. These students, many of them well heeled, set out an abundance of useful items (desks, chairs, futons, couches, filing cabinets, microwaves, lava lamps . . . anything you might find in the IKEA catalog that can fit in a dorm room makes its way to the street) as the young intelligentsia makes it way out of town for the summer, or into the real world forever. Keep your eyes open.

will be around to take away the merchandise. It's best to do your hunting the night before scheduled pickups. You'll generally start to notice piles appearing in the late afternoon and early evening.

3. **WHEN IN DOUBT, DON'T LEAVE IT OUT:** If you're considering an item, take it. Undoubtedly it will not be there if you decide to come back for it. But if you take it and it doesn't work or fit your need, you can always redonate it. Nothing ventured, nothing gained.

4. **DON'T BE A HOG:** If you find something that turns out not to fit your need, set it back out on the street right away. The temptation is to hold on to this great find and hope you can find a use for it someday. The problem is, you'll end up cluttering up your small studio apartment with stuff you can't use, and the longer you hold on to it, the harder it will be to part with it. Just like ripping off that Band-Aid, do it quick and it will be less painful. And no doubt, someone else will pick it up and be very grateful to you.

5. **A LITTLE WORK GOES A LONG WAY:** Repaint it, refinish it, change the knobs, or reupholster the cushion and presto! It's good as new!

6. **CLEAN IT.** (Hey, you never know.)

7. **ENJOY IT.**

HAPPY HUNTING!

The Big Salvation (Army)!

Not that I'm endorsing the idea of spending cash, but there are times when you can't wait to stumble across that perfect headboard, desk, or butcher-block countertop and money must be spent. The best option is always to shop at any of New York's many thrift stores. While whole books have been written on this subject alone, there are some standout shops to head for when you're in the market for furniture, appliances, or knickknacks of any kind. Most local thrift stores offer a smattering of sofas, chairs, and china, but their space is limited, so the selection is as well. Still, in each borough you'll find a main Salvation Army Thrift Store (usually connected to a warehouse) with huge assortments of goods. While these stores may not be around the corner, the prices and selection make them worth the trip. For some other shopping ideas, see the Shopping chapter, and for a good list of thrift stores throughout the city, check out the Web site www.salvationarmy.usaeast.org. Here are the super Salvation Army stores in each borough:

MANHATTAN: 536 West 46th Street (between Tenth and Eleventh Avenues); (212) 757-2311.

BROOKLYN: 436 Atlantic Avenue (between Bonds and Nevens Streets); (718) 834-1562.

22 Quincy Street (between Clausson and Downing Streets); (718) 622-5686.

THE BRONX: 4109 Park Avenue (at 175th Street); (718) 583-3500.

QUEENS: 34-02 Steinway Street (between Thirty-fourth and Thirty-fifth Avenues); (718) 472-2414.

STATEN ISLAND: 2053 Clove Road (at Mosel Avenue); (718) 442-3080.

"I always say shopping is cheaper than a psychiatrist."
—Tammy Faye Bakker

SHOPPING:
A TALE OF TWO STREETS

IF YOU *MUST* SPEND MONEY—and as a rule I do not endorse the practice—there are a couple of streets you should know about to keep this awful habit in check. Of course, there are thousands of stores throughout the city where you can find "a deal." There are also tons of books that tell you where to find these stores, but I'm just going to include a few of the best. On 17th and 32nd Streets, you'll find clusters of some of my favorite shops in New York City—the places where I shop almost to the exclusion of any other stores in town. What makes them so great? You guessed it: great stuff, really cheap.

On West 32nd Street you will find three stores that can supply you with all the essentials of life (food, dishes, books, clothes, furnishings, office supplies, cosmetics, electronics, toys . . .) and many of the absurdities of life ("As seen on TV" items, last year's fad items, "has-been" pop star paraphernalia, and more) at ridiculously low prices. West 17th Street is the place to head to check out three of the best thrift stores around. These secondhand shops are not necessarily the cheapest in the five boroughs, but you can snag some amazingly high-quality finds at very respectable prices at these shops. And most days they run specials that make it all the more worthwhile.

32ND STREET: BARGAIN PARADISE

JACK'S 99¢ STORES
110 West 32nd Street (between Sixth and Seventh Avenues)
(212) 268–9962
You may have come across other 99-cent stores in your travels, but Jack's is hands-down the best there is. This huge store is overflowing with bargains, from the frozen foods section to every household item or office supply you could ever need. While some of the goods are made by companies you may not recognize, a surprisingly large amount of the merchandise is brand name. The wares change on a daily basis, so you could walk the aisles every day and be almost guaranteed of finding something you can't live without (for 99 cents, that is). There's also a location at 16 East 40th Street (between Fifth and Madison Avenues) that has much the same selection, but isn't quite as exciting a shopping experience.

WEBBERS CLOSEOUTS
116 West 32nd Street (between Sixth and Seventh Avenue)
(212) 564–3606
Just a couple of doors down from Jack's, Webbers has also taken on the challenge of selling everything you can imagine for 99 cents. Also a huge store, though the selection isn't quite as vast as Jack's; still, there are plenty of good deals to be had if you're willing to do a little work sifting through the schlock. There are many other Webbers located throughout the city, but this is the only one that sell items exclusively for 99 cents.

ODD-JOB STORES
149 West 32nd Street (between Sixth and Seventh Avenues)
(212) 564–7370
www.oddjobstores.com
A little farther down the block, you'll find an Odd-Job. This is a large chain of closeout stores throughout New York, New Jersey, and the Northeast. They specialize in providing higher-ticket brand-name items at low prices.

Fruit of the Streets

Over the last few years, fruit stands have begun to sprout up on almost every street corner in the city. And generally you can get pretty decent deals on your apples, oranges, and green beans from these vendors, but one seems to stand above all others as the place to get more bananas for your buck. A guy named Smiley or "The Fruit Nazi" (depending on whom you talk to) runs a few Midtown stands where you're likely to find the kind of produce you don't usually see other street vendors selling: plump strawberries, mangos, mesclun, kiwis, as well as the usual apples, tomatoes, peppers, and more. The catch is that he sells them for pennies, but only in large quantities—10 large tomatoes for $1.00, four pounds of grapes for $2.00, five pounds of gourmet salad mix for $3.00. Also, he doesn't take too kindly to you picking out the fruit (hence "The Fruit Nazi"). Let him pick your pears and you'll stay on his good side. The main stand is on 48th Street, just east of Sixth Avenue. His other stands are at 42nd Street and Third Avenue, and 47th Street and Sixth Avenue. These stands are open for business Monday through Friday, after 3:00 P.M. He also has a Web site that doesn't give you much information, but does lay out his strict fruit-handling philosophy: www.expage.com/smileysproduce.

It's always worth a stroll down the aisles to see what you might find. Their selection includes housewares, stationery, books, health and beauty aids, food, toys, hardware, giftware, electronics, and garden supplies. Brand names carried may include, at any given time, Black and Decker, Hershey, Keebler, Mars, Mattel, Mikasa, Rubbermaid, and Sony. They have many other locations throughout the city, all with much the same merchandise.

17TH STREET: FIRST IN SECONDHAND

HOUSING WORKS THRIFT SHOPS
143 West 17th Street (between Sixth and Seventh Avenues)
(212) 366–0820
www.housingworksthrift.com

Think of Housing Works Thrift Shops as the Bergdorf Goodman of second-hand. The designer clothing, furniture, housewares, art, antiques, books, CDs, and records are certainly a cut above what you would find in your neighborhood Salvation Army or Goodwill. The prices are also a bit higher, but not much. They often run daily specials making the place a steal. There are three other locations around the city (202 East 77th Street, between Second and Third Avenues; 306 Columbus Avenue, between 74th and 75th Streets; 157 East 23rd Street, between Third and Lexington Avenues). Housing Works is New York's largest provider of housing and supportive services to homeless, formerly homeless, and at-risk men, women, and children living with HIV and AIDS.

ANGEL STREET
118 West 17th Street (between Sixth and Seventh Avenues)
(212) 229–0546
www.angelthriftshop.org
Continue along 17th Street a bit farther and you'll come across Angel Street. Much like Housing Works, it gets great high-quality donations but with more of an emphasis on furnishings and accessories than clothes (though the clothes they do sell, they sell very cheaply). You'll also find enticing daily specials at this boutiquelike shop. All proceeds from Angel Street benefit individuals and families affected by substance abuse, HIV, AIDS, and mental illness.

17 @ 17 THRIFT STORE
17 West 17th Street (between Fifth and Sixth Avenues)
(212) 727–7516
Walk farther down the street. Okay, you do actually have to cross an avenue to get to this thrift store, but since you're in the neighborhood, it's worth stopping in. This store is almost always so overflowing with fur-niture, clothes, and tchotchkes that you can pretty much count on them having a 50 to 75 percent off sale going on. All proceeds benefit the Women's Campaign of the UJA-Federation of New York, helping Jewish people in need around the world.

"And the turtles, of course . . .
all the turtles are free.

As turtles and, maybe, all
creatures should be."

—Dr. Seuss

PETS: CANINE, FELINE, BOTTOM LINE

WHETHER YOUR preference is cats or dogs (or hamsters, rabbits, or even the occasional turtle), there are plenty of little companions to be had for the asking. By opting for an adopted pet, you will not only be saving a cage full of cash and giving a home to a needy (and loving) buddy, but you will also be doing your part to put an end to the puppy mills that churn out unhealthy dogs and cats for pet stores. Most of the shelters around the city do require some "donation" to offset their expenses, but here are some ways to increase the size of your household without decreasing the size of your bank account. Also, here are some suggestions on where to go to keep your Pekinese in the pink without spending much green.

Surfing for Pets

Here are a few good Web sites to checkout for free pet adoptions. There is also no charge to list pets on these sites for adoptions.

WWW.LOOTUSA.COM, *the Web version of the classified ads newspaper* Loot, *is free and has more listings than the paper version (cost $1.00). Their pet section includes free private adoptions as well as pricey animals for sale. You can place an add in the paper and on the Web site in any category for free.*

WWW.PETFINDER.ORG, *a national clearinghouse for shelters and rescue organizations that lists thousands of animals by breed and locations. Many of these shelters do suggest donations ranging from $30 to $100.*

GET A PET

NORTH SHORE ANIMAL LEAGUE
25 Davis Avenue
Port Washington, Long Island
(516) 883–7575
www.nsalamerica.org

 They ask for a donation of any amount, but you aren't required to make one.

This huge shelter is overflowing with hundreds of dogs and cats at any given time, both purebreds and mixed breeds. It's a short forty-five-minute ride from Manhattan on the Long Island Railroad—and it's worth the trip. Not only is this the only shelter that will let you adopt a pet for free (or for whatever donation you feel like making), but all pets are spayed or neutered, vaccinated, and have ID tags. You also get free medical care for your pet for thirty days, free training advice for the life of the pet, very low-cost training classes, and a free starter kit when you take your new pal home (worth $100!). They will check you out before they let you adopt a pet, so bring two picture IDs and phone numbers of references. If you can't make it to Long Island, they'll come to your neighborhood. Their mobile adoption center travels throughout the city and the tristate area. Check the Web site or call for schedule and details. The shelter is open for adoptions seven days a week from 10:00 A.M. to 9:00 P.M.

PET POSTINGS

Another way to find a free companion is to check out the bulletin boards and windows of local pet stores and veterinarians for notices from your neighbors who need to give up their pets. Whether it's because they're moving and can't take the Tonkinese to Tupelo, or their Labrador just had a litter, or the new hubby is allergic to the husky, often owners and their pets must be parted. Here are some places where you're sure to find postings:

EAST SIDE

ANIMAL ATTRACTIONS, 343 East 66th Street (at First Avenue); (212) 734–8400.

CALLING ALL PETS, 1590 York Avenue (at 84th Street); (212) 249–7387.

CALLING ALL PETS, 301 East 76th Street (at Second Avenue); (212) 734–7051.

THE COUNTRY VET, 430 East 75th Street (between First and York Avenues); (212) 535–3250.

THE NATURAL PET, 238 Third Avenue (between 19th and 20th Streets); (212) 228–4848.

PETCO, 560 Second Avenue (at 31st Street); (212) 779–4550.

PETCO, 860 Broadway (at East 17th Street); (212) 358–0692.

WEST SIDE

ANIMAL GENERAL, 558 Columbus Avenue (at 87th Street); (212) 501–9600.

BARKING ZOO, 172 Ninth Avenue (between 20th and 21st Streets); (212) 255–0658.

CLINTON VETERINARY CENTER, 357 West 52nd Street (between Eighth and Ninth Avenues); (212) 333–5548.

NEW YORK DOG SPA, 145 West 18th Street (between Sixth and Seventh Avenues); (212) 243–1199.

PAWS INN, 189 Ninth Avenue (between 21st and 22nd Streets); (212) 646–7297.

PET BOWL, 440 Amsterdam Avenue (at 81st Street); (212) 595–4200.

PET MARKET, 210 West 72nd Street (between Broadway and West End Avenue); (212) 799–4200.

PET STOP, 564 Columbus Avenue (between 87th and 88th Streets); (212) 580–2400.

SIT. STAY. PLAY., 140 West 67th Street (between Broadway and Amsterdam Avenue); (212) 712–9535.

SPOILED BRATS, 340 West 49th Street (between Eighth and Ninth Avenues); (212) 459–1615.

WESTSIDE ANIMAL HOSPITAL, 733 Ninth Avenue (between 49th and 50th Streets); (212) 247–8600.

DOWNTOWN WEST

BEASTY FEAST, 237 Bleecker Street (between Carmine and Leroy Streets), (212) 243–3261.

PARROTS AND PUPS, 45 Christopher Street (east at Seventh Avenue), (212) 352–8777.

PET BAR, 132 Thompson Street (between Prince and Houston Streets), (212) 253–9250.

DOWNTOWN EAST

ANIMAL CRACKER, 26 First Avenue (at 2nd Street); (212) 614–6786.

MIKEY'S PET SHOP, 130 East 7th Street (between First Avenue and Avenue A); (212) 477–3235.

PET GARDEN, 239 East 5th Street (between Second and Third Avenues); (212) 533–5304.

WHISKERS, 235 East 9th Street (between Second and Third Avenues); (212) 979–2532.

LOW-COST PET HEALTH CARE

ASPCA
Berg Memorial Animal Hospital & Clinic

424 East 92nd Street (between York and First Avenues);
(212) 876–7700

2336 Linden Boulevard (between Shepherd Avenue and Essex
Street), Brooklyn; (718) 272–7200

www.aspca.org

Charges $40 for an appointment with a doctor and $50 for an emergency visit.

The granddaddy of all humane organizations, the ASPCA's clinic and hospital provide low-cost health care for your little loved ones. They provide the full range of medical care for pets, including spaying and neutering ($40 to $65), vaccines, and an on-site pharmacy. They also offer adoptions of all sorts of pets for a $75 donation. The adoption package includes microchip ID, spaying or neutering, follow-up exams, medical support, vaccines, literature, private behavior counseling, and starter equipment.

BIDE-A-WEE
410 East 38th Street, second floor (between First Avenue and
FDR Drive)
(212) 532–5884
www.bideawee.org

Charges $32.50 for exams and $42.50 for emergency visits.

This full-service veterinary clinic provides everything to keep your feline feeling fine. Appointments are available about a week in advance. They also have a large shelter and offer adoptions for a $30 to $55 donation.

THE FUND FOR ANIMALS
Have-A-Heart Spay & Neuter Clinic
355 West 52nd Street (between Eighth and Ninth Avenues)
(212) 977–6877
www.fund.org

Charges $25 for cats and $35 for dogs; vaccinations are $15.

This nonprofit organization offers low-cost spay and neuter services for all cat and dogs throughout the year. A couple of times a year, they have special free days for cats and pit bulls—usually around Halloween and Valentine's Day. Check the Web site or call for details.

Section 3:

EXPLORING NEW YORK

"Afoot and lighthearted I take to the open road,

Healthy, free, the world before me,

The long brown path before me, leading wherever I choose."

—Walt Whitman

WALKING TOURS: THE FREEDOM TRAIL

WHETHER YOU'RE a visitor to New York or a native, there is always so much to discover about every corner of the city. The best way to get to know New York is to walk the streets with someone who knows it well. There are free guided tours of every fashion: leisurely strolls; historical, architectural, and nature tours; one-on-one explorations and groups. Most of the tours happen at regularly scheduled times every week, and some can be scheduled at your convenience.

WALKING TOURS BY THE WEEK

TIME	MONDAY	TUESDAY	WEDNESDAY	THURSDAY	FRIDAY	SATURDAY	SUNDAY
9:00 A.M.	NYSE (9:00 A.M.–4:30 P.M.)	NYSE (9:00 A.M.–4:30 P.M.)	NYSE (9:00 A.M.–4:30 P.M.)	NYSE (9:00 A.M.–4:30 P.M.)	NYSE (9:00 A.M.–4:30 P.M.)		
9:30 A.M.	Federal Reserve Bank (9:30 A.M.–2:30 P.M.)	Federal Reserve Bank (9:30 A.M.–2:30 P.M.)	Federal Reserve Bank (9:30 A.M.–2:30 P.M.)	Federal Reserve Bank (9:30 A.M.–2:30 P.M.)	Federal Reserve Bank (9:30 A.M.–2:30 P.M.)		
10:00 A.M.							
10:30 A.M.							
11:00 A.M.	Columbia University NYPL	Columbia University Lincoln Square spring-fall WNET NYPL	Columbia University NYPL WNET	Columbia University NYPL WNET	Columbia University NYPL	NYPL	Orchard Street March–December
11:30 A.M.						8th Street June–September (selected dates)	
12:00 NOON				Wall Street	Times Square	Brooklyn Brewery (12:00–5:00 P.M.) Wall Street	
12:30 P.M.	Pennsylvania Station 4th Monday of month		Grand Central Station	34th Street	The Grand Tour		
1:00 P.M.		WNET	WNET	WNET			
1:30 P.M.							
2:00 P.M.	Columbia University NYPL Trinity Church	Columbia University NYPL Trinity Church	Columbia University NYPL Trinity Church	Columbia University NYPL Trinity Church	Columbia University NYPL Trinity Church	Union Square NYPL Trinity Church	Trinity Church
2:30 P.M.							
3:00 P.M.						Prospect Park Ravine April–November	Prospect Park Ravine April–November
3:30 P.M.							
4:00 P.M.							
4:30 P.M.							

AMERICAN STOCK EXCHANGE

86 Trinity Place (between Rector and Thames Streets)
(212) 306–1000
www.amex.com

Before September 11, they offered a thirty-minute tour of the trading floor. At press time the tours had been put on hiatus, and it's not certain if or when they will begin again. Call for details.

BATTERY PARK CITY WALKING TOURS

Battery Park City Parks Conservancy
2 South End Avenue (at West Thames Street)
(212) 267–9700
www.bpcparks.org
Various dates from spring through fall.
They offer a variety of walking tours, including nature walks, garden tours, river walks, art tours, and historic tours. Some tours are offered weekly, others on occasion. Check the Web site or call for schedules.

BIG APPLE GREETERS

1 Centre Street, Room 2035 (at Chambers Street)
(212) 380–8159
www.bigapplegreeter.org
Any day, any place, year-round.
This is your dream-come-true tour of New York. You choose the time and day, you choose the place, and you don't pay anything—in fact, they'll even give you a one-day unlimited-use Fun Pass for the subway. You think I'm kidding, don't you? Well, I'm not. Friendly and knowledgeable New Yorkers volunteer their time for this amazing organization to show you around any neighborhood in the city. They usually live in the area they show, so they can give you firsthand accounts of the area's history, off the-beaten-trail spots, and great tips for finding some tasty (and cheap!) food and drink. Walks can run from two hours to all day. They don't accept tips, but if you offer to buy them lunch, they probably won't argue with you. Call at least two weeks in advance.

BROOKLYN BREWERY

79 North 11th Street (between Wyeth and Levit Streets)
Williamsburg, Brooklyn
(718) 486–7422
www.brooklynbrewery.com
Saturday noon–5:00 P.M. (last tour at 4:30).
Brooklyn's mom-and-pop brewery walks you through the process of mixing up a batch of beer in intricate detail, right down to the molecular physics. And somehow it seems so very interesting once you've been plied full of generous samples of their fine (and fresh!) brew. Also, on Friday night they have free music and cheap beer.

CENTRAL PARK

Central Park Conservancy
(212) 360–2727 (tour hot line)
www.centralparknyc.org

Various days and times throughout the week, year-round.
Explore the wilds of New York City with the many tours led by volunteers for the Central Park Conservancy. With a wealth of knowledge about the flora, fauna, history, trivia, secret passageways, and hidden trails of Central Park, these tours are always worthwhile for natives and visitors alike. Call the hot line for schedule information.

COLUMBIA UNIVERSITY
213 Low Library (116th Street and Broadway)
(212) 854–4900
www.columbia.edu
Monday through Friday, 11:00 A.M. and 2:00 P.M., year-round.
One-hour tour of one of New York's two Ivy League schools (NYU is the other)—but the only one that actually has ivy.

8th STREET WALKING TOUR
The Village Alliance
(212) 777–2173
www.villagealliance.org
Every other Saturday at 11:30 A.M., late June through September.
The ninety-minute tour called "Discover Places, Tidbits & Gossip That Even New York's Cognoscenti Don't Know" delivers just what it promises as it traipses through the East and West Village. The tour meets at the northwest corner of Second Avenue and St. Marks Place (8th Street). Call or check the Web site for the schedule.

THE FEDERAL RESERVE BANK
33 Liberty Street (between Nassau and William Streets)
(212) 720–6130
www.newyorkfed.org
Monday through Friday at 9:30 A.M., 10:30 A.M., 11:30 A.M., 1:30 P.M., 2:30 P.M.; make a reservation two weeks ahead.
You've heard the sayings "Follow the money" and "Show me the money," right? Well, here's your chance to do both. This sixty-minute tour of the richest bank in the world takes you through their gold vaults, tells you all about the Fed's cash processing procedures, and even gives you some free money at the end of the tour! Okay, so it happens to be shredded. You can't have everything.

GRAND CENTRAL TERMINAL
42nd Street and Vanderbilt Avenue
(212) 439–1049
www.mas.org

Wednesday at 12:30 P.M., year-round.

While there's no charge for the tour, they do ask for a donation of any amount, though you aren't obligated to give one.

For more than twenty-five years, the Municipal Art Society has been show-ing folks around this Beaux Arts landmark. The tour includes the history of the terminal as well as a look at the major restorations completed in 1998. The tour runs a little over one hour and meets at the main infor-mation booth on the main level of Grand Central.

THE GRAND TOUR: GRAND CENTRAL STATION AREA
42nd Street and Vanderbilt Avenue
(212) 883-2420
www.grandcentralpartnership.org
Every Friday at 12:30 P.M., year-round.
This free ninety-minute walking tour organized by the Grand Central Partnership leaves from the Philip Morris Building across the street from Grand Central. This walk points out some of the architectural splendors of East 42nd Street, including Grand Central Station, the Chrysler Building, the Chanin Building, and many others, as well passing along some of the area's rich history and curious events.

JOHN J. HARVEY FIREBOAT
Pier 63 (Hudson River and 23rd Street)
www.fireboat.org
Various days and times, year-round.
Since she was put into service in 1931, the *John J. Harvey* fireboat has greeted every passenger cruise ship that has made its way into New York Harbor with a spectacular water display. But this boat wasn't made just for show. To this day, although she was officially retired from service by the New York City Fire Department in 1994, she remains one of the most pow-erful and fastest fireboats ever to take to the water. The ship is now under private ownership and does not rest on her impressive laurels. She's now pressed into action for tours up and down the Hudson and around New York Harbor. The schedule of events is erratic, but they go on throughout the year (more from spring through fall and less in the winter). Some tours have themes and knowledgeable guides, like their "History of Garbage" tour and a tour of historic fires the *Harvey* worked on. Other tours are just pleas-ant days on the water. All are free, because the boat doesn't meet the strict

standards set by the U.S. Coast Guard for the carriage of passengers for hire. If you come on board, it's as private guests of the boat, and you may be asked to sign a release to this effect. Trips are limited to the first fifty passengers. And yes, they do "fire up" the powerful hoses at some point on every trip. For schedule information, check out the Web site or sign up for their mailing list though the Web site.

LINCOLN SQUARE
Columbus Circle fountain (59th Street and Broadway)
(212) 581–3774
www.lincolnbid.org
Tuesday at 11:00 A.M., spring through fall.
This ninety-minute tour (that can actually run as long as three hours) explores the historic Lincoln Square district, which has become a world center for arts and entertainment—and is also full of historic treasures, architectural jewels, peaceful green areas, and surprising enclaves of public art. The tour meets at the Columbus Circle fountain.

NEW YORK CITY HALL
Murray Street and Broadway
(212) 788–6865
www.nyclink.org
Monday through Friday, year-round.
Stroll through this early-nineteenth-century Federal-style building that's home to the mayor's office and city council chambers and is chock-full of historic American portraits and artifacts. Since the September 11 attack, tours have been limited to school groups only, but they plan on returning to public tours in the future. Call for details and schedule.

NEW YORK PUBLIC LIBRARY (NYPL)
Humanities and Social Science Library, 476 Fifth Avenue
(entrance at 42nd Street)
(212) 930–0501
www.nypl.org
Monday through Saturday at 11:00 A.M. and 2 P.M., year-round.
The lions welcome you to a one-hour walk through the stunningly renovated main branch of the public library. They also offer guided tours through their major art exhibits daily at 12:30 and 2:30 P.M.

NEW YORK STOCK EXCHANGE
20 Broad Street (between Wall Street and Exchange Place)
(212) 656–5165
www.nyse.com

Monday through Friday, 9:00 A.M.–4:30 P.M. (at forty-five-minute intervals), year-round.
A visit to the NYSE Education Center includes a view of the tumultuous activity on the trading floor as well as interactive exhibits and presentations. They start handing out free tickets at 8:45 A.M. for timed entrances throughout the day. Get there early, as they are often sold out by mid-morning.

ORCHARD STREET WALKING TOUR
Katz's Deli
205 East Houston Street (at Ludlow Street)
(212) 226–9010
www.lowereastsideny.com
Sunday at 11:00 A.M., March through December.
From pushcarts to pulsing beats, this tour explores a neighborhood that started out as a hub for immigrants from Russia and Eastern Europe and is now turning into the newest chic area on the isle of Manhattan. Tours run about ninety minutes.

PENNSYLVANIA STATION TOURS
34th Street Partnership tourist information kiosk
32nd Street and Seventh Avenue
(212) 719–3434
www.members.aol.com/pennsy
The fourth Monday of every month at 12:30 P.M., year-round.
Tour the grandeur that once was New York's Penn Station. Lorraine B. Diehl, author of *The Late, Great Pennsylvania Station,* resurrects this behemoth by using vintage photographs and surviving remnants to tell the story of New York's lost railroad station. This ninety-minute walk tells the tale from Penn Station's turn-of-the-twentieth-century beginnings to the forces that brought about its destruction in the 1960s.

PROSPECT PARK RAVINE TOUR
9th Street and Cross Park Drive
(718) 965–8999
www.prospectpark.org
Saturday and Sunday at 3:00 P.M., April through November.
Visit Brooklyn's only forest with a gorge and waterfall (it would be Brooklyn's only forest even without a gorge and waterfall).

SURVEILLANCE CAMERA OUTDOOR WALKING TOURS (SCOWT)

(212) 561–0106

www.notbored.org/scowt.html

Various days, times, and locations throughout the year.

An anarchist organization (hmmm . . .) concerned about our emerging surveillance society leads groups around various "heavily surveilled neighborhoods" in Manhattan, pointing out the many cameras aimed in your direction. Tours last about sixty minutes and go on rain or shine.

TAKE A WALK, NEW YORK!

(212) 379–8339

www.walkny.org

Various locations throughout the five boroughs, year-round.

Your government thinks you're getting too fat. So they want you to hit the streets and start exercising. This federally funded local group organizes guided walks all around the city that aim to stimulate you intellectually and visually so they can sucker you into walking, walking, walking. This is a great chances to explore sections of the city you've never visited before (or may not have even known existed). The walks are always easily accessible by public transportation, led by knowledgeable guides, and free.

THIRTEEN/WNET

450 West 33rd Street (between Ninth and Tenth Avenues)

(212) 560–2711

www.thirteen.org

Tuesday, Wednesday, and Thursday at 11:00 A.M. and 1:00 P.M., year-round; reservations required.

A fascinating one-hour peek inside the country's largest public television station.

34TH STREET HISTORY TOUR

Empire State Building

350 Fifth Avenue (between 33rd and 34th Streets)

(212) 719–3434

www.34thstreet.org

Thursday at 12:30 P.M., year-round.

This ninety-minute architectural history tour of 34th Street tells the stories behind such buildings as the Empire State Building and Macy's, and introduces you to characters and events like "Andy Warhol versus Con Edison," architect Stanford White, and "Mary Murray's Tea Party." The tour meets at the Fifth Avenue entrance to the Empire State Building, and is led by noted architectural historians.

TIMES SQUARE WALKING TOUR
Times Square Visitors Center
1560 Broadway (between 46th and 47th Streets)
(212) 768–1560
www.timessquarebid.org
Friday at noon, year-round.
What was once a center for horse trading has now become the center of the commercial theater world. This two- to three-hour tour fills you in on all the history, intrigue, and ever-changing architecture of Broadway and its surrounding areas. The visitor center also offers free Internet access, loads of information, and clean bathrooms!

TRINITY CHURCH
Broadway and Wall Street
(212) 602–0800
www.trinitywallstreet.org
Daily at 2:00 P.M., year-round.
A short fifteen- to twenty-minute tour that covers the long history of one of New York's oldest churches (established 1697). Concerts are also offered every Thursday at 1:00 P.M. (free during the summer; $2.00 suggested donation the rest of the year).

UNION SQUARE WALKING TOUR
16th Street between Union Square East and West (Park Avenue and Broadway)
(212) 460–1200
www.unionsquarenyc.org
Saturdays at 2:00 P.M., year-round.
Take a ninety-minute opinionated, totally interactive tour of Union Square's past, present, and future. Meet at the Lincoln statue midpark at 16th Street.

URBAN PARK RANGERS
Parks throughout the five boroughs
(866) NYC–HAWK (692–4295)
www.nyc.gov/parks
Various times, days, and locations, year-round.
Yogi Bear has nothing on New York. Yes, we have our own pack of park rangers, and they're a useful bunch of folks to know. They run an extensive and ever-changing array of walks, hikes, nature explorations, canoe trips, and even camping trips. Call to get a schedule or check out the Web site.

WALL STREET WALKING TOUR
Museum of the American Indian
1 Bowling Green (at the end of Broadway, across from Battery Park)
(212) 606–4064
www.downtownny.com
Thursday and Saturday at noon, year-round.
Explore this area that takes in everything from Founding Fathers of the United States to the financial capital of the world. This free ninety-minute tour weaves together the history, events, architecture, and people of downtown with stops at the U.S. Custom House, Trinity Church, New York Stock Exchange, and many other sites along the way. No two walks are ever the same, so join in often.

" We're gonna see America.
We take no map. We'll
follow the sun. Stay in
cheap motels and steal what
we need along the way."

—Al Bundy

TRAVEL: FREE-WHEELIN'

JUST BECAUSE YOU'RE LOW on cash is no reason to sit at home. Whether it's getting around the city or getting out of town, there are some great options. Of course, the best way to get to see New York is the cheapest—by foot (biking and in-line skating are great choices as well). More than any other place in America, New York is a walking city—logically laid out, compact, lots to see, and plenty of people to bump into along the way (figuratively and literally). While New York is undoubtedly a big city, as you walk the streets you realize that it's also very much a small town. There may be 8 million people, but you'll be amazed at how many friends and acquaintances you'll run into on the streets and how many familiar faces in the crowds you'll see over and over again. When walking is out of the question, though, the subway is the answer. The unlimited-use Metro Pass ($4.00 for one day, $17.00 for one week, $63.00 for one month) makes getting from here to there a bargain. The Metro Pass is good for all subways and buses (see below). Here are some other suggestions for getting around and out of New York.

GETTING AROUND NEW YORK

FREECAR MEDIA
11990 San Vicente Boulevard, Suite 350
Los Angeles, CA 90049
(310) 566–4000
www.freecar.com

 Your application must be chosen, and you drive around in a car that is completely covered in advertising.

This national company gives you—yes, *gives* you!—a free new car for you to drive around for two years. They generally give away SUVs and mini-vans, and you are responsible for the cost of insurance and gas. This car will be completely covered from front bumper to tailpipe in a very eye-catching advertisement for a company such as Sega, Pringles, IHOP, Microsoft, or maybe even Playboy. They choose their drivers depending on the demographics requested by the advertisers, which vary from product to product. Fill out your application at their Web site. As you might imagine, a lot of people apply, so the more detailed the information, the better your chance of getting chosen. If you have a car already, you can have them "wrap" it in an advertisement; they'll pay you $400 a month. They run advertising campaigns in New York and in many other cities around the country.

MTA NEW YORK CITY TRANSIT
(718) 330–1234
www.mta.nyc.ny.us/nyct
Okay, I know I'm not offering you any special deals here. Yes, you do have to pay to get on the trains. This isn't Germany; there ain't no such thing as an honor system on these trains. You pay your fare and you ride your train. You will be ticketed if you hop the turnstiles. Don't try it. But the unlimited-use MetroCards make it easy and cheap to get to anywhere in the five boroughs by subway and/or bus.

Hacking It in New York

You won't be surprised by this recommendation: Don't ever take a cab. Besides the fact that it's expensive (just hopping in a cab seems to always cost you at least $5.00), the wild ride will invariably take you longer than grabbing the nearest subway. Fahgeddaboutit!

STATEN ISLAND FERRY
Whitehall Terminal (at Whitehall and South Streets)
(718) 815–BOAT (2628)
www.ci.nyc.ny.us/html/dot/html/get_around/ferry/statfery.html
www.si-web.com/SI-Ferry.html

This not-to-be-missed trip runs about every twenty-minutes most times, but once an hour late at night. It's absolutely free, and with the spectacular views of Lower Manhattan and the Statue of Liberty, how can you pass it up? Particularly dramatic views at sunset, but any time of day it's an awe-inspiring voyage.

GETTING OUT OF NEW YORK

AUTO DRIVEAWAY COMPANY
225 West 34th Street, #1201 (between Seventh and Eighth Avenues)
(212) 967–2344
www.autodriveaway.com

 There's a $15 registration fee and a $300 refundable deposit. The registration fee is good for one year and at all locations.

Forget about flying, Greyhound, or Amtrak; here's your chance to see America the way it was meant to be seen, behind the wheel of your very own gas guzzling, pedal-to-the-metal, "where the hell is the next rest stop" automobile. With sixty-four locations throughout the United States and Canada, these folks can provide you with the free use of a late-model car to practically any major city you want to visit. If your plans are somewhat flexible, this is a great way to drive yourself around the states. The deal is: ADC acts as a kind of matchmaker between people or companies that need vehicles moved from place to place and drivers who want to get from here to there. Call them up to see what's available, pay your registration and deposit, and hit the road. Cars go on a first-come, first-served basis to drivers twenty-one years or older with two photo IDs. They give you time to do plenty of sight-seeing along the way by allotting you extra time to get to where you're going (four days to Florida, for instance, and ten days to the West Coast). When you deliver your car, you get back your deposit and call the nearest ADC office to see when you can get a car back or off to your next destination. The looser your travel plans, the better this system will work for you. The cars come with a free first tank of gas; otherwise, all gas and lodging costs along the way are your responsibility.

AUTO CARRY, INC.
300–2 Route 17 South
Lodi, NJ 07622
(973) 777–8100 or (888) 659–9903
www.autocarry.com

 $200 deposit ($35 is kept for auto insurance; $165 is refundable).

Similar to Auto Driveaway, though not as extensive a network, Auto Carry primarily sends drivers to California and is busiest during the summer. They do have two offices in Southern California, where you can try your luck for a car back east. Drivers must be twenty-one or over and have three forms of ID, including a driver's license and major credit card.

CLUB GETAWAY
Kent, Connecticut
(800) 643–8292

You must have the ability to teach something fun, or provide some useful service to campers in exchange for free weekends.

This summer camp for adults is a "Club Med in Connecticut" and is always on the lookout for volunteers to commit to spending some weekends with their swinging singles. If you can offer some useful service to the paying campers—teaching yoga, arts and crafts, or in-line skating, say, or even cooking-up a killer pie—they will give you room, board, and free run of the extensive grounds and facilities in exchange for the time you spend working with the campers. Even if you don't necessarily think you have some great expertise, they're pretty open to any idea; it's definitely worth a shot. The camp has been rated "one of the top ten hottest destinations

The Virtual Thumb

There are a number of Web sites where you can find yourself a free ride out of town or a companion to ride with you wherever you're going. These Ride Share listings are a great way to travel to or from New York, save a load of cash, and maybe even make a good friend along the way. You are usually expected to split the cost of gas, but not always. Check out these sites for details:

www.erideshare.com

www.newyork.craigslist.org

www.collegerideboard.com

www.hitchhikers.org

for singles" by the Travel Channel and has everything you need to do almost any sport under the sun.

GODSTOW RETREAT CENTER
Redding, Connecticut
(203) 938–2330 or (212) 475–7752
www.world-view.org
godstow@world-view.org

 Help with the upkeep of the grounds through such duties as trimming trees and foliage, planting, pruning, raking, cleaning, making repairs, or painting.

Escape the hustle and bustle of the city for a couple of days of contemplative meditation and housecleaning. This newly restored mansion is run as a retreat for the Asian Classics Institute of New York and is situated on ninety-eight beautiful acres of woods and meadows, rolling hills, streams, and ponds. Volunteers spend part of their time helping to keep the center looking beautiful and are free to enjoy the grounds for the rest of their stay. Volunteers are welcome weekends or weekdays.

KRIPALU CENTER FOR YOGA & HEALTH
Lenox, Massachusetts
(413) 448–3123
www.kripalu.org

 Volunteers work forty hours per week in exchange for a stay at this yoga retreat.

This world-renowned center for karma yoga offers free one- to four-week stays at the breathtaking mountain retreat to volunteers through the Seva Program. In exchange for a vigorous forty-hour workweek that could include chopping vegetables, cleaning bathrooms, washing dishes, or performing basic maintenance tasks, you can take part in all the class and activities that are part of their Retreat and Renewal schedule, including classes in hatha yoga, meditation, Kripalu DansKinetics, and more. They will also provide you with a dormitory room and three vegetarian meals a day. The weeks are scheduled from Sunday to Sunday. And if you want more once your stay is over, they also offer other longer-term volunteer programs that could run from three to twenty-one months.

ROWE CAMP & CONFERENCE CENTER
Rowe, Massachusetts
(413) 339–4954
www.rowecenter.org

> **THE CATCH** Chop wood and carry water in exchange for a peaceful week in the mountains.

For one week every spring and fall, the Rowe Center holds "Work Weeks" where folks from far and wide, both young and old, come to help spiff up the grounds and have a great time. This community-oriented camp offers lots of fun activities and free room and board for all those helping out these weeks. Throughout the year they also offer various conferences on a wide variety of artistic and spiritual subjects, and you can work off the cost of these programs through other work-study programs. Check the Web site for more details and schedule.

THE TRAIN TO THE PLANE

Getting to New York's three major airports can be an expensive affair. It can cost you $35 by cab, $18 by shuttle van, or $13 by bus service, but it can be done for next to nothing if you have some time and patience.

KENNEDY AIRPORT
This is the easiest and most user-friendly airport to get to by public transportation. Take the A train to the Howard Beach subway station and catch the free shuttle bus to the airport terminals. Travel time from Manhattan is sixty to ninety minutes. Another route is to take the E or F train to the

Kew Gardens/Union Turnpike subway station and grab the Q10 to the airport. The train ride is a lot shorter this way, but the bus takes longer. The total travel time ends up being about the same sixty to ninety minutes. Both ways will take longer nights and weekends. Cost: regular subway fare ($1.50 or MetroCard).

LA GUARDIA AIRPORT

Getting here can be an adventure, but it can be done for the cost of subway token as well. From 106th Street and Broadway or 125th Street and Lenox Avenue, hop on the M60 bus. The bus winds its way around Upper Manhattan and Queens and takes you directly to the airport. Travel time is forty-five to ninety minutes (depending on traffic). Another option is

Next Year in Jerusalem

How about an all-expenses-paid ten-day trip to Israel? Well, if you're between eighteen and twenty-six years old, Jewish, and have never been to the Holy Land before, Birthright Israel wants to take you for free.

Sound inviting? To date they have sent more than 30,000 people from all around the county (including many groups from New York City), and they're looking for more every year. The aim is to build a strong link between young American Jews and Israel. While they try to keep the proselytizing to a minimum, there are many discussions of all things Jewish while you visit historic sites like Masada, the Wailing Wall, and the Dead Sea. Of course, they wouldn't mind you spending your own cash to come back to Israel in the future, or even deciding to settle in Israel, but there's no pressure to do either.

Birthright Israel puts together more than thirty groups to make the trip each winter and spring. These trips take into account the full spectrum of ideological, religious, educational, and cultural backgrounds of the Jewish community. There are groups for those who are nonobservant, Reform, Conservative, and Orthodox. Some trips have a traditional hotel and sight-seeing agenda, while others are for those with special interests like biking, sports, or history. In recent years they have also begun to coordinate their activities with the Israeli government to ensure the safety and security of those on the trips. For more information, stop by the Birthright Israel offices at 521 Fifth Avenue, twenty-seventh floor (at 43rd Street); call (888) 99–ISRAEL (994–7723); or check the Web site www.birthrightisrael.com.

to take the E or the F train to the 74th Street and Roosevelt Avenue stop, then catch the Q33 bus. This isn't a shuttle to the airport, so this bus makes many stops before it gets to the main terminal, and it doesn't have any special luggage racks. You won't be making friends with your fellow passengers if you block the aisle with your steamer trunk. For information on all MTA buses and subways, call (718) 330–1234 or check the Web site www.mta.nyc.ny.us/nyct.

NEWARK AIRPORT

Making it to Newark cheaply can be relatively easy on weekdays, but give yourself plenty of extra time on the weekends. Take the PATH train to Newark Penn Station ($1.50), then catch the New Jersey Transit bus #62 ($1.00) which runs about every twenty minutes and takes about twenty minutes to get to the terminals (depending on traffic). Another route from Newark Penn Station is the Airlink Train ($6.60) which runs about every twenty to thirty minutes and gets you to the terminals in about fifteen minutes. During the week, give yourself sixty to seventy-five minutes to get there, and on the weekends plan on two hours. For schedules and more information, call (973) 762–5100 or check the Web site www.panynj.gov/aviation/ewrframe.

"Your first job is to prepare the soil. The best tool for this is your neighbor's motorized garden tiller. If your neighbor does not own a garden tiller, suggest that he buy one."

—Dave Barry

GARDENS AND GARDENING: DIRT CHEAP

G ARDENS MAY NOT BE the first thing you think of when you think of New York, but there's a surprising amount of greenery to be found within this urban jungle—and I'm not just talking about fire-escape gardens. From quaint community gardens to grand botanical gardens, you can delight in some to the most stunning horticulture anywhere in the world within the city limits. Not only can you partake in the sights and smells of the gardens, but you can also produce some lovely flowers and vegetables yourself. Cultivate your own free plot of land in one of New York's many community gardens, get free bulbs and cuttings, or develop your own green thumb through free gardening classes around town.

PUBLIC GARDENS

THE BROOKLYN BOTANIC GARDEN (BBG)

1000 Washington Avenue (at Flatbush Avenue)
(718) 623–7200 (info) or (718) 623–7333 (events hot line)
www.bbg.org

 Free admission all day Tuesday, and on Saturday from 10:00 A.M. to noon; seniors are also free on Friday.

Hailed by the *New York Times* as "the premier horticultural attraction in the region," the BBG's endless gardens and greenhouses will bring your senses to life. They also provide free gardening and composting classes and workshops throughout the year (see below for details).

THE CENTRAL PARK CONSERVATORY GARDENS

105th Street and Central Park West
(212) 360–2766 or 310–6658
www.centralparknyc.org

Always free, this is the only formal garden in Manhattan open to the public. It covers a relatively small area (when compared to the other botanical gardens in New York) but provides a welcome escape from the clamor of city life. They offer free tours of the gardens from spring through fall on Saturday at 11:00 A.M. Also be on the lookout for their annual plant giveaways—tulips in May and mums in November.

THE NEW YORK BOTANICAL GARDEN

200th Street and Kazimirov Boulevard
The Bronx
(718) 817–8700
www.nybg.org

 Free admission all day Wednesday, and on Saturday from 10:00 A.M. to noon.

Who could want anything more than 250 acres of flora from every corner of the world, including forty-eight gardens and plant collections and fifty acres of forestland? This is one of the oldest and largest gardens in the world and should not be missed. They also run an extensive adult education curriculum, which you can get free or at reduced tuition by taking part in their work-study program.

THE QUEENS BOTANICAL GARDEN (QBG)
Flushing Meadows Park, 43–50 Main Street (at Dahlia Avenue)
(718) 886–3800
www.queensbotanical.org
Always free admission to this twenty-acre garden (closed Monday). QBG also presents a free concert series during the summer and many free classes throughout the year.

THE STATEN ISLAND BOTANICAL GARDEN
1000 Richmond Terrace
(718) 273–8200
www.sibg.org

THE CATCH **Free admission to the garden grounds, but a $5.00 charge for Chinese Scholar's Garden.**

This is a small garden when compared to the big guys in the Bronx and Brooklyn, but it makes a lovely place to take a respite. Admission to the garden grounds is free every day, but you will need to pay your way into the enticing and well-regarded Chinese Scholar's Garden.

WAVE HILL PUBLIC GARDEN AND CULTURAL CENTER
675 West 252nd Street (enter at 249th Street and
Independence Avenue)
The Bronx
(718) 549–3200
www.wavehill.org

THE CATCH **Free admission all day Tuesday, and on Saturday from 10:00 A.M. to noon.**

This former private estate, now a city-owned garden, offers some outstanding views of the Hudson River and New Jersey (yes, it is possible), and some gorgeously maintained gardens.

GARDENING EDUCATION

BROOKLYN GREENBRIDGE & URBAN COMPOSTING PROJECT
Brooklyn Botanic Gardens
1000 Washington Avenue (at Flatbush Avenue)
(718) 623–7250 or (718) 623–7209;
Compost Help Line (718) 623–7290
www.bbg.org

 Classes and workshops are free, but you must register at least one week in advance.

Classes and workshops offered throughout the year in such topics as "Composting in the City," "Perennial Flowers Basics," "Introduction to Horticulture Therapy," "Gardening with Native Plants," and "Battle the Asian Long Horn Beetle!" The classes are targeted toward community gardeners, but all are welcome.

NEW YORK BOTANICAL GARDEN SCHOOL OF CONTINUING EDUCATION
200th Street and Kazimirov Boulevard
The Bronx
(718) 817–8610
www.nybg.org/edu/conted

 Work-study is available: Perform administrative duties in exchange for free or discounted classes. The math: 1 hour of work = 33 percent reduction in price per classroom hour; 2 hours of work = 66 percent reduction in price per classroom hour; 3 hours of work = 1 free classroom hour.

Choose from more than 700 courses in botanical art and illustration, botany, crafts, floral design, gardening, commercial horticulture, landscape design, and horticultural therapy. Take a short how-to class, explore a topic in depth, or pursue a new career in one of their seven certificate programs.

Get the Dirt

Every New Yorker is entitled to up to thirty pounds of free com-
post compliments of the Department of Sanitation and the vari-
ous botanical gardens of New York City. There are four scheduled
days (two in the spring and two in the fall) when you can show
up at locations in each borough to shovel yourself a load of this
messy but useful and nutrient-rich organic plant food. They also
sell discounted compost bins for $20 ($70 retail price). For
give-back days, check the Web site www.nyccompost.org or call:

THE BRONX AND MANHATTAN: *(718) 817–8543*

BROOKLYN: *(718) 623–7290*

QUEENS: *(718) 539–5296*

STATEN ISLAND: *(718) 273–0629*

COMMUNITY GARDENS

Community gardens are generally free to join. They provide you with a plot of land to plant in and all the supplies and materials you need, from seeds and soil to how-tos and hothouses. Some long-established, centrally located gardens have long waiting lists, while newer, off-the-beaten-trail gardens have many spots available. These gardens are not only a good place to grow rutabagas, but also great gathering spots for the communities they are in. Many of the gardens have full schedules of free classes, perform-ances, and activities for all.

GREEN GUERILLAS

151 West 30th Street, tenth floor (between Sixth and Seventh Avenues)

(212) 594–2155

www.greenguerillas.org

A good starting point to find a community garden in your neighborhood to participate in.

GREENTHUMB
49 Chambers Street, Room 1020 (between Broadway and
Center Street)
(212) 788–8070
www.greenthumb.org
This organization has more than 650 member community gardens in practically every neighborhood in the five boroughs. The Web site also has a
great events calendar where you will find all kinds of free goings-on in the
gardens: classes (tai chi, writing, yoga, drawing), concerts, barbecues,
community gatherings, film screenings, and more. Check the Web site or
call for the community garden near you.

NEW YORKERS FOR PARKS
457 Madison Avenue, sixth floor (between 50th and 51st Streets)
(212) 838–9410
www.parkscouncil.org
Free bulbs and shrub giveaways every winter and spring for community
gardeners, block associations, churches, schools, and anyone who does
gardening in public spaces. Call to get on the mailing list for giveaway
invitations.

"I hate flowers. I paint them
because they're cheaper than
models and they don't move."
—Georgia O'Keeffe

ART GALLERIES:
SHOW ME THE MONET

NEW YORK IS HOME to hundreds, perhaps thousands of art galleries, and every one of them is free for you to wander through. In this city where space is at a premium, many of these are small single-room galleries with limited exhibition space, yet there are others that rival some of the major museums around town in the caliber of artists they show and their vast spaces. In some cases, in fact, the line between *commercial gallery* and *museum* is hard to define. Ultimately, though, the prime difference between the two remains simple and clear: money. You will never pay an admission charge at a commercial gallery, because everything you see hanging on the walls, lying on the floor, and dangling from the ceiling is for sale. Does the Gap charge you to browse? New York being the center of the art world, the artists you'll find at these galleries are the same ones you'd see at any major contemporary or modern art museum around the world. The styles of works you will find in these galleries run the full spectrum from fine art to the kind of contemporary installations that keep right-wing Republicans in business.

While there are galleries scattered all over the city, you'll find a large concentration of them clustered in just a few neighborhoods: Chelsea, Soho, and Williamsburg, Brooklyn. Each of these areas caters to a different clientele and mind-set, but all have a huge variety of styles, techniques, and talents within their own worlds. The galleries I'm including in this listing are those where you're sure to find some of the most intriguing, world-class, cutting-edge, or otherwise eye-opening works in these neighborhoods and around the city. Don't take this list as the comprehensive survey of galleries in the five boroughs, but as a jumping-off point. Galleries generally change shows every four to six weeks. The best way to take them in is to wander these neighborhoods with an open mind (but you can keep the purse closed).

CHELSEA

Chelsea has become the most popular area in Manhattan for galleries. Most of those located here are considered blue-chip galleries that work with lists of established, well-known, high-profile artists. In other words, the galleries can charge thousands of dollars for any given work. There are about 150 galleries crammed into a ten-block area, and most are open Tuesday through Saturday, 10:00 A.M. to 6:00 P.M. Below are some of the big-shot galleries you don't want to miss, but the best way to discover a favorite spot is to walk the streets and check out everything that looks inviting. Most of the galleries are located between 21st and 26th Streets, and between Tenth and Eleventh Avenues.

BARBARA GLADSTONE GALLERY
515 West 24th Street (between Tenth and Eleventh Avenues)
(212) 206–9300
www.gladstonegallery.com
Known for presenting high-minded shows with a focus on conceptual sculpture.

CHEIM & READ
547 West 25th Street (between Tenth and Eleventh Avenues)
(212) 242–7727

A Feast for the Eyes (With an Open Bar!)

You are cordially invited to rub shoulders with the hoi polloi of the New York art scene, be the first to see what's happening at the happening galleries, and grab yourself a glass (or three) of fine wine or a few bottles of beer. Whenever you stop in to view a gallery, be sure to put your name on their mailing list, and you will start receiving invitations to their upcoming shows, including information about the opening reception. Every gallery holds an opening reception a couple of days before the show opens to the public, where anyone has a chance to meet the artist(s), mix and mingle, drink, and sometimes even eat. These events are almost always open to anyone in the know, and now that means you. Another way to find out about openings is to check out the Web site dks.thing.net. This site is run by Douglas Kelly, whose public access TV show, the Douglas Kelly Show *(every other Friday at midnight on channel 34), covers art gallery openings and receptions. You can also get on his mailing list at the Web site and receive a weekly calendar of art openings and events.*

This large gallery represents the works of such artists as Diane Arbus, Louise Bourgeois, Robert Mapplethorpe, and Andy Warhol.

DCA GALLERY
525 West 22nd Street (between Tenth and Eleventh Avenues)
(212) 255–5511
www.dcagallery.com
Owned by the Danish Ministry of Culture, this is the home of contemporary Danish art in New York.

FEATURE INC.
530 West 25th Street (between Tenth and Eleventh Avenues)
(212) 675–7772
www.featureinc.com
Specializes in contemporary artists that they consider to be on the cutting edge.

Where Else to (van) Gogh

Stop into any gallery along the way and pick up a copy of ChelseArt and Art Now's Gallery Guide. ChelseArt is a concise map and up-to-date listing of all the goings-on in the Chelsea area. The Gallery Guide is a monthly publication of happenings at every major gallery in the Manhattan and selected listings in the other boroughs and beyond. You can get both of these free at any gallery. You may notice the $3.00 price tag on the Gallery Guide, but don't pay any attention; everyone gives it away for free. You can also check out the Web site www.galleryguide.org for more information.

GAGOSIAN GALLERY

555 West 24th Street (between Tenth and Eleventh Avenues)
(212) 741–1111
www.gagosian.com
Shows are always headline grabbing, and the huge space allows them to present works on a grand scale.

GALERIE LELONG

528 West 26th Street (between Tenth and Eleventh Avenues)
(212) 315–0470
www.artnet.com/lelong.html
The gallery's long history includes a dedication to abstract and minimalist paintings, contemporary sculpture, and contemporary Latin American artists.

LUHRING AUGUSTINE GALLERY

531 West 24th Street (between Tenth and Eleventh Avenues)
(212) 206–9100
www.luhringaugustine.com
Cutting-edge, big-budget shows.

MATTHEW MARKS GALLERY

522 West 22nd Street (between Tenth and Eleventh Avenues)
523 West 24th Street (between Tenth and Eleventh Avenues)
(212) 243–0200
www.mmarks.com
One of the first galleries to settle in Chelsea, its two spaces are always home to an unpredictable but intriguing array of works.

METRO PICTURES
519 West 24th Street (between Tenth and Eleventh Avenues)
(212) 206–7100
www.metropicturesgallery.com
Primarily presents photography shows by such artists as Cindy Sherman and Robert Longo.

PACEWILDENSTEIN
534 West 25th Street (between Tenth and Eleventh Avenues)
(212) 929–7000
www.artnet.compacewildenstein.html
The list includes such artists as Chuck Close, Isamu Noguchi, Pablo Picasso, Robert Rauschenberg, Mark Rothko, and Julian Schnabel.

303 GALLERY
525 West 22nd Street (between Tenth and Eleventh Avenues)
(212) 255–1121
www.303gallery.com
Represents a battery of young artists working in a variety of forms, including photography, film, painting, sculpture and whatever else moves them.

SOHO

Soho is the original art gallery neighborhood of New York, and while gentrification and skyrocketing real estate prices have forced many galleries to relocate, it still remains well populated by galleries presenting vital work. The galleries are often smaller than those in Chelsea, but they display works that are generally more cutting edge and riskier. The spaces are sometime storefronts and clearly marked, but they're often up a few flights and out of the way. Most galleries are open Tuesday through Saturday, 11:00 A.M. to 6:00 P.M. You will find most of the galleries located between West Broadway and Mercer, from Grand to Houston. There's a good map and extensive area listings in the *Gallery Guide,* available free at any gallery. Here are some of the highlights.

A.I.R. GALLERY
40 Wooster Street (between Broome and Grand Streets)
(212) 966–0799
www.airnyc.org
Generally exhibits works by female artists working in photography, sculpture, crafts, painting, drawing, video, and performance.

ARTISTS SPACE

38 Green Street (between Grand and Broome Streets)
(212) 226–3970
www.artistsspace.org

This nonprofit gallery is often the first stop in a professional career for artists. Since 1972, this large gallery has played host to the first works of many artists who've gone on to international recognition working in almost any style and medium.

DEITCH PROJECTS

18 Wooster Street (between Canal and Grand Streets)

76 Grand Street (between Wooster and Greene Streets)

(212) 343–7300

These two galleries play host to wildly diverse solo and group shows of contemporary artists.

DIA CENTER FOR THE ARTS

393 West Broadway (between Spring and Broome Streets)

141 Wooster Street (between Prince and Houston Streets)

www.diacenter.org

Without giving too much away about these two long-term installations, they are worth viewing if only to ponder the question, *What would Starbucks give to get this real estate?* These two works, the Earth Room and the Broken Kilometer, have been on display in these spaces since 1977 and 1979, respectively. Open Wednesday through Saturday noon to 6:00 P.M., but closed from 3:00 to 3:30 P.M.

THE DRAWING CENTER

35 and 40 Wooster Street (between Grand and Broome Streets)
(212) 219–2166
www.drawingcenter.org

A cross between a museum and a gallery, this is the only institution in the United States dedicated exclusively to the exhibition, study, and promotion of the medium of drawing. The larger space at 40 Wooster is home to major historical and contemporary shows. They do occasionally ask for "suggested donations" for large historical shows. The smaller space across the street at 35 Wooster always shows contemporary works and is always free to view.

JACK TILTON/ANNA KUSTERA GALLERY

49 Green Street (between Broome and Grand Streets)
(212) 941–1775
www.jacktilongallery.com

You're sure to have a visceral experience at the shows at this gallery. They focus on emerging international artists working in video, installations, and photography—and the shows are often startling and unnerving.

RONALD FELDMAN FINE ARTS
31 Mercer Street (at Grand Street)
(212) 226-3232
www.feldmangallery.com
One of the oldest and best-respected galleries in Soho, they have a strong focus on performance, installation, political, and conceptual works from both emerging and long-established artists. Among the collection is the largest selection of Andy Warhol prints of any gallery.

ROSENBERG + KAUFMAN FINE ART
115 Wooster Street (between Prince and Spring Streets)
(212) 431-4838
Up four flights, you'll find this small gallery that's well worth the haul. Working with emerging and midcareer artists, the studio specializes what it calls contemporary contemplative art. They seek out art that reveals itself slowly to the viewer, operating under the motto, "The more you look, the more you see."

SHAKESPEARE'S FVLCRVM
480 Broome Street (between Wooster and Green Streets)
(212) 966-6848
Here's a new excuse for not cleaning up after yourself: "I'm making art!" A style dubbed "Actual Art" is on display at this most unusual gallery. What is it? Anything from dust gathering on a windowpane to rusty pieces of metal might be called art here. The sign on the door warns, NO ONE ADMITTED WITHOUT AN OPINION. Trust me, you'll have one.

WILLIAMSBURG, BROOKLYN

The Williamsburg art galleries are the newest and freshest additions to the New York art world. Since the late 1990s, a set of young, brash, daring, less serious, more innovative galleries has begun to sprout up in some unusual settings in this formerly industrial/working-class, now artsy-hip neighborhood. Spread throughout the area, there are about forty spaces located in lofts, storefronts, even a backyard toolshed. The spaces are a mix of larger studios and some closet-sized galleries that are not always clearly marked, and

Beer Here!

If your style is more Budweiser than Beaujolais, Williamsburg art may be right up your alley. At these decidedly less pretentious Brooklyn galleries, beer is the official drink of choice for the opening receptions. So chugalug your way down to these opening nights for some free beer and intriguing art. For information on openings, check out the calendar at www.wburg.com or put your name on each gallery's mailing list to receive invitations.

can be off the beaten trail, but a hearty stroll around the neighborhood should give you a chance to see most of the sights. There is a good continually updated map of all the area galleries at the Web site www.wburg.com. Most galleries are open Friday through Monday or just on weekends. Here are some of the area galleries where you can always count on seeing something interesting.

HOLLAND TUNNEL
61 South 3rd Street (between Berry and Wythe Avenues)
(718) 384–5738
Hours: Saturday and Sunday, 1:00–5:00 P.M.
You might call it intimate, petite, confined, even claustrophobic, but whatever you call it there's no getting around the fact that this gallery started out in life as a toolshed from Home Depot. This space has gained quite a reputation partly because of the space itself, but also because of its daring programming. At times, this two-by-four of a gallery has hosted as many as one hundred artists in a single show.

MOMENTA ART
72 Berry Street (between North 9th and 10th Streets)
(718) 218–8058
www.momentaart.org
Hours: Friday through Monday, noon–6:00 P.M.
Momenta is not-for-profit gallery dedicated to giving opportunities to emerging artists. Many exhibitions are the first solo shows by these artists.

MONK GALLERY
301 Bedford Avenue (between South 1st and 2nd Streets)
(718) 782–2458
www.monkgallery.com
Hours: Saturday and Sunday, noon–7:00 P.M.

You may find yourself walking past this space a couple of times before you even realize it's a gallery. Specializing in installation art, this storefront gallery could be camouflaged as a water boutique, crime scene, bodega, or anything else you can imagine, but look closely and you'll discover the humor and the serious points of view behind the set dressings.

PIEROGI 2000
177 North 9th Street (between Bedford and Driggs Avenues)
(718) 599–2144
www.pierogi2000.com
Hours: Friday through Monday, noon–6:00 P.M.
One of the oldest, best-respected, and most spacious of the area galleries, Pierogi 2000 highlights the works of Brooklyn artists in a series of mostly solo shows.

PLUS ULTRA
235 South 1st Street (between Roebling Avenue and Havermeyer Street)
(718) 387–3844
www.plusultragallery.com
Hours: Saturday and Sunday, noon–6:00 P.M.
A recent addition to the neighborhood, this small gallery has begun to make a big splash with its experimental group shows and down-to-earth attitude.

ROEBLING HALL
390 Wythe Avenue (at South 4th Street)
(718) 599–5352
www.brooklynart.com
Hours: Friday through Monday, noon–6:00 P.M.
Considered one of the powerhouses of the area, Roebling Hall displays the works of neighborhood and international artists working in all forms. The shows are always daring, insightful, filled with humor, and thought provoking.

SCHROEDER ROMERO
173A North 3rd Street, second floor (between Bedford and Driggs Avenues)
(718) 486–8992
Hours: Friday through Sunday, noon–6:00 P.M.
One of the original Williamsburg galleries (first under the name Feed), this large loft gallery presents provocative group and solo shows from emerging and established artists.

OTHER GALLERIES AND SHOWS AROUND NEW YORK

BROADWAY WINDOWS
Broadway at East 10th Street
(212) 998–5751
www.nyu.edu/pages/galleries
Hours: 24/7.
Five innocent-looking shop windows that serve as a gallery. They display a wide range of styles including paintings, sculpture, and site-specific work. Be careful when walking in this neighborhood: People are forever crashing into each other, because they can't take their eyes off these often surprising windows.

BWAC PIER SHOW
141 Beard Street
Red Hook, Brooklyn
(718) 596–2507
www.bwac.org
Hours: Saturday and Sunday, noon–6:00 P.M., May and June only.
The Brooklyn art scene is brought to the public's eye at this annual event showcasing more than 200 emerging and established artists. Painting, sculpture, installation art, photography, and experimental forms are on display. It's a bit of a haul to get there, but the Civil War–era warehouse location, amazing view of the Statue of Liberty, passing barge traffic, and enough art to fill the Louvre all make it worth the effort.

80 WASHINGTON SQUARE EAST GALLERIES
New York University
80 Washington Square East
(212) 998–5748
www.nyu.edu/pages/galleries
Hours: Tuesday, 10:00 A.M.–7:00 P.M.; Wednesday and Thursday,
10:00 A.M.–6:00 P.M.; Friday and Saturday, 10:00 A.M.–5:00 P.M.
Eight galleries consisting of different solo shows or one group show. Don't miss the "Small Works" international competition every February.

KENKELEBA GALLERY
214 East 2nd Street (between Avenues B and C)
(212) 674–3939

Hours: Wednesday through Saturday, 11:00 A.M.–6:00 P.M.
This gallery specializes in works by African American and third-world artists, emerging artists, and experimental works.

LOFT LAWYERS

145 Hudson Street, ninth floor (between Beach and Hubert Streets)
(212) 431–7267
Hours: Monday through Friday, 9:30 A.M.–5:00 P.M.
This is a working law firm located in Tribeca that has a fifteen-year tradition of displaying "interesting" contemporary artists on the wall of their office space. The offices are open to the public, but you may be asked to do some filing while you browse.

PAINTING SPACE 122 ASSOCIATION

150 First Avenue (entrance on 9th Street)
(212) 228–4249
Hours: Thursday through Sunday, noon–6:00 P.M.
The gallery wing of the birthplace of downtown performance art, where you'll find shows of paintings, photography, drawings, sculptures, videos, installations, multimedia, and many other things sure to piss off Jesse Helms. You can also volunteer usher to see performances here for free. (See the first chapter, Theater: Free Speech, for details.)

THE ROTUNDA GALLERY

33 Clinton Street (at Pierrepont Street)
Brooklyn
(718) 875–4047
www.brooklynx.org/rotunda
Hours: Tuesday through Friday, noon–5:00 P.M.; Saturday,
11:00 A.M.–4:00 P.M.
Exhibits all Brooklyn-based artists working in all forms, from painting and sculpture to installations and performance art.

SOCRATES SCULPTURE PARK

Broadway at Vernon Boulevard
Long Island City Queens
(718) 956–1819
www.Socratessculpturepark.org
Hours: Daily, 10:00 A.M.–sunset.
This four-and-a-half-acre stretch of land along the Queens side of the East River has been transformed into a delightful green space that highlights the works of up-and-coming artists. They also offer free tours and occa-

sionally free films and music as well. Call or check the Web site for details and schedule.

THE SPANISH INSTITUTE GALLERY
684 Park Avenue (between 68th and 69th Streets)
(212) 628-0420
www.spanishinstitute.org
Hours: Monday through Friday, 10:00 A.M.–6:00 P.M.; Saturday, 11:00 A.M.–6:00 P.M.
Focuses on the culture and history of Spain through exhibitions of artists both classical and contemporary.

WEST SIDE ARTS COALITION
On the mall at Broadway and 96th Street
(212) 316-6024
Hours: Saturday and Sunday, noon–6:00 P.M.; Wednesday, 6:00–8:00 P.M.
From cheesy kitsch to winsome watercolors, you never know what you'll find at this little gallery showcasing the works of community artists in the middle of the road, literally (it's located on the median between the traffic running up and down Broadway). Stop by and take a look; it'll just take you a minute, again, literally.

WHITE COLUMNS
320 West 13th Street (enter on Horatio Street, between Eighth Avenue and Hudson Street)
(212) 924-4212
www.whitecolumns.org
Hours: Wednesday through Sunday, noon–6:00 P.M.
Specializing in large-scale installations by emerging and underrepresented artists, White Columns was the first to commission works by many artists who have gone on to international fame (and infamy), including William Wegman and Andres Serrano.

"I went to the museum where they had all the heads and arms from the statues that are in all the other museums."
—Stephen Wright

MUSEUMS: FREE TO SEE

THE MUSEUMS OF New York City are world class, abundant—and most of these collections can be seen free of charge. Whatever your taste or interest, whatever your age, background, or curiosities, there are museums to satisfy you. Many are completely free of charge at all times, while others have specific days and hours when they allow the public in for free or "Pay What You Want" (and you know what I want to pay!). Chances are, if the institution you would like to visit does not fit into one of those two catagories, the admission charge is a "suggested donation." (Can you guess what I suggest you donate?)

ALWAYS FREE

AMERICAN FOLK ART MUSEUM
Eva and Morris Feld Gallery
2 Lincoln Square (Columbus Avenue, between 65th and 66th
Streets)
(212) 595–9533
www.folkartmuseum.org
Hours: Monday 11:00 A.M.–6:00 P.M.; Tuesday through Sunday
until 7:30 P.M.
While much of the Folk Art Museum has moved down to fancier digs on
53rd Street where they charge you to get in (except Friday evening), they
still maintain these galleries at the original location of the museum, filled
with enticing selections from their extensive permanent collection as well
as temporary exhibitions. It's always a joy to take a walk through these
halls and see what new treasures they have discovered. A sign at the front
desk suggests a $3.00 donation, but no one seems to take any notice of
that, and the staff doesn't stop you and ask for any cash. (See page 246
for more information on the 53rd Street location.)

AUDUBON TERRACE
American Numismatic Society Museum, (212) 234–3130;
www.amnumsoc.org
Hispanic Society of America, (212) 926–2234;
www.hispanicsociety.org
American Academy of Arts and Letters, (212) 368–5000;
Broadway, between 155th and 156th Streets
Hours: Tuesday through Friday 10:00 A.M.–4:30 P.M.
These three regal buildings in Upper Manhattan are home to three small
but impressive collections. The Numismatic Society Museum traces the history of civilization through the development of money, from rocks to paper
to plastic and beyond. The Hispanic Society is an impressive collection of
paintings, sculpture, archaeological finds, textiles, rare books, and manuscripts from Spain, Portugal, and Latin America dating as far back as the
seventh century B.C. These two museums are always free and open to the
public. The Academy of Arts and Letters is a private organization of 250
preeminent American writers, composers, painters, sculptors, and architects. The building is home to many of the works of these artists and is
free, but it's open to the public only for exhibitions during the spring and
fall. Call for a schedule and details.

CARNEGIE HALL

The Rose Museum
154 West 57th Street, second floor (between Sixth and Seventh Avenues)
(212) 903–9629
www.carnegiehall.org
Hours: Thursday through Tuesday, 11:00 A.M.–4:30 P.M., and during concert intermissions.

Explore the history of the architectural splendor and acoustical wonder that is Carnegie Hall. From Toscanini's baton to Benny Goodman's clarinet, this museum has hundreds of artifacts, photographs, and memorabilia from its legendary past.

CASTLE CLINTON

Battery Park
(212) 344–7220
www.nps.gov/cacl
Hours: Daily, 8:30 A.M.–5:00 P.M.

Originally built in 1811 as the vanguard in the defense of New York Harbor off the shores of the southwest tip of Manhattan, Castle Clinton has over its long history served as a fort, an opera house, and the New York Aquarium; it was finally saved from destruction and returned to its original fort design to serve as a national monument. A small museum and video display tell you about the long and varied history of the building, as does a well-marked self-guided tour. Before the September 11 attack, guided tours were offered every hour by the park rangers, but because of added security needs, the staff have been diverted to other functions. They hope to resume tours, but as of press time were not sure of the schedule. Call for details.

DAHESH MUSEUM OF ART

601 Fifth Avenue (between 48th and 49th Streets)
(212) 759–0606
www.dahesh.org
Hours: Tuesday through Saturday, 11:00 A.M.–6:00 P.M.

"Make the painters copy everything beautiful in Rome, and when they are done, if possible, make them do it again" was the philosophy of the French Academy up through the nineteenth and early twentieth centuries. This collection specializes in this academic art by artists working to emulate Renaissance masters like da Vinci and Michelangelo with their works depicting classical mythology and biblical images.

FASHION INSTITUTE OF TECHNOLOGY MUSEUM
Shirley Goodman Resource Center
Seventh Avenue between 27th and 28th Streets
(212) 217-5800
www.fitnyc.suny.edu
Hours: Tuesday through Friday, noon–8:00 P.M.;
Saturday, 10:00 A.M.–5:00 P.M.
Located in the fashion district, this school museum is home to the largest collection of costumes, textiles, and apparel dating from the eighteenth century in the world. You won't find all their finery on display at all times, though; exhibitions change throughout the year. Still, whatever they have on display is sure to thrill any fashion bug.

FEDERAL HALL NATIONAL MEMORIAL
26 Wall Street (at Broad Street)
(212) 825-6888
www.nps.gov/feha
Hours: Monday through Friday, 9:00 A.M.–5:00 P.M.
The site of George Washington's first inauguration as president and the first home of the U.S. Congress, this building now houses a museum about its role in the early history of the city and country. Free guided tours at 11:00 A.M. and 3:00 P.M.

FORBES MAGAZINE GALLERIES
62 Fifth Avenue (at 12th Street)
(212) 206-5548
Hours: Tuesday, Wednesday, Friday, and Saturday,
10:00 A.M.– 4:00 P.M.
The world's second largest collection of Fabergé eggs, along with thousands of toy soldiers and a toy boat collection.

THE GARIBALDI-MEUCCI MUSEUM
420 Thomkins Avenue (at Chestnut Avenue)
Staten Island
(718) 442-1608
community.silive.com/cc/GaribaldiMeucci
Hours: Tuesday through Sunday, 1:00–4:30 P.M.
Think you know who invented the telephone? Well, think again, because back in 1850, while Alexander Graham Bell was still a child in Scotland, Giuseppe Garibaldi and Antonio Meucci were burning up the wires in Staten Island. Visit the historic home where the real first telephone conversation

took place, and find out more about these two men's long list of accomplishments.

GENERAL GRANT'S NATIONAL MONUMENT
Riverside Drive and 122nd Street
(212) 666–1640
www.nps.gov/gegr
Hours: Daily, 9:00 A.M.–5:00 P.M.
Here you'll finally get an answer to that age-old question: Who's buried in Grant's Tomb? You can also see some exhibits out about U. S. Grant's life (childhood, the Civil War years, and the presidency) as well as some pretty stunning views of the Hudson River.

HALL OF FAME FOR GREAT AMERICANS
Hall of Fame Terrace
181st Street and University Avenue
The Bronx
(718) 289–5161
Hours: Daily, 10:00 A.M.–5:00 P.M.
If there was a Hall of Fame for Halls of Fame, this one would certainly be in it, because this is where the whole idea began. On this covered walkway you'll find bronze busts of great American political leaders, scientists, soldiers, and authors.

LOUIS ARMSTRONG ARCHIVES
Queens College
65–30 Kissena Boulevard (at the Long Island Expressway)
(718) 997–3670
www.satchmo.net
Hours: Monday through Friday, 10:00 A.M.–5:00 P.M.
Home to more than 5,000 photographs, home recordings, scrapbooks, music, and instruments from the home of one of the (if not *the!*) greatest trumpet players in the history of jazz. They will also begin leading tours through the Armstrong house at 34–57 107th Street in Corona, Queens, in the near future (though probably for a fee). Call for details.

MUSEUM OF AMERICAN ILLUSTRATORS
128 East 63rd Street (between Park and Lexington Avenues)
(212) 838–2560
www.societyillustrators.org
Hours: Tuesday, 10:00 A.M.–8:00 P.M.; Wednesday through Friday, 10:00 A.M.–5:00 P.M.; Saturday, noon–4:00 P.M.

This East Side town house is home to a private club for illustrators, but the public is always invited to explore their two gallery spaces. They put up anywhere from fifteen to twenty-two shows a year from their extensive permanent collection of historical book and magazine covers and illustrations. Some of the true prizes of the collection reside in the upstairs dining room, which is not officially open to the public. If you ask nicely, though, they'll be happy to let you up there to see the Norman Rockwell, Maxfield Parrish, and other treasures.

NATIONAL MUSEUM OF THE AMERICAN INDIAN
1 Bowling Green Place (between State and Whitehall Streets)
(212) 514–3700
www.si.edu/nmai
Hours: Daily, 10:00 A.M.–5:00 P.M.; Thursday until 8:00 P.M.
A branch of the Smithsonian Institution, this museum is overflowing with dazzling artifacts, interactive displays, firsthand oral histories, music, and crafts of Native Americans. The changing exhibits explore the histories, beliefs, customs, and cultures of these once vast civilizations. The museum offers free workshops in such things as traditional basket weaving and beadwork (small materials fees are required), and free guided tours at 2:00 P.M. every day. If you miss the official guided tour, drop by the information desk on the second floor anytime—there's usually someone available to show you around free of charge. They also have a schedule of free films and live performances. Call or check the Web site for a schedule and details.

NEW YORK UNEARTHED
17 State Street (at Pearl Street)
(212) 748–8628
www.southstseaport.org
Hours: Monday through Friday, noon–6:00 P.M.
Explore 5,000 years of New York history in fifteen minutes at this free branch of the South Street Seaport Museum.

NICHOLAS ROERICH MUSEUM
319 West 107th Street (between Broadway and Riverside Drive)
(212) 864–7752
www.roerich.org
Hours: Tuesday through Sunday, 2:00–5:00 P.M.
Houses more than 200 works by the artist Nicholas Roerich that deal mainly with Himalayan scenery and spiritual subject matter.

QUEENS COUNTY FARM MUSEUM
73–50 Little Neck Parkway
Floral Park, Queens
(718) 347–FARM (3276)
www.queensfarm.org
Hours: Monday through Friday, 9:00 A.M.–5:00 P.M. (outside only);
Saturday and Sunday, 10:00 A.M.–5:00 P.M.
Where the City Mouse meets the County Mouse. This forty-seven-acre
working farm is the last remaining tract of undisturbed farmland in New
York City and dates back to the seventeenth century. On the weekend take
a free guided tour of the farmhouse and greenhouse, wander the farmyards
and *hey!* they even have hay rides (for $2.00).

TIBET HOUSE NEW YORK
22 West 15th Street (between Fifth and Sixth Avenues)
(212) 807–0563
www.tibethouse.org
Hours: Monday through Friday, noon–5:00 P.M; Saturday, 2:00–5:00 P.M.
The galleries host exhibitions of artworks having to do with the culture,
beliefs, history, and mythology of Tibetan Buddhism. They also hold open
meditations every Tuesday evening, with talks afterward. They ask for a
$7.00 donation or "whatever you like."

URBAN CENTER
Architectural League of New York;
(212) 753–1722; www.archleague.org
The Municipal Art Society;
(212) 935–3960; www.mas.org
457 Madison Avenue (between 50th and 51st Streets)
Hours: Monday through Wednesday, Friday, and Saturday, 11:00 A.M.–
5:00 P.M.
The galleries on the first two floors of the Urban Center play host to
exhibitions from both of these organizations. The Municipal Art Society
works usually highlight the city as a work of art, while the Architectural
League's shows concentrate on the art of making the city.

WHITNEY MUSEUM AT PHILIP MORRIS
120 Park Avenue (at 42nd Street)
(917) 663–2453
www.whitney.org
Hours: Monday through Wednesday and Friday, 11:00 A.M.–6:00 P.M.;
Thursday until 7:30 P.M.

A branch of the Whitney Museum, this small gallery and atrium plays host to four or five shows a year with a focus on contemporary emerging artists. There isn't much gallery here, but it's a nice indoor public space for a brown-bag lunch. They also host a series of performances every spring.

SOMETIMES FREE

AMERICAN CRAFT MUSEUM
40 West 53rd Street (between Fifth and Sixth Avenues)
(212) 956–3535
www.americancraftmuseum.org
Hours: Daily, 10:00 A.M.–6:00 P.M.; Thursday, until 8:00 P.M.
When free: Thursday 6:00–8:00 P.M. is "Pay What You Want"
An elegant three-story museum that essentially serves as an excuse for a very popular gift shop. The museum displays functional objects hand-crafted by contemporary American artists working in such areas as glass, baskets, quilts, furniture, instruments, utensils, and even boats, kites, brooms, and snowshoes. And yes, many of the artists on display in the museum have pricey items available at the gift shop.

AMERICAN FOLK ART MUSEUM
45 West 53rd Street (between Fifth and Sixth Avenues)
(212) 265–1040
www.folkartmuseum.org
Hours: Tuesday through Sunday, 10:00 A.M.–6:00 P.M.;
Friday until 8:00 P.M.
When free: Friday, 6:00 P.M.–8:00 P.M.
This glorious new building is home to a huge collection of American folk art. The works on display from their permanent collection or from temporary exhibitions are created by artisans and artists from all walks of life throughout American history to the present time. These mostly self-taught artists have created pieces that are often whimsical and surprising, and could be anything from weather vanes or painted furniture to handwoven Shaker rugs or duck decoys. The Lincoln Center gallery is open seven days a week and always free. (See page 240 for details on the museum's other location at 2 Lincoln Square.)

ASIA SOCIETY
725 Park Avenue (between 70th and 71st Streets)
(212) 288–6400
www.asiasociety.org

Hours: Tuesday through Saturday, 10:00 A.M.–6:00 P.M.; Friday, 10:00 A.M.–9:00 P.M.; Sunday, noon–5:00 P.M.

When free: Friday, 6:00–9:00 P.M.

A terrifically modern museum with exhibits from every corner of Asia that encompasses antiquities as old as humankind as well as the most starling new technologies and contemporary art commissions. They offer free guided tours and audio tours on Free Fridays as well.

FREE OR PAY-WHAT-YOU-WISH DAYS AT MUSEUMS

MUSEUM	MONDAY	TUESDAY	WEDNESDAY	THURSDAY	FRIDAY	SATURDAY	SUNDAY
American Craft Museum				6:00–8:00 P.M.			
American Folk Art Museum					6:00–8:00 P.M.		
Asia Society					6:00–9:00 P.M.		
Bartow-Pell Mansion Museum							First Sunday of Every Month 12:00–4:00 P.M.
Bronx Museum of the Arts			NOON–9:00 P.M.				
Brooklyn Museum of Art						First Saturday of Every Month 5:00–11:00 P.M.	
Cooper-Hewitt, National Design Museum		5:00–9:00 P.M.					
Guggenheim Museum					6:00–8:00 P.M.		
International Center of Photography					5:00–8:00 P.M.		
Jewish Museum				5:00–8:00 P.M.			
Museum for African Art							NOON–6:00 P.M.
Museum of Modern Art (MoMA)					4:30–8:15 P.M.		
New York Hall of Science				2:00–5:00 P.M. (EXCEPT JULY AND AUGUST)	2:00–5:00 P.M. (EXCEPT JULY AND AUGUST)		
The Studio Museum in Harlem						First Saturday of Every Month 10:00 A.M.–6:00 P.M.	
Whitney Museum					6:00–9:00 P.M.		

BARTOW-PELL MANSION MUSEUM
895 Shore Road North
Pelham Bay Park, the Bronx
(718) 885-1461
www.bartowpellmansionmuseum.org
Hours: Wednesday, Saturday, and Sunday, noon–4:00 P.M.
When free: The first Sunday of every month.
Travel back to the early part of the nineteenth Century, when living in the Bronx was considered living in the country. The estate predates the signing of the Declaration of Independence, and the mansion was built and furnished in early 1800s. The museum has returned the home, carriage house, and gardens to their original splendor. You are welcome to make yourself at home free of charge the first Sunday of every month.

BRONX MUSEUM OF THE ARTS
1040 Grand Concourse (at 165th Street)
The Bronx
(718) 681-6000
www.bxma.org
Hours: Wednesday, noon–9:00 P.M.; Thursday through Sunday until 6:00 P.M.
When free: Wednesday.
Primarily shows twentieth-century contemporary art by African, African American, Latino, and Asian artists as well as any artists who have lived in the Bronx.

BROOKLYN MUSEUM OF ART
200 Eastern Parkway
(718) 638-5000
www.brooklynmuseum.org
Hours: Wednesday through Friday, 10:00 A.M.–5:00 P.M.; Saturday and Sunday, 11:00 A.M.–6:00 P.M.
When free: The first Saturday of every month, 5:00–11:00 P.M.
Don' t miss the First Saturday event every month: free theater, free music, free movies, free dancing, free art, free guided tours. What a night!

COOPER-HEWITT, NATIONAL DESIGN MUSEUM
2 East 91st Street (at Central Park East)
(212) 849-8400
www.si.edu/ndm
Hours: Tuesday, 10:00 A.M.–9:00 P.M.; Wednesday through

Saturday, 10:00 A.M.–5:00 P.M.; Sunday, noon–5:00 P.M.

When free: Tuesday, 5:00 P.M.–9:00 P.M.

The former Carnegie mansion is a the home to the Smithsonian Institution's National Design Museum, where you'll find entertaining exhibits about anything that has ever been designed that affects our daily lives. Many things that you may never have thought of as art become fascinating displays when the Cooper-Hewitt folks get their hands on them. You'll find exhibitions on anything from toasters, can openers, furniture and dishes to glass art, architecture, even light itself—nothing is out of bounds for this museum. Be sure to get to the museum by 5:30 on Tuesday night for the lively free guided tour of the exhibitions.

GUGGENHEIM MUSEUM

1071 Fifth Avenue (at 89th Street)

(212) 423–3500

www.guggenheim.org/new_york_index.html

Hours: Sunday through Wednesday, 9:00 A.M.–6:00 P.M.; Friday and Saturday until 8:00 P.M.

When free: Friday 6:00–8:00 P.M. is "Pay What You Want."

The art museum that is a work of art itself. Designed by Frank Lloyd Wright, the building houses modern works that are sometimes controversial, sometimes commercial, but always worth seeing.

INTERNATIONAL CENTER OF PHOTOGRAPHY

1133 Avenue of the Americas (at 43rd Street)

(212) 857–0000

www.icp.org

Hours: Tuesday through Thursday, 10:00 A.M.–5:00 P.M.; Friday until 8:00; Saturday and Sunday until 6:00 P.M.

When free: Friday 5:00–8:00 P.M. is "Pay What You Wish."

The huge gallery spaces of the ICP mount shows that celebrate the art, craft, and images caught in the blink of an eye by the finest photographers from around the world and throughout the history of this ever-evolving art form.

JEWISH MUSEUM

1109 Fifth Avenue (at 92nd Street)

(212) 423–3200

www.jewishmuseum.org

Hours: Sunday through Wednesday, 11:00 A.M.–5:45 P.M.; Thursday until 8:00 P.M.

When free: Thursday 5:00–8:00 P.M. is "Pay What You Wish."

Ancient traditions and modern sensibilities clash, collide, and mesh in this museum that follows the development and culture of the Jewish experience from antiquity to the present day. The walls are full of rare artifacts, interactive displays, and intriguing works of art that span the centuries.

MUSEUM FOR AFRICAN ART

593 Broadway (between Houston and Prince Streets)
(212) 966–1313
www.africanart.org
Hours: Tuesday through Friday, 10:30 A.M.–5:30 P.M.; Saturday and Sunday, noon–6:00 P.M.
When free: Sunday.
This museum is the only one in the United States devoted entirely to originating and traveling exhibitions of African art. The changing exhibits explore the relationship between the arts and crafts across the African continent and people's daily lives, cultures, and rituals. They also offer a free Family Day of readings and storytelling one Saturday afternoon each month. Call or check the Web site for the Family Day schedule.

MUSEUM OF MODERN ART (MoMA)

11 West 53rd Street (between Fifth and Sixth Avenues)
(212) 708–9480
www.moma.org
Hours: Saturday through Tuesday and Thursday, 10:30 A.M.–5:45 P.M.; Friday until 8:15 P.M.
When free: Friday, 4:30 P.M.–8:15 P.M.
From Monet to milk cartons, everything modern can be found here. Films, gallery talks, and jazz in the sculpture garden as well as high-profile temporary exhibitions and the permanent collection are all available during the Free Friday hours.

NEW YORK HALL OF SCIENCE

47–01 111th Street
Flushing Meadows–Corona Park, Queens
(718) 699–0005
www.nyhallsci.org
Hours: Monday through Wednesday, 9:30 A.M.–2:00 P.M.; Thursday through Saturday until 5:00 P.M.
When free: Thursday and Friday, 2:00–5:00 P.M., except July and August.
Kids of all ages love this place. A lot of hands-on science experiments, space stuff, and a big glowing brain—who could ask for anything more?

THE STUDIO MUSEUM IN HARLEM
144 West 125th Street (between Lenox and Seventh Avenues)
(212) 864–4500
www.studiomuseuminharlem.org
Hours: Wednesday and Thursday, noon–6:00 P.M.; Friday,
noon–8:00 P.M.; Saturday and Sunday, 10:00 A.M.–6:00 P.M.
When free: The first Saturday of each month.
The leading museum dedicated to the works of African American artists.

WHITNEY MUSEUM OF AMERICAN ART
943 Madison Avenue (at 75th Street)
(212) 570–3600
www.whitney.org
Hours: Tuesday through Thursday, Saturday, and Sunday,
11:00 A.M.–6:00 P.M.; Friday 1:00–9:00 P.M.
When free: Friday 6:00–9:00 P.M. is "Pay What You Want."
One of the most impressive collections of modern art in the world, the permanent collection follows the developments of modern work from Hopper to Pollock and from Rauschenberg to today's cutting-edge artists. A couple of floors of the museum are always reserved for changing shows, from historic solo works to daring group shows. Drop by any Friday for pay-what-you-want night and also take in the free live music, guided and audio tours.

MUSEUMS WITH SUGGESTED DONATIONS

A large selection of major and smaller museums in New York operate under a "Suggested Donation" system. So, while they may "suggest" a $12 "donation," you are under no obligation to make that specific donation. There's no reason to feel bad about giving less than they ask or as little as you can afford. The fact of the matter is, most of these institutions are members of the Cultural Institutions Group (CIG) and receive a tremendous amount of money from the city of New York. One of the obligations that go along with this cash from the city is that they have to let folks into their museums for whatever they are willing to pay. In essence, you've already paid your admission when you pay your taxes. You can get away with giving as little as a penny. My standard contribution is a quarter (see, I can be generous).

AMERICAN MUSEUM OF NATURAL HISTORY, Central Park West (at 79th Street); (212) 769-5100; www.amnh.org.

BROOKLYN CHILDREN'S MUSEUM, 145 Brooklyn Avenue (between St. Marks and Prospect Streets), Brooklyn; (718) 735-4400; www.brooklynkids.org.

CHINATOWN HISTORY MUSEUM, 70 Mulberry Street, second floor (at Bayard Street); (212) 619-4785; www.moca-ny.org.

THE CLOISTERS, Fort Tryon Park, Washington Heights; (212) 923-3700; www.metmuseum.org.

EDGAR ALLAN POE COTTAGE, Kingsbridge Road and Grand Concourse, the Bronx; (718) 881-8900; www.bronxhistoricalsociety.org.

EL MUSEO DEL BARRIO, 1230 Fifth Avenue (at 105th Street); (212) 831-7272; www.elmuseo.org.

METROPOLITAN MUSEUM OF ART, 1000 Fifth Avenue (at 82nd Street); (212) 535-7710; www.metmuseum.org.

MUSEUM OF AMERICAN FINANCIAL HISTORY, 28 Broadway (at Bowling Green); (212) 908-4110; www.financialhistory.org.

MUSEUM OF THE CITY OF NEW YORK, 1220 Fifth Avenue (at 103rd Street); (212) 534-1672, www.mcny.org.

NEWHOUSE CENTER FOR CONTEMPORARY ART, Snug Harbor Cultural Center, 1000 Richmond Terrace, Building C, Staten Island; (718) 448-2500, ext. 260; www.snug-harbor.org.

NEW YORK CITY POLICE MUSEUM, 100 Old Slip (between Water Street and FDR Drive); (212) 480-3100; www.nycpolicemuseum.org.

NEW YORK FIRE MUSEUM, 278 Spring Street (between Varick and Hudson Streets); (212) 691-1303; www.nycfiremuseum.org.

NEW YORK HISTORICAL SOCIETY, 2 West 77th Street (at Central Park West); (212) 873-3400; www.nyhistory.org.

NOGUCHI GARDEN MUSEUM, 32-37 Vernon Boulevard (at 33rd Road), Queens; (718) 204-7088; www.noguchi.org.

P.S. 1 CONTEMPORARY ART CENTER, 22–25 Jackson Avenue (at 46th Avenue), Queens; (718) 784–2084; www.ps1.org.

QUEENS MUSEUM OF ART, Flushing Meadows Park; (718) 592–9700; www.queensmuse.org.

STATEN ISLAND INSTITUTE OF ARTS AND SCIENCES, 75 Stuyvesant Place (at Wall Street); (718) 727–1135; www.siiasmuseum.org.

VALENTINE VARIAN HOUSE, 32–66 Bainbridge Avenue (at 208th Street), the Bronx; (718) 881–8900; www.bronxhistoricalsociety.org.

ZOOS: BORN FREE

I T USED TO BE THAT THE BEST place to see the wildlife for free in New York was to walk around Times Square on any late night. But now that 42nd Street has gotten its facelift, the closest you will come to seeing anything too wild on those streets are the fake furs and leather worn by visitors to the Disney Shop and Madam Tussaud's. So for some real roars, New York offers some fine collections of everything from African lions, Chilean flamingos, Indian elephants, and Australian lizards to grizzly bears, Goliath beetles, lowland gorillas, and Grevy's zebras. You will find zoos in each of the Boroughs, but the only ones that have free hours are the Bronx and Staten Island Zoos. Free days for both zoos are on Wednesdays.

THE BRONX ZOO

Fordham Road and the Bronx River Parkway
(718) 367–1010
www.wcs.org/home/zoos/bronxzoo

 Wednesday is "Donation Day," when you pay what you want. Regular admission is $9.00 for adults, $5.00 for children.

The rain forest of the Congo or the African savannah may not be what you expect to see in the Bronx, but at this, the largest metropolitan zoo in the country, you'll find more than 6,000 animals and exhibits set in startlingly realistic natural habitats. As part of the Wildlife Conservation Society, the Bronx Zoo has played an integral part in saving such endangered species as the snow leopard, the American bison, lowland gorillas, Chinese alligators, Mauritius pink pigeons, and more than 40 other species. And bring the family by on any Wednesday to save a fistful of cash. Wednesday is Donation Day and everyone gets in for whatever they want to pay, even if that's nothing. Some exhibits do have additional charges (even on Wednesdays).

STATEN ISLAND ZOO

614 Broadway (off Glenwood Avenue)
(718) 442–3100
www.statenislandzoo.org

Free on Wednesday after 2:00 P.M.

Particularly well known for its collection of snakes and other reptiles, this small zoo also boasts an aquarium, children's zoo, rain forest, and African savannah habitats and free parking.

"If you want to say it with flowers, a single rose says: 'I'm cheap!'"

—Delta Burke

APPENDIX A
ROMANCE: CHEAP DATES

HEY, EVEN CHEAP BASTARDS need love. And while it's true that introducing yourself as a "Cheap Bastard" may not be the most successful way to get a date, being a Cheap Bastard shouldn't get in the way of having a great time. In fact, you might even score extra points by coming up with some original ideas for romantic liaisons around New York. Here are some great ways to spend days and evenings with that special someone that won't cost you a thing (except maybe your heart).

THE UNTRADITIONAL TRADITIONAL DATE: Why not put a twist on the usual date by seeing a free movie? In the summer there are any numbers of star-lit nights for you to set out a blanket and cuddle while you watch the stars of Hollywood twinkle on the screen. My personal favorite romantic setting is the Brooklyn Bridge Park Film Festival—not too crowded, the skyline of New York as a backdrop, and fun films on the screen. During the cooler months move indoors with the free screenings at Axis Company and Void. For more details and other film ideas, see the chapter titled Film: Cheap Shots.

THE SWEEP-HER-OFF-HER-FEET DATE: Swing down to the Moondance at Pier 25 any Sunday during the summer for dancing under the stars to live music. Show up early for a free lesson. During the cooler months, stick a rose in her mouth and heat things up by going down to Chelsea Market to do the Dance of Love any Saturday afternoon, when they offer a traditional Argentinean tango *milonga*. For details and more dance ideas, see the chapter titled Dance: Free Expression.

THE SURE-WAY-TO-SCORE DATE: Spend a day of fun and games in Central Park by borrowing a free Field Day Kit from the folks at the North Meadow Recreation Center. They throw in all kinds of equipment for almost any sport you can think of. Your big sack of fun includes a basketball, bats, Wiffle balls, football, Nerf ball, horseshoe set, Frisbee, jump rope, and even hula hoops. If that doesn't get the two of you working up a sweat, nothing will. For more information, see page 271–72.

THE THIS-ISN'T-QUITE-VENICE-BUT-HEY-YOU-AREN'T-QUITE-SOFIA-LOREN DATE: Your gondola awaits you at the Downtown Boathouse on Pier 26 or Pier 64. The bad news is, you have to do all the rowing and serenading yourself; the good news is, it's free. Borrow a kayak for you and your love to paddle up and down the Hudson any weekend from May through October. For details, see pages 169–70.

THE TROUBADOUR DATE: If you don't have the voice to serenade your sweetheart by yourself, here's the next best thing. Catch one of the very intimate performances at the Postcrypt Coffee House on the campus of Columbia University any Friday or Saturday night during the school year. Any candlelit evening of acoustic music is the perfect setting for a romantic evening for two. And hey, there's even free popcorn. For details see page 31.

THE MAKE-'EM-LAUGH DATE: A surefire way to win someone's heart is to put a smile on their face, and there are many free funny nights every week around the city. During the week you'll find some unusual comedy performances at PSNBC, and on Saturday night don't miss Felber's Frolics at Ye Olde Tripple Inn. For more details and other comedy destinations, see the chapter titled Comedy: Cheap Jokes.

THE LOVE-BIRDS DATE: See if a walk among the birds and the bees inspires anything for you. Stop by Belvedere Castle in Central Park and borrow a free Birding Kit for a delightful stroll through the wilds of the park. Your kit comes equipped with your very own set of binoculars, a field guide, a sketch pad, and colored pencils. For more details, see page 133.

THE PRETENTIOUS DATE: Show your date you can bandy around words like *cubist, conceptual, minimalistic,* and *postmodernist* with the best of them at any of the many art gallery openings that go on every week. If that doesn't have any effect, maybe all the free wine or beer will. For more details, see the chapter titled Art Galleries: Show Me the Monet.

THE FUN-IN-THE-SUN DATE: A day at any one of the local beaches. An old reliable free day. Sorry, they can't all be gems. See pages 172–74 for beaches.

THE SHOW-'EM-YOU-GOT-CLASS DATE: Take in a museum on one of the many free, suggested donation, or pay-what-you-want nights. The best one is First Saturday Night at the Brooklyn Museum—free live music and dancing, free films, and, oh yeah, there's some art there, too. For more museum details, see the chapter titled Museums: Free to See.

THE NOT-QUITE-THE-GREAT-WHITE-WAY DATE: Take my advice: If you want a second date, don't try this on a first date. If you've been dating for a while, though, and it's clear that you're both Cheap Bastards, then why not pick a Broadway or Off Broadway show for you to volunteer usher at together? For a list of theaters to usher at, see the chapter titled Theater: Free Speech. If you don't want to seem chintzy, get free tickets to a production or concert at Julliard or NYU or any of the other free theaters listed on pages 20–25.

THE YOU-THINK-*WE'VE*-GOT-PROBLEMS? DATE: Hitting one of those rough patches in the relationship? Well, there's nothing like reveling in someone else's misery to make you feel good about your own life. Take your date to see a taping of *The Montel Williams Show, Ricki Lake,* or *Maury* and by comparison your troubles will surely seem insignificant. Though if you start to feel more like you should be a guest on any of these shows, it may be time to check out *Change of Heart.* For details and more TV taping ideas, see the chapter titled Television Tapings: Public Access.

THE GETTING-TO-KNOW-YOU DATE: Why not take the time to get to know each other as you get to know a bit of New York? There are some great walking tours that will give you the time to walk and talk your way around the city. Check out Take a Walk New York, urban park rangers tours, or the delightful jaunts through Central Park given by the Central Park Conservancy. For more details, see the chapter titled Walking Tours: The Freedom Trail.

THE HEY-THIS-IS-GOING-PRETTY-SWELL-I-MAY-JUST-WANT-TO-KISS-YOU SPECIAL ADD-ON TO ANY DATE: It may not be as romantic as the *Titanic,* but a ride on the Staten Island Ferry will leave you feeling like you're "on top of the world." Particularly if you end that date with a romantic kiss on the boat while you ride by the dramatic New York skyline with the wind in your hair. For more details, see page 215.

FINDING A CHEAP DATE . . .

Um, I mean *finding a date, cheap*. It's a big city with lots of single folks out there trying to find each other, but hanging out in bars or going to "singles" parties and events can be costly, not to mention depressing. Here are a couple of alternative ways to make the connection by volunteering and just being your own cheap self.

DATE BAIT
(212) 971–1084
www.datebait.com
DateBaitNYC@netscape.net

 Volunteers arrive forty-five minutes early help with registration and stay a few minutes after to help with cleanup, but they fully participate in the event.

These are structured, results-oriented mixers for single people. The way it works is that when you register, you get a name tag with a number. Once the whole group has gathered—and these events do attract large crowds—everyone gets up to one minute to introduce themselves in front of the assembled. Then there's time to mingle and get to know each other; at the end of the night, you hand in a card with the numbers of those people you're interested in having a date with. If you're on their card as well, it's a match. If not . . . well, at least there was no face-to-face rejection. They have straight, gay, and lesbian events almost every week, and they're always surprisingly unintimidating, fun, and well put together. Call or e-mail at least a few weeks in advance to make a reservation to volunteer.

SPEEDDATING
(646) 365–0030
www.aish.com/speeddating

 Volunteers help with registration and organization. They aren't guaranteed a chance to participate in the speeddating, but can mingle and meet potential dates.

Got seven minutes? Have a date, or seven! These mixers are for straight Jewish singles only. The evening consists of two parts. There's some of the usual mix-and-mingle you'd expect at any singles soiree, but what makes this different is that you're guaranteed seven dates during the night. Each date consists of a seven-minute conversation where you two can get to know the basics about each other and see if you might be interested in the real thing. If you both check off "yes" on your date card, Speeddating will give you each other's phone numbers and let nature take its course. Volunteers get to participate in the one-on-one dates only when there's an odd number of men and women (provided you even out the count) and if you fit into the age group for the evening. Otherwise, you're always welcome to participate in the mix-and-mingle.

APPENDIX B
PUBLIC LIBRARY BRANCH LOCATIONS

MANHATTAN

MID-MANHATTAN LIBRARY, 455 Fifth Avenue (at 40th Street); (212) 340–0833; www.nypl.org; Telephone Reference, (212) 340–0849, ext.3

EAST SIDE

58TH STREET, 127 East 58th Street; (212) 759–7358

67TH STREET, 328 East 67th Street; (212) 734–1717

96TH STREET, 112 East 96th Street; (212) 289–0908

125TH STREET, 224 East 125th Street; (212) 534–5050

AGUILAR, 174 East 110th Street; (212) 534–2930

EPIPHANY, 228 East 23rd Street; (212) 679–2645

HAMILTON FISH PARK, 415 East Houston Street; (212) 673–2290

MACOMB'S BRIDGE, 2650 Adam Clayton Powell Jr. Boulevard; (212) 281–4900

OTTENDORFER, 135 Second Avenue; (212) 674–0947

ROOSEVELT ISLAND, 524 Main Street; (212) 308–6243

TERENCE CARDINAL COOKE-CATHEDRAL, 560 Lexington Avenue; (212) 752–3824

WEBSTER, 1465 York Avenue; (212) 288–5049

YORKVILLE, 222 East 79th Street; (212) 744–5824

WEST SIDE

115TH STREET, 203 West 115th Street; (212) 666–9393

ANDREW HEISKELL LIBRARY FOR THE BLIND AND PHYSICALLY HANDICAPPED, 40 West 20th Street; (212) 206–5400; voice mail (212) 206–5425; TDD (212) 206–5458

BLOOMINGDALE, 150 West 100th Street; (212) 222–8030

COLUMBUS, 742 Tenth Avenue; (212) 586–5098

COUNTEE CULLEN, 104 West 136th Street; (212) 491–2070

DONNELL LIBRARY CENTER, 20 West 53rd Street; (212) 621–0618

FORT WASHINGTON, 535 West 179th Street; (212) 927–3533

GEORGE BRUCE, 518 West 125th Street; (212) 662–9727

HAMILTON GRANGE, 503 West 145th Street; (212) 926–2147

HARLEM, 9 West 124th Street; (212) 348–5620

INWOOD, 4790 Broadway; (212) 942–2445

JEFFERSON MARKET, 425 Avenue of the Americas; (212) 243–4334

KIPS BAY, 446 Third Avenue; (212) 683–2520

MORNINGSIDE HEIGHTS, 2900 Broadway; (212) 864–2530

MUHLENBERG, 209 West 23rd Street; (212) 924–1585

RIVERSIDE, 127 Amsterdam Avenue; (212) 870–1810

ST. AGNES, 444 Amsterdam Avenue;
(212) 877-4380

SEWARD PARK, 192 East Broadway;
(212) 477-6770

WASHINGTON HEIGHTS, 1000 St.,
Nicholas Avenue; (212) 923-6054

DOWNTOWN

CHATHAM SQUARE, 33 East
Broadway; (212) 964-6598

EARLY CHILDHOOD RESOURCE &
INFORMATION CENTER (ECRIC),
66 Leroy Street; (212) 929-0815

HUDSON PARK, 66 Leroy Street;
(212) 243-6876

NEW AMSTERDAM, 9 Murray Street;
(212) 732-8186

TOMPKINS SQUARE, 331 East 10th
Street; (212) 228-4747

STATEN ISLAND

ST. GEORGE LIBRARY CENTER, 5
Central Avenue; (718) 442-8560

DONGAN HILLS, 1617 Richmond
Road; (718) 351-1444

GREAT KILLS, 56 Giffords Lane; (718)
984-6670

HUGUENOT PARK, 830 Huguenot
Avenue; (718) 984-4636

NEW DORP, 309 New Dorp Lane; (718)
351-2977

PORT RICHMOND, 75 Bennett Street;
(718) 442-0158

RICHMONDTOWN, 200 Clarke Avenue;
(718) 668-0413

SOUTH BEACH, 21-25 Robin Road;
(718) 816-5834

STAPLETON, 132 Canal Street; (718)
727-0427

TODT HILL-WESTERLEIGH, 2550
Victory Boulevard; (718) 494-1642

TOTTENVILLE, 7430 Amboy Road;
(718) 984-0945

WEST NEW BRIGHTON, 976 Castleton
Avenue; (718) 442-1416

THE BRONX

FORDHAM LIBRARY CENTER, 2556
Bainbridge Avenue (at Fordham
Road); (718) 579-4244; Bronx
Reference Center, (718) 579-4257

ALLERTON, 2740 Barnes Avenue;
(718) 881-4240

BAYCHESTER, 2049 Asch Loop North;
(718) 379-6700

BELMONT LIBRARY-ENRICO FERMI
CULTURAL CENTER, 610 East
186th Street; (718) 933-6410

CASTLE HILL, 947 Castle Hill Avenue;
(718) 824-3838

CITY ISLAND, 320 City Island
Avenue; (718) 885-1703

CLASON'S POINT, 1215 Morrison
Avenue; (718) 842-1235

EASTCHESTER, 1385 East Gun Hill
Road; (718) 653-3292

EDENWALD, 1255 East 233rd Street;
(718) 798-3355

FRANCIS MARTIN, 2150 University
Avenue; (718) 295-5287

GRAND CONCOURSE, 155 East 173rd
Street; (718) 583-6611

HIGH BRIDGE, 78 West 168th Street;
(718) 293-7800

HUNT'S POINT, 877 Southern
Boulevard; (718) 617-0338

JEROME PARK, 118 Eames Place
(718) 549-5200

KINGSBRIDGE, 280 West 231st
Street; (718) 548-5656

MELROSE, 910 Morris Avenue;
(718) 588-0110

MORRISANIA, 610 East 169th Street;
(718) 589-9268

MOSHOLU, 285 East 205th Street; (718) 882-8239

MOTT HAVEN, 321 East 140th Street; (718) 665-4878

PARKCHESTER, 1985 Westchester Avenue; (718) 829-7830

PELHAM BAY, 3060 Middletown Road; (718) 792-6744

RIVERDALE, 5540 Mosholu Avenue; (718) 549-1212

SEDGWICK, 1701 Dr. Martin Luther King Jr. Boulevard; (718) 731-2074

SOUNDVIEW, 660 Soundview Avenue; (718) 589-0880

SPUYTEN DUYVIL, 650 West 235th Street; (718) 796-1202

THROG'S NECK, 3025 Cross Bronx Expressway Extension; (718) 792-2612

TREMONT, 1866 Washington Avenue; (718) 299-5177

VAN CORTLANDT, 3874 Sedgwick Avenue; (718) 543-5150

VAN NEST, 2147 Barnes Avenue; (718) 829-5864

WAKEFIELD, 4100 Lowerre Place; (718) 652-4663

WESTCHESTER SQUARE, 2521 Glebe Avenue; (718) 863-0436

WEST FARMS, 2085 Honeywell Avenue; (718) 367-5376

WOODLAWN HEIGHTS, 4355 Katonah Avenue; (718) 519-9627

WOODSTOCK, 761 East 160th Street; (718) 665-6255

BROOKLYN

CENTRAL LIBRARY, Grand Army Plaza (Flatbush Avenue and Eastern Parkway); (718) 230-2100; www.brooklynpubliclibrary.org; Telephone Reference, (718) 230-2100, ext. 5

ARLINGTON, Arlington Avenue at Warwick Street; (718) 277-6105

BAY RIDGE, Ridge Boulevard at 73rd Street; (718) 748-5709

BEDFORD, Franklin Avenue at Hancock Street; (718) 623-0012

BEDFORD LEARNING CENTER, (718) 623-0028

BOROUGH PARK, 43rd Street near Thirteenth Avenue; (718) 437-4085

BRIGHTON BEACH, Brighton First Road (near Brighton Beach Avenue); (718) 946-2917

BROOKLYN HEIGHTS, 280 Cadman Plaza West (at Tillary Street); (718) 623-7100

BROWER PARK, St. Marks Avenue near Nostrand Avenue; (718) 773-7208

BROWNSVILLE, Glenmore Avenue at Watkins Street; (718) 498-9721

BUSHWICK, Bushwick Avenue at Seigel Street; (718) 602-1348

CANARSIE, Rockaway Parkway near Avenue J; (718) 257-6547

CARROLL GARDENS, Clinton Street at Union Street; (718) 596-6972

CLARENDON, Nostrand Avenue near Farragut Road; (718) 421-1159

CLINTON HILL, Washington Avenue near Lafayette Avenue; (718) 398-8713

CONEY ISLAND, Mermaid Avenue near West 19th Street; (718) 265-3220

CONEY ISLAND LEARNING CENTER; (718) 265-3880

CORTELYOU, Cortelyou Road at Argyle Road; (718) 693-7763

CROWN HEIGHTS, New York Avenue at Maple Street; (718) 773-1180

CYPRESS HILLS, Sutter Avenue at Crystal Street; (718) 277-6004

DEKALB, Bushwick Avenue at DeKalb Avenue; (718) 455-3898

DYKER, Thirteenth Avenue at 82nd Street; (718) 748-6261

EASTERN PARKWAY, Eastern Parkway at Schenectady Avenue; (718) 953-4225

EASTERN PARKWAY Adult Learning Center; (718) 778-9330

EAST FLATBUSH, 9612 Church Avenue near Rockaway Parkway; (718) 922-0927

FLATBUSH, Linden Boulevard near Flatbush Avenue; (718) 856-0813

FLATBUSH ADULT LEARNING CENTER; (718) 856-2631

FLATLANDS, Flatbush Avenue at Avenue P; (718) 253-4409

FORT HAMILTON, Fourth Avenue at 95th Street; (718) 748-6919

GERRITSEN BEACH, Gerritsen Avenue at Channel Avenue; (718) 368-1435

GRAVESEND, Avenue X near West 2nd Street; (718) 382-5792

GREENPOINT, Norman Avenue at Leonard Street; (718) 349-8504

HIGHLAWN, West 13th Street at Kings Highway; (718) 234-7208

HOMECREST, Coney Island Avenue near Avenue V; (718) 382-5924

JAMAICA BAY, Seaview Avenue at East 98th Street; (718) 241-3571

KENSINGTON, Ditmas Avenue near East 5th Street; (718) 435-9431

KINGS BAY, Nostrand Avenue near Avenue W; (718) 368-1709

KINGS HIGHWAY, Ocean Avenue near Kings Highway; (718) 375-3037

LEONARD, Devoe Street at Leonard Street; (718) 486-3365

MACON, Lewis Avenue at Macon Street; (718) 573-5606

MAPLETON, 60th Street at Seventeenth Avenue; (718) 256-2117

MARCY, DeKalb Avenue near Nostrand Avenue; (718) 935-0032

MCKINLEY PARK, Fort Hamilton Parkway at 68th Street; (718) 748-8001

MIDWOOD, East 16th Street near Avenue J; (718) 252-0967

MILL BASIN, Ralph Avenue near Avenue N; (718) 241-3973

NEW LOTS, New Lots Avenue at Barbey Street; (718) 649-0311

NEW UTRECHT, 1783 86th Street (at Bay 17th Street); (718) 236-4086

PACIFIC, Fourth Avenue at Pacific Street; (718) 638-1531

PAERDEGAT, East 59th Street near Flatlands Avenue; (718) 241-3994

PARK SLOPE, Sixth Avenue near 9th Street; (718) 832-1853

RED HOOK, Wolcott Street at Dwight Street; (718) 935-0203

RUGBY, Utica Avenue near Tilden Avenue; (718) 566-0054

RYDER, Twenty-third Avenue at 59th Street; (718) 331-2962

SARATOGA, Thomas S. Boyland Street at Macon Street; (718) 573-5224

SHEEPSHEAD BAY, East 14th Street near Avenue Z; (718) 368-1815

SPRING CREEK, Flatlands Avenue near New Jersey Avenue; (718) 257-6571

STONE AVENUE, 581 Mother Gaston Boulevard at Dumont Avenue; (718) 485-8347

SUNSET PARK, Fourth Avenue at 51st Street; (718) 567-2806

ULMER PARK, Bath Avenue at Twenty-sixth Avenue; (718) 265-3443

WALT WHITMAN, 93 St. Edwards Street (at Auburn Place); (718) 935-0244

WASHINGTON IRVING, Irving Avenue at Woodbine Street; (718) 628-8378

WILLIAMSBURG, 240 Division Avenue (at Marcy Avenue); (718) 302-3485

WILLIAMSBURG ADULT LEARNING CENTER, (718) 302-3489

WINDSOR TERRACE, East 5th Street at Fort Hamilton Parkway; (718) 686-9707

QUEENS

CENTRAL LIBRARY, 89-11 Merrick Boulevard (between Eighty-ninth and Ninetieth Avenues); (718) 990-0700; www.queenslibrary.org; Telephone Reference, (718) 990-0714 or (718) 990-0728

ARVERNE, Beach 54th Street; (718) 634-4784

ASTORIA, 14-01 Astoria Boulevard; (718) 278-2220

AUBURNDALE, 25-55 Francis Lewis Boulevard; (718) 352-2027

BAISLEY PARK, 117-11 Sutphin Boulevard; (718) 529-1590

BAYSIDE, 214-20 Northern Boulevard; (718) 229-1834

BAY TERRACE, 18-36 Bell Boulevard; (718) 423-7004

BELLEROSE, 250-06 Hillside Avenue; (718) 831-8644

BRIARWOOD, 85-12 Main Street; (718) 658-1680

BROAD CHANNEL, 16-26 Cross Bay Boulevard; (718) 318-4943

BROADWAY, 40-20 Broadway; (718) 721-2462

CAMBRIA HEIGHTS 220-20 Linden Boulevard; (718) 528-3535

CORONA, 38-23 104th Street (between Thirty-eighth and Thirty-ninth Avenues); (718) 426-2844

COURT SQUARE, 25-01 Jackson Avenue; (718) 937-2790

DOUGLASTON/LITTLE NECK, 249-01 Northern Boulevard; (718) 225-8414

EAST ELMHURST, 95-06 Astoria Boulevard; (718) 424-2619

EAST FLUSHING, 196-36 Northern Boulevard; (718) 357-6643

ELMHURST, 86-01 Broadway; (718) 271-1020

FAR ROCKAWAY, 1637 Central Avenue; (718) 327-2549

FLUSHING, 41-17 Main Street; (718) 661-1200

FOREST HILLS, 108-19 Seventy-first Avenue; (718) 268-7934

FRESH MEADOWS, 193-20 Horace Harding Expressway; (718) 454-7272

GLENDALE, 78-60 73rd Place; (718) 821-4980

GLEN OAKS, 256-04 Union Turnpike; (718) 831-8636

HILLCREST, 187-05 Union Turnpike; (718) 454-2786

HOLLIS, 202-05 Hillside Avenue; (718) 465-7355

HOWARD BEACH, 92-06 156th Avenue; (718) 641-7086

JACKSON HEIGHTS, 35-51 81st Street; (718) 899-2500

KEW GARDENS HILLS, 72-33 Vleigh Place; (718) 261-6654

LANGSTON HUGHES, 100-01 Northern Boulevard; (718) 651-1100

LAURELTON, 134-26 225th Street; (718) 528-2822

LEFFERTS, 103-34 Lefferts Boulevard; (718) 843-5950

LEFRAK CITY, 98-25 Horace Harding Expressway; (718) 592-7677

MASPETH, 69-70 Grand Avenue; (718) 639-5228

MCGOLDRICK, 155–06 Roosevelt Avenue; (718) 461–1616

MIDDLE VILLAGE, 72–31 Metropolitan Avenue; (718) 326–1390

MITCHELL–LINDEN, 29–42 Union Street; (718) 539–2330

NORTH FOREST PARK, 98–27 Metropolitan Avenue; (718) 261–5512

NORTH HILLS, 57–04 Marathon Parkway; (718) 225–3550

OZONE PARK, 92–24 Rockaway Boulevard; (718) 845–3127

PENINSULA, 92–25 Rockaway Beach Boulevard; (718) 634–1110

POMONOK, 158–21 Jewel Avenue; (718) 591–4343

POPPENHUSEN, 121–23 Fourteenth Avenue; (718) 359–1102

QUEENSBORO HILL, 60–05 Main Street; (718) 359–8332

QUEENSBRIDGE, 10–43 Forty-first Avenue; (718) 937–6266

QUEENS VILLAGE, 94–11 217th Street; (718) 776–6800

RAVENSWOOD, 35–32 21st Street; (718) 784–2112

REGO PARK, 91–41 63rd Drive; (718) 459–5140

RICHMOND HILL, 118–14 Hillside Avenue; (718) 849–7150

RIDGEWOOD, 20–12 Madison Street; (718) 821–4770

ROCHDALE VILLAGE, 169–09 137th Avenue; (718) 723–4440

ROSEDALE, 144–20 243rd Street; (718) 528–8490

ST. ALBANS, 191–05 Linden Boulevard; (718) 528–8196

SEASIDE, 116–15 Rockaway Beach Boulevard; (718) 634–1876

SOUTH HOLLIS, 204–01 Hollis Avenue; (718) 465–6779

SOUTH JAMAICA, 108–41 Guy R. Brewer Boulevard; (718) 739–4088

SOUTH OZONE PARK, 128–16 Rockaway Boulevard; (718) 529–1660

STEINWAY, 21–45 31st Street; (718) 728–1965

SUNNYSIDE, 43–06 Greenpoint Avenue; (718) 784–3033

WHITESTONE, 151–10 14th Road; (718) 767–8010

WINDSOR PARK, 79–50 Bell Boulevard; (718) 468–8300

WOODHAVEN, 85–41 Forest Parkway; (718) 849–1010

WOODSIDE, 54–22 Skillman Avenue; (718) 429–4700

APPENDIX C
BEACON PROGRAM LOCATIONS

The Beacon programs are school-based community centers located throughout the city. Program offerings vary from location to location but usually include youth-oriented classes and activities ranging from tutoring to arts and crafts to sports. Evening activities are also available for teens and adults. Here is a listing of all Beacon program locations. For more information on Beacon schools, see page 122–23.

MANHATTAN

CENTRAL HARLEM, MS 54, 103 West 108th Street; (212) 866-5579

CENTRAL HARLEM, IS 88, 215 West 114th Street; (212) 932-7895

CHELSEA, IS 70, 333 West 17th Street; (212) 243-7574

CHINATOWN, IS 131, 100 Hester Street; (212) 219-8393

EAST HARLEM, JHS 45, 2351 First Avenue, Room 154; (212) 410-4227, ext. 226

EAST HARLEM, JHS 99, 410 East 100th Street; (212) 987-8743

EAST VILLAGE, JHS 60, 420 East 12th Street; (212) 598-4533

HARLEM, PS 194, 242 West 144th Street; (212) 234-4500

LOWER EAST SIDE, JHS 22, 145 Stanton Street, (212) 505-6338

ROOSEVELT ISLAND, IS 217, 585 Main Street; (212) 527-2505

UPPER EAST SIDE, PS 198, 1700 Third Avenue; (212) 828-6342

UPPER WEST SIDE, IS 118, 154 West 93rd Street; (212) 866-0009

WASHINGTON HEIGHTS, JHS 64, 401 West 164th Street; (212) 927-7251

WASHINGTON HEIGHTS/INWOOD, JHS 143, 515 West 182nd Street; (212) 928-4992

WEST HARLEM, IS 195, 625 West 133rd Street; (212) 368-1827 or (212) 368-1622

BROOKLYN

BAY RIDGE, IS 259, 7301 Fort Hamilton; (718) 836-3620

BEDFORD/STUYVESANT, IS 35, 272 Macdonough Street; (718) 453-7004

BENSONHURST, IS 96, 99 Avenue P; (718) 232-2266

BOROUGH PARK, IS 220, 4812 Ninth Avenue; Room 252; (718) 633-8200, ext. 262

BROWNSVILLE, IS 263, 210 Chester Street; (718) 498-7030

BROWNSVILLE, JHS 275, 985 Rockaway Avenue, Room 111; (718) 485-2719

BUSHWICK, IS 111, 35 Starr Street; (718) 417-1702

BUSHWICK, IS 291, 231 Palmetto Street; (718) 573-7702 or (718) 573-7703

BUSHWICK, IS 296, 125 Covert Street, Room 49B; (718) 919-4453

CONEY ISLAND, PS 288, 2950 West 25th Street; (718) 714-0103

EAST FLATBUSH, IS 68, 956 East 82nd Street; (718) 241-2555

EAST FLATBUSH, IS 232, 905 Winthrop Street; (718) 221-8880

EAST FLATBUSH, IS 285, 5909 Beverly Road; Room 107; (718) 451-4088

EAST FLATBUSH/MIDWOOD, IS 271, 1137 Herkmimer Street; (718) 345-5904

EAST NEW YORK, JHS 166, 800 Van Sicklen Avenue; (718) 257-7003

EAST NEW YORK, IS 218, 370 Fountain Avenue; (718) 277-1928

EAST NEW YORK, IS 302, 350 Linwood Street; (718) 277-3522

FLATBUSH, MS 2, 655 Parkside Avenue; (718) 826-2889

FLATBUSH/MIDWOOD, JHS 126, 424 Leonard Street, Room 105; (718) 388-5546

FORT GREENE/BROOKLYN HEIGHTS, JHS 265, 101 Park Avenue; (718) 694-0601

MIDWOOD, PS 269, 1957 Nostrand Avenue; (718) 462-2597

RED HOOK, PS 15, 71 Sullivan Street; (718) 522-6910

SHEEPSHEAD BAY, IS 14, 2424 Batchelder Street; (718) 743-5065

SOUTH SUNSET PARK, PS 314, 330 59th Street; (718) 439-5986

SUNSET PARK, JHS 136, 4004 Fourth Avenue; (718) 788-4972

WILLIAMSBURG, IS 50, 183 South 3rd Street; (718) 486-3936

WILLIAMSBURG, Eastern District HS, 850 Grand Street; (718) 387-2800, ext. 313

THE BRONX

CROTONA/MORRISANIA, IS 148, 3630 Third Avenue; Room 227; (718) 293-5454

EASTCHESTER, MS 142, 3750 Baychester Avenue; (718) 798-6670

EAST TREMONT, JHS 117, 1865 Morris Avenue; (718) 466-1806

EAST TREMONT, IS 200, 1970 West Farms Road, Room 146; (718) 991-6338

FORDHAM, MS 45, 2502 Lorillard Place; (718) 367-9577

HIGHBRIDGE/MELROSE, CES 11, 1257 Ogden Avenue; (718) 590-0101

HUNTS POINT, IS 74, 730 Bryant Avenue; (718) 542-6850

HUNTS POINT, IS 192, 650 Hollywood Avenue; (718) 239-4080

KINGSBRIDGE HEIGHTS/BEDFORD PARK, PS 86, 2756 Reservoir Avenue; (718) 563-7410

MORRISANIA, IS 116, 977 Tiffany Street; (718) 589-6509

MOTT HAVEN, IS 139, 345 Brook Avenue; (718) 585-3353

NORWOOD, MS 80, 149 East Mosholu Parkway; (718) 882-5929

WILLIAMSBRIDGE, MS 113, 3710 Barnes Avenue; (718) 654-5881

QUEENS

ASTORIA, JHS 204, 36-41 28th Street; (718) 433-1989

BAYSIDE, MS 158, 46-35 Oceania Street; (718) 423-2266

CORONA, PS 19, 99th Street/ Roosevelt Avenue; (718) 651-4656

FAR ROCKAWAY, IS 43, 160 Beach 29th Street; (718) 471-7875

FAR ROCKAWAY, JHS 198, 365 Beach 56th Street; (718) 945-7845

FLORAL PARK, MS 172, 81-14 257th Street; (718) 347-3279

FLUSHING, IS 5, 50–40 Jacobs Street; (718) 429–8752

FLUSHING, JHS 189, 144–80 Barclay Avenue; (718) 961–6014

FLUSHING, JHS 194, 154–60 Seventeenth Avenue; (718) 747–3644

HILLCREST/FRESH MEADOWS, IS 168, 158–40 76th Road; (718) 820–0760

HILLCREST/FRESH MEADOWS, JHS 216, 64–20 175th Street; (718) 445–6983

JACKSON HEIGHTS, IS 10, 45–11 Thirty-first Avenue; (718) 777–9202

JACKSON HEIGHTS, JHS 141, 37–11 Twenty-first Avenue; (718) 777–9200

JACKSON HEIGHTS, PS 149, 93–11 Thirty-fourth Avenue; (718) 426–0888

JAMAICA/HOLLIS, IS 72, 133–25 Guy R. Brewer Boulevard; (718) 276–7728

LAURELTON, JHS 231, 145–00 Springfield Boulevard; (718) 528–1743

OZONE PARK, IS 210, 93–11 101st Avenue; (718) 659–7710

REGO PARK/FOREST HILLS, JHS 190, 68–17 Austin Street; (718) 830–5233

RIDGEWOOD, IS 93, 66–56 Forest Avenue; (718) 628–8702

SOUTH JAMAICA, New Preparatory School for Technology (JHS 8), 108–35 167th Street; (718) 523–7338

SOUTH OZONE PARK, JHS 226, 121–10 Rockaway Boulevard; (718) 848–2890

STATEN ISLAND

MID ISLAND/SOUTH 50/51, IS 2, 33 Midland Avenue; (718) 668–9176

MID ISLAND/SOUTH 50/51, Tottenville HS, 100 Luten Avenue; (718) 984–9225

STAPLETON, IS 49, 101 Warren Street, B–33; (718) 556–1565

WEST BRIGHTON; PS 18, 221 Broadway; (718) 448–4834

APPENDIX D
NEW YORK CITY RECREATION CENTERS

CHIEF OF RECREATION'S OFFICE: (212) 408-0243

ALFRED EAST SMITH (LOWER EAST SIDE)

80 Catherine Street (off Cherry Street, between Madison and South Streets); (212) 285-0300

Hours: Monday through Friday, 7:00 A.M.–10:00 P.M.; Saturday, 9:00 A.M.–5:00 P.M.; Sunday 2:00–6:00 P.M. (fitness room closed).

Dance classes, open basketball, badminton, gardening club, basic computer courses, kickboxing and karate classes.

ASSER LEVY (MIDTOWN EAST SIDE)

East 23rd Street and Asser Levy Place (at FDR Drive); (212) 447-2020

Hours: Monday through Friday, 6:30 A.M.–9:30 P.M.; Saturday and Sunday, 8:00 A.M.–4:45 P.M.

Indoor and outdoor pool, group fitness classes, martial arts classes, swim classes, guitar lessons, yoga, seniors programs.

CARMINE (WEST VILLAGE/SOHO)

1 Clarkson Street (near Seventh Avenue South and Houston Street); (212) 242-5228

Hours: Monday through Friday, 7:00 A.M.–10:00 P.M.; Saturday and Sunday, 9:00 A.M.–5:30 P.M.

Very popular center. Indoor and outdoor pools, handball courts, two fitness rooms, indoor track, boccie court, fitness classes, basketball and flag football leagues.

EAST 54 (UPPER EAST SIDE)

348 East 54th Street (between First and Second Avenues); (212) 408-0243

Hours: Temporarily closed for renovations; call for hours.

Before they closed for renovations, they offered an extensive schedule of fitness and dance classes, indoor track, fitness room, basketball, tennis, and seniors programs. Call to check when they will reopen.

HAMILTON FISH (LOWER EAST SIDE)

128 Pitt Street (at East Houston Street); (212) 387–7687

Hours: Monday through Friday, 8:00 A.M.–9:00 P.M.; Saturday, 10:30 A.M.–5:00 P.M.; Sunday, 10:00 A.M.–3:00 P.M.

Olympic-sized outdoor pool, game room, fitness room, basketball courts, wrestling, computer classes, karate class.

HANSBOROUGH (CENTRAL HARLEM)

35 West 134th Street (between Lenox and Fifth Avenues); (212) 234–9603

Hours: Monday through Friday, 9:00 A.M.–9:30 P.M.; Saturday, 10:00 A.M.–5:30 P.M.

Outdoor rooftop sundeck, indoor pool, outdoor and indoor track, aerobic classes, fitness room, seniors programs.

HIGHBRIDGE (WASHINGTON HEIGHTS)

Amsterdam Avenue and West 173rd Street; (212) 927–2400

Currently undergoing renovations, and offers only after-school programs.

JACKIE ROBINSON (WEST HARLEM)

89 Bradhurst Avenue (at 146th Street); (212) 324–9607

Hours: Monday through Friday, 9:00 A.M.–10:00 P.M.; Saturday until 5:00 P.M.

Olympic-sized outdoor pool, fitness room, computer classes, volleyball, teen cooking classes, after-school program.

J. HOOD WRIGHT (WASHINGTON HEIGHTS)

351 Fort Washington Avenue (at 174th Street); (212) 927–1563

Hours: Monday through Thursday, 9:00 A.M.–10:00 P.M.; Friday and Saturday, 10:00 A.M.–4:00 P.M.

Fitness room, computer center, softball and basketball tournaments, game room, two athletic fields, tennis court, handball courts, teen and seniors programs.

MORNINGSIDE PARK (WEST HARLEM)

410 West 123rd Street (at Morningside Avenue); (212) 280–0209

Hours: Monday, 8:00 A.M.–4:00 P.M.; Tuesday through Friday, 10:00 A.M.–6:00 P.M.

Operates primarily as an after-school and seniors center.

NORTH MEADOW (UPPER EAST AND WEST SIDE)

Central Park (midpark at 97th Street); (212) 348–4867

Hours: Monday through Friday, 10:00 A.M.–6:00 P.M.; Saturday and Sunday until 4:30 P.M.

Open to all, with no membership required. Tai chi and yoga classes, youth adventure programs, climbing wall (open-climbing hours are free for eight- to twelve-year-olds; adults $5.00), basketball clinics, and Field Day Kits. (Borrow a sack of equipment from them for a fun day in the park. The kit includes a basketball, ten cones, three bats, a horseshoe set, playground ball, Nerf ball, football, Frisbee, two handballs, a soccer ball, jump rope, two Wiffle balls, and hula hoops.)

PELHAM FRITZ (WEST HARLEM)

18 Mount Morris Park West (at 122nd Street); (212) 860–1380

Hours: Monday through Friday, 8:30 A.M.–9:30 P.M.; Saturday, 10:00 A.M.–4:00 P.M.

Outdoor pool, computer room, aerobics classes, dance classes, drumming, extensive seniors programs, game room, basketball courts.

REC 59 (MIDTOWN WEST)

533 West 59th Street (between Tenth and Eleventh Avenues); (212) 397–3159

Hours: Monday through Friday, 11:00 A.M.–10:00 P.M.; Saturday, 10:00 A.M.– 6:00 P.M.

Indoor pool, small fitness room.

THOMAS JEFFERSON (EAST HARLEM)

2180 First Avenue (at East 112th Street); (212) 860–1383

Hours: Monday through Friday, 10:00 A.M.–9:30 P.M.; Saturday, 9:00 A.M.– 3:30 P.M.

Olympic-sized outdoor pool, fitness room, basketball courts, athletic fields, martial arts classes, aerobic classes, boxing, handball courts, game room.

BROOKLYN

CHIEF OF RECREATION'S OFFICE: (718) 965–8941

BROOKLYN SENIOR CENTER (FORT HAMILTON)

9941 Fort Hamilton Parkway (at 100th Street); (718) 439–4296

Hours: Monday through Saturday, 9:00 A.M.–5:00 P.M.

Line dancing, tap dancing, social dancing, arts and crafts, day trips, bingo, computer access.

BROWNSVILLE

1555 Linden Boulevard (between Mother Gaston and Christopher Streets); (718) 345–2706

Hours: Monday, Wednesday, and Friday, 9:00 A.M.–10:00 P.M.; Tuesday and Thursday until 11:00 P.M.; Saturday until 6:00 P.M.

Indoor pool, computer center, aerobics classes, martial arts classes, game room, basketball clinics, handball courts, track and field, music studio.

METROPOLITAN POOL AND FITNESS CENTER (WILLIAMSBURG)

261 Bedford Avenue (at Metropolitan Avenue); (718) 599–5707

Hours: Monday through Friday, 7:00 A.M.–10:00 P.M.; Saturday, 9:00 A.M.– 5:30 P.M.

Indoor pool, fitness room, computer center, computer and digital video classes, play schoolroom, and "arguably the best indoor pool in New York City," says the Village Voice.

RED HOOK

155 Bay Street (between Henry and Clinton Streets); (718) 722–3211

Hours: Monday through Friday, 10:00 A.M.–9:00 P.M.

Outdoor pool, computer center and classes, aerobics, martial arts, yoga.

ST. JOHN'S RECREATION CENTER

1251 Prospect Place (at Schenectady Avenue); (718) 771–2787

Hours: Monday through Friday, 9:00 A.M.–10:00 P.M.; Saturday, 10:00 A.M.–6:00 P.M.

Indoor pool, computer center and classes, fitness room, aerobics, tai chi, SAT classes, quilting, seniors programs.

SUNSET PARK

Seventh Avenue and 43rd Street (at 42nd Street); (718) 965–6533

Hours: Monday through Friday, 2:00–10:00 P.M.; Saturday, 10:00 A.M.– 6:00 P.M.

Outdoor pool, computer center, fitness room, boxing room, aerobics classes, tae bo classes, game room.

VON KING CULTURAL ARTS CENTER

670 Lafayette Avenue (between Marcy and Tompkins Avenues); (718) 622–2082

Hours: Monday through Friday, 9:00 A.M.–9:00 P.M.; Saturday, 10:00 A.M.–6:00 P.M.

Computer center, aerobics classes, game room, dance room, athletic fields, handball courts.

THE BRONX

CHIEF OF RECREATION'S OFFICE: (718) 430–1858

CROTONA PARK

East 173rd Street and Fulton Avenue (at Crotona Park East); (718) 731–0984

After-school programs.

HAFFEN PARK

Hammersly Avenue at Ely, Gunther, and Burke Avenues; (718) 379–8347

Hours: Daily, 7:00 A.M.–3:30 P.M.

Outdoor pool, tennis courts, seniors center, handball courts.

KINGSBRIDGE

3101 Kingsbridge Terrace (between Perot and Sedwick Streets); (718) 884–0700

Hours: Monday through Thursday, 8:00 A.M.–10:00 P.M.; Friday, 8:00 A.M.–9:00 P.M.; Sunday, 9:00 A.M.–2:00 P.M.

After school teen and senior programs, computer and back-to-work classes.

MULLALY
East 164th Street (at River Avenue); (718) 822–4191
Outdoor skate park.

ST. JAMES
2530 Jerome Avenue (at 192nd Street); (718) 822–4271
Hours: Monday through Friday, 9:00 A.M.–10:00 P.M.; Saturday until 5:00 P.M.
Computer center, tennis courts, basketball courts, handball courts, teen and seniors programs.

ST. MARY'S
450 St. Ann's Avenue (at 145th Street); (718) 402–5160
Hours: Monday through Friday, 9:00 A.M.–10:00 P.M.; Saturday until 5:00 P.M.
Indoor pool, computer center, fitness room, basketball courts, aerobics classes, boxing, cooking, karate, tae kwon do, teen programs, scuba classes, tennis courts, athletic field.

WEST BRONX
1527 Jessup Avenue (at 172nd Street); (718) 293–5934
Hours: Monday through Friday, 3:00–8:00 P.M.; Saturday, 2:00–6:00 P.M.
After school programs, basketball courts, weight room, and tae kwon do classes.

WILLIAMSBRIDGE OVAL
3225 Reservoir Oval East (between 208th Street and Bainbridge Avenue); (718) 543–8672 or (718) 822–4508
Hours: Monday through Friday, 9:00 A.M.–8:00 P.M.; Saturday until 5:00 P.M.
Fitness room, tennis courts, basketball courts, handball courts, outdoor track, play schoolroom, karate classes, twenty-two acre playground, seniors programs.

ZIMMERMAN PLAY–SCHOOL
Olinville and Barker Avenues; (718) 881–7564
Hours: Monday through Friday, 8:00 A.M.–4:00 P.M.
Toddler play school.

QUEENS

CHIEF OF RECREATION'S OFFICE: (718) 520–5936

DETECTIVE KEITH L. WILLIAMS (JAMAICA)
173rd Place and Liberty Avenue (at 106th Street); (718) 523–6912
Hours: Monday through Friday, 10:00 A.M.–6:00 P.M.
Outdoor pool, tennis courts, handball courts, cooking classes, garden, arts and crafts.

LOST BATTALION HALL (REGO PARK)

93–29 Queens Boulevard (at Sixty-second Avenue); (718) 263–1163

Hours: Monday through Friday, 9:00 A.M.–10:00 P.M.; Saturday, 10:00 A.M.–5:00 P.M.

Computer center, boxing room, fitness center, karate, kickboxing, rhythmic gymnastics, Gymboree, seniors program.

LOUIS ARMSTRONG (CORONA)

108th Street and Northern Boulevard; (718) 446–8010

Hours: Monday through Friday, 9:00 A.M.–5:00 P.M.

Fitness room, karate classes, dance classes, boxing, GED program, community groups, basketball, handball.

PASSERELLE

Flushing Meadows Corona Park (between National Tennis Center and Shea Stadium); (718) 699–4236

Hours: Open by appointment; call for details.

Fitness room, computer center, REACH program for the handicapped. "We are more like a visitor center. We invite groups to come to us—school groups, organizations, seniors, et cetera."

ROY WILKINS FAMILY CENTER (ST. ALBANS)

177th Street at Baisley Boulevard; (718) 276–8686

Hours: Monday through Friday, 10:00 A.M.–10:00 P.M.; Saturday until 5:00 P.M.

Indoor pool, fitness room, outdoor track, extensive seniors program.

SORRENTINO (FAR ROCKAWAY)

18–48 Cornaga Avenue (at Beach 19th Street)

(718) 471–4818

Hours: Monday through Friday, 9:00 A.M.–9:45 P.M.; Saturday until 4:45 P.M.

Fitness room, computer center, double Dutch program, computer classes, play school, seniors programs.

STATEN ISLAND

CHIEF OF RECREATION'S OFFICE: (718) 390–8020

CROMWELL CENTER

Pier 6 and Hannah Street; (718) 816–6172

The center is undergoing renovations and scheduled to reopen in the spring of 2002.

INDEX

About the Author

Born and bred in New York City, **Rob Grader** is a writer, actor, and massage therapist and has lived in four out of the five boroughs (he'll make it to Staten Island one of these days). As an actor, Rob has appeared at many regional theaters across the country; on the television shows *Law & Order, The Job, All My Children, Who's the Boss,* and in the HBO film *American Splendor;* and in a number of national commercials. He's a graduate of the American Repertory Theater's Institute for Advanced Theater Training at Harvard University. In other creative pursuits, Rob has written scripts for the NPR series *Jazz from Lincoln Center.* As a massage therapist, he has rubbed many sore and aching backs around New York. Rob currently lives, works, and does his darndest not to spend any money in Manhattan.